MW00772231

THE SOFT POWER OF CULTURE

Other works by Jonathan Sklar

Landscapes of the Dark: History, Trauma, Psychoanalysis (Karnac, 2011)

Balint Matters: Psychosomatics and the Art of Assessment (Karnac, 2017)

Dark Times: Psychoanalytic Perspectives on Politics, History and Mourning (Phoenix, 2019)

THE SOFT POWER
OF CULTURE
Art, Transitional Space, Death and Play

Jonathan Sklar

KARNAC

firing the mind

First published in 2024 by
Karnac Books Limited
62 Bucknell Road
Bicester
Oxfordshire OX26 2DS

Copyright © 2024 by Jonathan Sklar

The right of Jonathan Sklar to be identified as the author of this work has been asserted in accordance with §§ 77 and 78 of the Copyright Design and Patents Act 1988.

All rights reserved. No part of this publication may be reproduced, stored in a retrieval system, or transmitted, in any form or by any means, electronic, mechanical, photocopying, recording, or otherwise, without the prior written permission of the publisher.

British Library Cataloguing in Publication Data

A C.I.P. for this book is available from the British Library

ISBN: 978-1-80013-248-1 (paperback)
ISBN: 978-1-80013-249-8 (e-book)
ISBN: 978-1-80013-250-4 (PDF)

Typeset by Medlar Publishing Solutions Pvt Ltd, India

www.firingthemind.com

To Ilana, Zack, Sam and Eddie

Contents

List of figures

About the author

Dr Jonathan Sklar, MBBS, FRCPsych is an Independent training and supervising psychoanalyst of the British Psychoanalytical Society. Originally trained in psychiatry at Friern and the Royal Free Hospitals, he also trained in psychotherapy in the adult department of the Tavistock Clinic, London. For many years, he was consultant psychotherapist and head of the psychotherapy department at Addenbrooke's and Fulbourn hospitals in Cambridge.

As well as lecturing widely across the world, he has taught psychoanalysis annually in South Africa for over ten years, and termly in Chicago for ten years until 2018, as well as regularly across Eastern Europe and in Peru.

From 2007 to 2011, he was vice president of the European Psychoanalytic Federation, with special responsibility for seminars for recently qualified analysts as well as the development of new analytic groups in East Europe. He was a board member of the International Psychoanalytical Association from 2015 to 2019. He is an honorary member of the South African Psychoanalytic Society and the Serbian Psychoanalytic Society, and established and chaired the Independent Psychoanalytic Trust.

He works in analytic practice in London.

Prologue

Serendipity is the great finder. As I was assembling and editing these chapters I chanced upon the so-far undiscovered title of this book in an extraordinary quote by Simon Schama.

Schama wrote about his 2022 BBC2 television series *History of Now* as

> the fruit of sombre, late-life reflection that the History of Now was prefigured in the History of Then; that what we had imagined to be things of the past have returned to shadow the present and the future. Shrieking, whether online or on platforms, is back; hate is sexy and stalks the world as 'disruption'.

Schama quipped the phrase "art against tyranny"—

> *the soft power of culture*—poetically charged words, images, music, all of which can, in some circumstances, exert a force beyond the workaday stuff of politics. Culture can do this because it can connect with human habits, needs and intuitions in ways that expose the inhuman hollowness of official propaganda. (Schama, 2022)

So those old battles need to be refought, and with the help of the unlikely weapons that once opened eyes and changed minds; I will add to his quote the *unconscious* as another place that is part of the human habitat where we can seek and find further reflections of history then and now, as well as those well-known particulates of psychoanalysis—Freud's free associations and the return of the repressed. And as such, psychoanalysis is another different and valuable tool to add in between the sciences and the arts to the already formidable array of human knowledge—history, economics, sociology, sexology and those humanities—painting, poetry, opera, music, dance, sport, and I will include as well as fiction, the depths of storytelling (which has its own long and ancient traditions of the imagination). All of these subjects contain unconscious hidden depths that can become insight and understanding and contribute to our human humanity as culture.

Cultural displays in art show multitudinous views of humans within their environment, and as time passes, how artists express and develop new views of life. From early times the Catholic church has utilised art on the walls of churches to show conception, as in the annunciation to the Madonna that she is pregnant, the birth of Christ, and within its schema is a haunting into the future of a death foretold. The Madonna carries the baby Christ on her lap, and after his crucifixion his dead body once again lies supported there. Alongside depictions of religious life that the people are invited to follow are potent frescoes of the allegories of Adam and Eve in Paradise and their expulsion, with an underlying split between good and bad. These transform into pictures of a good religious life inviting entry back to Paradise, but now with its interlocutor dwelling in Hell for evermore. And thus paintings educated the people into how the Church desires the lived life.

Later art forms developed the concept(ion) of *momenta mori*, with depictions of skulls that concentrate reflection on death. Hans Holbein the younger painted *The Ambassadors* in 1533[1] standing in front of a table on which are a celestial globe, a sundial and other scientific and musical instruments. There is a strange object on the floor that is an anamorphic—an intentional distortion—image of a skull, which, by the viewer moving around the painting, can come into vision as a clear motif of death and of separating scientific and cultural objects from us when we die. They are, and continue to be, available for the living. Similarly, paintings of still life, which began in northern Europe from the sixteenth century, contained the device of a vase of cut flowers beginning their decay from beauty and scent into death, and so back to earlier Christian paintings depicting the cycles of Christ's journey from birth to death.

There are architecturally special buildings containing culture that are seen to be important landmarks of a city or a country's achievements. When going abroad, these are places towards which tourists congregate, such as, in London, the British Museum, National Gallery, Royal Academy, the two Tates, opera, ballet and concert halls, and football stadiums. These are visited as some hallmark of cultural achievement and yet what has this got to do with us? Many citizens pass by or take for granted such cultural achievements. And the whole world adores football's World Cup, which is its own particular art form of skills leading to the "death" of the other team (and similar to the game of war, and chess, in the desire to win and be on the victorious side).

And when we cannot visit these special cultural places, as none of us around the world could during three years of Covid lockdown, people felt dismayed, emptier of purpose, sickly and depressed. The absence of culture was part of the emptiness of mind in lockdown. During the Second World War, London lived with the Blitz and its counterpoint the Blackout. Lunchtime concerts were played and organised by Myra Hess at the National Gallery a few weeks after the start of war. They were presented on Monday to Fridays for six and a half years without fail. If London was being bombed, the concert was moved to a smaller, safer room. Hess presented 1,698 concerts, playing in 150 herself. They were seen by 824,152 people.[2] Culture as valuable tool to boost morale.

And where are the origins of culture in the developing mind of the child? "The place where cultural experience is located is in the *potential space* between the individual and the environment (originally the object). The same can be said of playing. Cultural experience begins with creative living first manifested in play" (Winnicott, 1966b, p. 433). Winnicott theorised that the start of the infant's transitional object, which he labelled the first not-me possession, is "both the first use of a symbol and the first experience of play" (ibid., p. 431). This takes place in the inner world of unconscious phantasy, whilst simultaneously it is in the presence of, and by the reinforcement of, the actual mother, coming and going, returning to offer and develop her maternal care. What the baby can manage by way of internal mental representations of the losing of mother gradually extends in time, or the phantasy of mother develops a robustness and can be remembered as an image for when the object (mother) is gone. This can be observed in the longer periods for which a baby can play alone with his or her body or a toy. The length of managing this gradually extends if the mother is available in a good-enough way. The lack of mother for too long a period that is repetitive can eventually damage the baby's development of its internal mental representations of its objects, and leads in time to a profound lack of trust in the world.

As an exemplar of transitional space and play, Marion Milner, in conversation with Donald Winnicott, "conveyed the tremendous significance that there can be in the interplay of the edges of two curtains, or the surface of a jug that is placed in front of another jug" (Winnicott, ibid., p. 431). The act of looking at a painting means unconsciously being confronted with "something next to something else", which can resonate unconsciously with the observer. For example, look at the Cézanne still life *The Basket of Apples* (1893).

Figure 1. *The Basket of Apples*, Paul Cézanne, 1893

It is a strange picture to look at because the planes are vertiginous—if it were a mountain view one would be confronted with unsettling planes of view that seem to slip downwards (or upwards). Look at the table and trace its lines. One sees the upper right-hand corner as being much higher than the upper corner on the left, which is an unsettling surprise. The apples on the right-hand side of the table seem about to journey off it, down the plane of the higher corner—*but they do not.* They are in a state of suspension. This injects an uncanny element, as if by watching the canvas we are preparing for "the next second" of movement as the apples crash to the floor. Unstable certainly, as Cézanne is pointing out the singularity of that impending movement. He is taking hold of a movement in time and confronting the viewer with a *moment* prior to the fall. Who is about to fall? The apples, yes, but also the viewer may have to look at their impending next fall, like the moment prior to Adam and Eve having to leave Paradise. Or just when we see life being sort of level, the painting confronts us with the instability of

Figure 2. *Three Skulls on a Patterned Carpet*, Paul Cézanne, 1904

life's longitude. And perhaps the viewer, unsettled, just quickly passes by. And why not, as the unconscious play is an extraordinary comment about *momento mori*, which is true for all pictures of cut flowers in a vase or fruit in a basket, as they are but a moment on the path towards decay and death? Who now is unaware, as we emerge from our three impossible years of Covid lockdown, that life is unstable?

I think that is something that Milner was inviting us to notice in the banality of two opposing curtains meeting (or not) at an edge, or one object in front of the other, meaning that one object is *behind* the other. Would that, in a moment, be the baby in front of mother or mother in front? And how might that matter, depending on what has happened before that moment? Is mother more important than her baby for a moment or are there too many such narcissistic moments of mother leaving the baby in the shadows? As Schama (ibid.) states, "So those old battles need to be refought", but this time in one's unconscious object relational system, testing out if the world is still conforming to the earlier blueprint of life, or has developed away from a more nihilistic position to one containing trust and love.

In discussing that Cézanne painting, the Belgian painter Luc Tuymans writes in the catalogue for the 2022–2023 Tate Modern exhibition:

> the painting works as if it is being pushed to its breaking point. Here fragility becomes dangerous and obstinate—a moment frozen in time, purposely trying to destroy the unified image in order to recreate it … The painting functions as an echo chamber, incorporating the act of looking and separating the points of view of both eyes, combining the result into a single pictorial experience …
>
> All in all, I think Cézanne's quest was for the affirmation of his own eternity, driven by monumental persistence. The irony is that by using the most humble and unimportant subjects—such as an apple—Cézanne was able to crack depiction single-handedly. (Tuymans, 2022, p. 129)

Winnicott notes that "the use of an object symbolises the union of two now separate things, baby and mother, *at the point in time and space of the initiation of their state of separateness*" (ibid., p. 430, italics Winnicott's own). The plane that mother and baby are on is, like the painting, a union of separate humble things—apples, bottle, cloth, plate and basket on a table. They are together and apart; and have movement that includes being on the edge of the next (minor) catastrophe. And that edge can include needing a bit more of a feed, losing the nipple or the departed mother or toy. Baby care is an edgy business. In a similar fashion, "Psychotic patients are all the time hovering between living and not living" (ibid., p. 433), forcing us to look at this problem. Winnicott, in a discussion of what life is about, argues that it is more than psychoneurosis and that the problems of being on the psychotic edge are also part of being a human in greater or lesser amounts.

> I am claiming that these same phenomena that are life and death to our schizoid or borderline patients appear in our cultural experiences. It is these cultural experiences that provide the continuity in the human race that transcends personal existence. I am assuming that cultural experiences are in direct continuity with play, the play of those who have not yet heard of games. (ibid., p. 433)

Cézanne plays earnestly with the potentiality of the object falling at any moment and is in touch with the life–death moment for the observer to visualise before our very eyes, by looking at the basket of apples ('Conversation avec Picasso', *Cahiers d'art* special edition 1935, cited in T. J. Clark, 2022, p. 75). Nonetheless, another story tells an opposite view. Alex Danchev in his biography of Cézanne, writes about the art dealer Vollard who nodded off when Cézanne was painting his portrait. The artist did not mince his words: "Wretch. You've ruined the pose! I tell you in all seriousness you must hold it like an apple. Does an apple move?" (Danchev, 2013, p. 79).

This links to a chapter in this collection about the Bloomsbury Group being an early culture carrier of psychoanalysis in London. Maynard Keynes had persuaded the British Government to have an allocation of £20,000 to spend on art in Paris, and went with the Director of the National Gallery, Charles Holmes, to buy from Degas' collection following his death in 1918. The museum acquired a Corot, a Gauguin, a Rousseau, two Delacroix, two Manets and four Ingres, but to Keynes' immense frustration, not a single Cézanne. Keynes bought one Cézanne for himself and went directly to Charleston, the home of Duncan Grant and Vanessa Bell, where he revealed the small painting *Apples*, the first Cézanne to be in a British collection, and rapturously received by the Bloomsberries (Danchev, ibid., p. 128).

When we humans fall asleep, *the fall* is symbolic of falling back into mother and her womb where we originally lived. And there is an analogy in art and culture that connects womb and tomb, as if there is uncertainty that the place we surrender ourselves to return to each night will restore us the next day or will entrap us as the place of our death. This is a reason why so many people are too anxious to fall asleep, in case they never wake up again.

Dream: I am on the ocean in a box, a houseboat … We are drifting and I fall asleep. Then we land. I am onshore and awake. A woman is there.

Géza Róheim, the Hungarian anthropologist and psychoanalyst, interprets. Falling asleep in the box on the water simply symbolises the process of falling asleep, such as being in a box on the water with a woman(womb). Landing is being born, awakening, and to dream is a partial awakening … Falling asleep itself is a repetition of the womb situation but is sometimes symbolised by its opposite, being born. In this case we have both symbols: uterine regression and birth (Róheim, 1952, pp. 3–4).

And with the metaphor of birth there is its companion metaphor—death, linking womb and tomb. "A patient whose depression started at a very early age with the birth of his brother has the following hypnagogic fantasy: John and I are both in the grave. Even there I am trying to kill him" (ibid., p. 6).

Sleep and death are intimately connected, as are sleep and sex. The return to the inside of mother dream is so often about the return to mother *and* sex—being a reflection on the phallus that both enters and leaves the cave. The hero may die whilst falling asleep but is resurrected in the subsequent rising up, as the metaphor of the erection of the penis brings a return to being alive.

Or Winnicott quoting Tagore:

> On the seashore of endless worlds,
> Children play.

Winnicott then writes:

> When I first became a Freudian I *knew* what it meant. The sea
> and the shore represent endless intercourse between man and
> woman, and the child emerged from this union to have a brief
> moment before becoming in turn adult or parent. Then, as a
> student of unconscious symbolism, I *knew* (one always knows)
> that the sea is the mother, and onto the seashore the child is
> born. Babies come out of the sea and are spewed out upon the
> land, like Jonah from the whale. So now the seashore was the
> mother's body, after the child is born and the mother and
> the now viable baby are getting to know each other. (Winnicott,
> 1966b, p. 430)

All this description is to understand that this place is where play may
begin to form, between Milner's two edges, now the primordial sea
and the land—that evolutionary edge where Darwinian change happened, from sea creatures to those existing on land. And humans have a
trace of that sea world as the foetus develops within the sea of mother's
aquatic womb space.

Later Winnicott differentiates between *body functioning* and body
experience (ibid., p. 434) in developing the idea of play and its continuum as a potential space: play *becomes* culture. And as language
is being heard or misheard, its musicality and meanings are played
and shaped into metaphor, as I will discuss in the first chapter of this
book.

Hypnagogic states relate to immediately before falling asleep (from
the Greek *Hypnos*—sleep and *agogos*—to lead). Hypnopompic states are
the fleeting perceptual experiences from sleep to wakefulness. Róheim
examines the sensations of falling or sinking that are typical hypnagogic
sensations.

> In English we have the expression "to fall asleep", in Hungarian, *alomba merult*, "to dip under into sleep", as into water. But in German we have *einschlafen*, in French *endormir*, "to sleep in, to turn into oneself". If we condense these two ways of expressing sleep, we can say that the sleeper turns into himself and falls back into the womb, his own body being the material substratum of the dream-womb. (ibid., p. 7)

The Yukaghir shaman's drum is a lake into which he dives in order to descend into the spirit world (Czaplicka, 1914, p. 209). A patient reports a dream flash as "I am falling down a precipice into an endless depth". And Róheim related the falling into the womb dream at the start of *Alice in Wonderland* similarly as a falling asleep phantasy—"Alice was beginning to get very tired of sitting by her sister on the bank"—as the white rabbit leads her to the rabbit hole. "Either the well was very deep, or she fell very slowly, for she had plenty of time as she went down to look about her and to wonder what was going to happen next" (Carroll, 1865, p. 1).

Ideas associated with falling asleep and waking up, containing dream imagery of falling, felt in the body, caught up in words in our different languages and metaphors, are similarly found in the work of a Siberian Shaman, a late nineteenth-century French artist and a well-known British novelist. The hypnagogic thoughts as sleep returns us to the womb in our re-imagining falling into our origins, are expressed in our languages, imagery, and the novels of our culture, creating a soft power in linking to seemingly different things. Such capacities for unconscious linkage are made good use of in the invitation to the analysand to say whatever comes to mind without evasion or censorship. And what develops from a thread of two of these associations is a mycelium of interconnections, like the neurones themselves compacted into the brain.

These introductory remarks are by way of introducing the reader to the multi-layered chapters that follow. There are four long clinical descriptions of working with particular technical difficulties in analysing a heroin addict, a schizophrenic patient, reflecting on Freud's paper "A child is being beaten" (1919) to examine maternal cruelty; and an exploration of understanding Winnicott's "true and false self".

These provide a psychoanalytic matrix to think about human cruelty and nihilism, often dressed up as being "just a game". This is then reflected in a chapter on the violent apocalyptic times we live in and how psychoanalytic thinking can be seen as an essential perspective to examine our present "us and them" politics, with the world drifting into a vortex of deadly climate change as humans attack Mother Earth. Another chapter examines metaphor, particularly in the stranger who comes from beyond our comfortable life, and the present disdain for the past welcoming of the stranger into one's tent as we find ourselves in a paranoid politic.

And there are many interwoven reflections on art and society: a paper on Francis Bacon and the radicality of free association, and another on Velázquez and power, which leads into the tragedy of the collapse of psychoanalysis during Nazification in the Berlin and Vienna psychoanalytic Societies during the Third Reich and after. The latter is also about how Anne-Marie Sandler recovered depth analysis with those members, as well as re-finding her lost German tongue. Another chapter is on the art of William Tillyer via a free-associative examination of the painter's life through his art.

As T. S. Eliot wrote, "Birth, and copulation, and death. That's all the facts when you come to brass tacks" (1975, p. 115).[3] Cruelty, destruction and death stalk these chapters, and are found together in three small pieces of writing on our recent Covid times. There is also a thread running through the book about holding one's nerve, being alive in the moment, realising that enactment in clinical work can be another royal road to the unconscious. And Winnicott's observation of the child painting over their colourful picture by a total cover of black paint is a realisation that the death and destructive instinct as black is not the unconscious baseline, rather it indicates a necessity to descend beneath that clinical black layer to the colour and aliveness of the earlier true self, protected and still alive with the possibility of new creativity beneath the dark.

CHAPTER 1

Stranger, visitor, metaphor

Όλο τον κόσμο γύρισες μα τίποτα δεν είδες
You have been all around the world, but you saw nothing
Λυχνος του Αλλαδινου, Νίκος Καββαδίας
Nikos Kavvadias, *Alladin's Lamp*, 2006

In this chapter on *Xenos*, a word which means not only stranger or foreigner, but also ally, lifelong friend, guest as well as host,[1] I will be concentrating on ideas around the uses and functions of metaphor in language as a critical means of carrying the weight of the unconscious, which can transfer, as in transference, understanding and knowledge of that part of the mind. My particular focus will be an examination of the flow of associations from Xenos—foreigner, outsider, stranger and in particular *tramotane*—a person who lives on the other side of the mountain. And, in addition, Xenos means guest and hospitality. Thus, the Greek word is double-edged as the stranger is also the guest. The word contains a pair of opposites.

> It's not that what is past casts its light on what is present, or what is present its light on the past; rather, image is that wherein what

1

has been comes together in a flash with the now to form a con-
stellation. In other words, image is dialectics at a standstill. For
while the relation of the present to the past is a purely temporal,
continuous one, the relation of what-has-been to the now is dialectical: is not progression but image, suddenly emergent. Only
dialectical images are genuine images (that is, not archaic); and
the place where one encounters them is language. (Benjamin,
1927–1940, p. 462)

Metaphor

St Christopher, the patron saint of travellers, was in legend a 6.3 metre
giant who decided to serve "the greatest king there was". Noticing that
the king he found to serve crossed himself at the mention of the devil, he
realised that the king lived in fear, and so he departed to search out the
more powerful master. In time, learning that the Devil feared Christ,
he decided to serve Him. A hermit suggested that, given his bodily
strength, he could serve Christ by assisting people cross a dangerous
river. You probably know the story that a little child asked his help to get
across; however, despite the child's size, on crossing the river he felt that
his load weighed him down considerably. On reaching the far shore he
said that "the whole world could have been as heavy as you on my shoulders". The child Christ then revealed that, indeed, Christopher had had
the whole world on his shoulders as well as he who made it, revealing
that Christopher was now serving Christ the King by carrying all of it.

Holding that metaphor in mind, let us examine an oppositional
position.

Goethe wrote the poem "The Erl-King" ["*Erlkönig*"], which Schubert
then set to music—both wonderful evocations of something that is also
very disturbing. The poem depicts a father riding through a forest, holding to his chest his son, who is crying in fear of the Erl-King, the spirit
of wind and forest. The father dismisses his son's fears as mist, pressing
him closer to himself as he gallops faster. Arriving home, he discovers
his son dead in his arms. The exciting ride, the galloping horse, with the
father tightening his grip on the boy can be read as a cipher for paedophilia. The Erl-King, like the Pied Piper or the Rat Catcher of Hamelin,
is the pagan lover of children (Forrester, 2017, p. 99). This subject is covered up by mist and as such it is invariably invisible.

Figure 3. *Saint Christopher Carrying the Christ Child,* Hieronymus Bosch, c.1450–1516

I bring these two stories together as they both contain the metaphor of holding—the early holding required by the child that is the task of mother, which in time becomes the psychic frame containing/holding creative life. Its devil-opposite, as represented by the Erl-King, is the perverse erotism of holding directed to paedophilia and death.

It is in Winnicott's work that analytic holding has profound resonances of carrying/supporting a child with protectiveness, care, calm, and the maternal ecstasy of the burden. The good-enough mother provides and creates continuity in the baby's experience of the world. The dropping of the baby is the rupturing of continuity that needs to be mended and repaired by mother or not; later it becomes re-framed in analysis. Paedophilia is at an extreme obverse of loving and is the enactment of hatred without repair. Such unconscious negative states can become available for engagement in analysis.

In the countless images that exist of the Madonna and Child, the infant Christ is held/contained. These images represent the commencement of the journey from birth to death, re-found in the image of the Madonna in the *Pietà*, once again holding the body of her son, now transformed into the dead Christ. Here the structure of the early scene of Madonna and child finds its structural counterpart of her holding a dead grown-up man. "In the beginning is my end", as T. S. Eliot wrote in "East Coker" (1940), a metaphor for the inevitability of death as a known fact, whilst the rest in-between is the actuality of a life lived.

The analysand arrives in the psychoanalytic consulting room with some notion that he or she may just perhaps be able to find help to overcome disturbances. The psychoanalyst is a place of last resort, where monsters are to be found "in the sleep of reason" (*Los Caprichos*, plate 43, Goya, 1799, in the Metropolitan Museum of Art, New York). Goya does not judge monsters, rather he allows them to present the world of the night that is a characteristic of the *Los Caprichos* etchings. These can only emerge—to to be seen beyond their darkness in the unconscious—when reason sleeps. Bravery is required for such a process, certainly from the patient to dare to evoke and begin the process of taming the turbulent wildernesses of the mind. The same is required of the analyst, to allow his or her psyche–soma to be the sounding board of the patient's often-severe distresses, some of which, projected, need to be "caught" by the analyst to allow them to come into existence somewhere in and between the clinical dyad. Sometimes it is in the analyst's dreams or somatics that the "it" of the analysand is perceived. Perhaps in the gap between the rent and the patch in the ego; one or other will feel, know or enact the traumatic origins suffered by the child in the analysis of the adult (Ferenczi, 1931).

And so, St Christopher trying to help travellers cross the river, preventing their death by drowning, can but suffer the—at times—extremely heavy burden that he carries. A metaphor alongside St Christopher is Charon, the boatman carrying the souls of the dead across the River Styx to Hades. Brother of Thanatos and Hypnos, he makes possible the drift into sleep and enables the dream function. One metaphor carries another, layered beneath or alongside. This has relevance for the problem of deadness within an analysis that needs space to emerge without analysand or analyst being killed in the journey.

In the first metaphor, the Christ Child, carrying the world, is being carried by Christopher. For the patient, the analyst carries the weight of the lived life, and with some patients, the burden contains a fear of the impossibility of returning to life. Here I want to cite John Forrester's observation on the problem of holding. On one hand, the Madonna holds the body of her son, the alive child and the dead, thirty-three-year-old man. And in the Erl-King myth, the negative holding, an over-exciting ride, ends in a holding that suffocates to death—such a paedophilic direction fragments and continues to murder mental life. The Erl-King metaphor is sexual perversion at the heart of carrying across, as metaphor is contaminated when the erotic sphere is a "confusion of tongues between adults and the child" (Ferenczi, 1932).

Yet erotics are part of the mother holding the baby, containing profound "resonances of care, calm and maternal ecstasy of the burden" (ibid., p. 101). Some mothers fear that their holding may be an insufficient activity to prevent the death of their baby, thus turning the live, sleeping baby in their arms into an imaginary holding of a dead baby. This is the nightmare of the mother. Can I, with all that has happened in my life, be "good-enough" to nurture my baby into life? Of course, some mothers, perhaps visualising their baby as representing the environmental cruelties bestowed by their own mother, or grandmother, in a transgenerational maternal series, cannot bear the life of their baby and return to a suffocating feminine version of the Erl-King. More often, though, it is "the father who is aware that the baby, especially a baby son, has become his rival, as a starting point of an antagonism towards the favourite which is deeply rooted in the unconscious" (Freud, 1910c, p. 59).

It is perplexing to understand where St Christopher is standing as he carries the world—outside the earth, or in space? Or is standing, as the purveyor of "carrying over", precisely the work of the metaphor, concealed in language and culture. How, also, does psychoanalysis manage to have a secure foundation when its foot does not rest on the world, but instead rests on this thing, the unconscious? As Forrester acutely questions:

> Where does psychoanalysis' power to transform, to carry, to transfer come from? Freud's answer is not suggestion but transference. Winnicott's answer was "holding". Winnicott's answer, like Freud's, comes close to saying that there is a fundamental metaphoricity at the heart of such answers. What else is transference—the German *Ubertragung* (from *uber tragen* literally "to carry over", than a version of the Greek *meta-phorein*, literally, "carrying across"). (Forrester, 2017, p. 103)

So the metaphor of St Christopher, like the metaphor of psychoanalysis—metaphor, transference, holding—is but a metaphor. Perhaps we analysts have a task to restore metaphoricity to the metaphors, so that deeply understanding the language of the patient in its transmission of the monster's release is the place where our work stands.

The *flâneur* in analysis

What is important, the large or the small? I have argued elsewhere that, for Bacon and other artists, grass has its own intrinsic and even mystical value, perhaps transformed as the straw that one lies on and which holds one's body up when going to sleep. Walter Benjamin had a passion "for small, minute things"; his friend Gershon Scholem tells of his ambition to get one hundred lines onto one page of an ordinary notebook, and about his admiration for two grains of wheat in the Jewish section of the Musee Cluny "on which a kindred soul had inscribed the complete prayer *Schema Israel*. For him the size of an object was an inverse ratio of its insignificance" (Benjamin, 1970, p. 17). The small object passes by, seemingly insignificant, yet it can carry the very essence of, say, Judaism, in the metaphor of a grain of rice. Large things, such as ideas or ethics, can float in the ether of our lives. It is an idea that fits with psychoanalysis giving a similar status to a passing thought, the wisp of a dream or a touch of a memory that weaves in and out of our mind without being noticed, passed by for now. The integrity of what the little object contains is retained until another time, when its significance can be extracted.

The aimless stroll through the crowds in big cities is distinct from their hurried, purposeful activity; things reveal themselves in their secret meaning: the true picture of the past flits by and only the *flâneur*/psychoanalyst who idly strolls by receives the message in contrast. This is a reason for the power of Benjamin's position of being a *flâneur* in walking around a city. Of course, one can examine a guidebook of the major places to visit, but it requires a knowledge of where one will be going and is very different from finding something else, without knowing its place, just by passing by.

"Oh so here is that place. I did not expect to find it here!" (Arendt, 1968, p. 164). This is precisely the point that Freud (1913c) makes about free associations with his metaphor of looking at the passing vistas in the window of the train, until eventually one ends up at a place that neither analysand nor analyst had expected to be in.

Similarly to the *flâneur*, Benjamin's "Angel of History" (in his discussion of Paul Klee's 1920 *Angelus Novus* mono print, 1940) turns his back on the crowd even as he is propelled and swept by it; so the "Angel of History", who looks at nothing but the expanse of ruins of the past, is blown backwards into the future by the storm of progress.

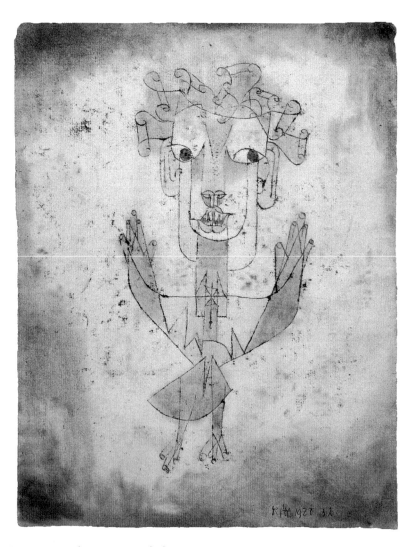

Figure 4. *Angelus Novus,* Paul Klee, 1940

In analysis, the analytic dyad re-finds the present in the past, and this can spark off an act of freedom. That is how the patient enters a "New Beginning" (Balint, 1968). The medium for this may be an interpretation given by the analyst or be found by the patient. It can also be a humble metaphor, which carries on a grain of a word the transfer of a sensually perceived connection that reveals an immediate insight. Arendt makes a link between metaphor and poetry, suggesting that they both re-create description and feelings. She gives a powerful and helpful quote from Kafka's *Diaries* about seeing from a different vantage point.

> Anyone who cannot cope with life while he is alive needs one hand to ward off a little his despair over his fate […] but with his other hand he can jot down what he sees among the ruins, for he sees different and more things than others; after all, he is dead in his own lifetime and the real survivor. (Kafka, 1975)

Often analysands complain of not remembering a dream that they know they have had. Jotting down thoughts of the dream and associations on awakening can be very helpful in grasping them before they return to the mist (in both senses).

Some patients, although they go through the motions of talking about their life, give the impression that they are living one that is dead. Such monologues can be very hard to bear, since the listener can only hear that nothing can be done. Did the parents not notice how the abandoned child was feeling? It is easy for such a child to take guilt onto him or herself and carry the fault as their own. Kafka's idea of making jottings amongst the ruins is a metaphor for the difficulty of analytic narratives. The analysand is surrounded by life's ruins. Nevertheless, we may have glimpses that, despite everything, they are a survivor and therefore alive.

In a similar metaphor, Arendt then quotes Benjamin: "Like one who keeps afloat on a shipwreck by climbing to the top of a mast that is already crumbling. But from there he has a chance to give a signal leading to his rescue" (Arendt, 1968, p. 172).[2] Experiences viewed from the top of the mast, brought to an analysis, enable a concomitant affect of impending disaster. Many neurotic symptoms are already attached to the unconscious knowledge of the disasters of upbringing and other traumatic events in life's journey. For instance, generalised anxiety may be attached to the danger of holding onto the top of the mast as the ship is sinking. Now it is no longer a generalised, unattached and massive anxiety. Similar may be found in obsessional holding onto the mast, leading to being pitched into the sea, unable to swim.

These metaphors, or what I can call poetics, allow the analyst to realise where the patient is speaking from, and accepting this, instead of simply registering the analysand's anxiety and possible fear with their difficulties of describing where they are in themselves. In addition, the analysand is making a big effort to speak from a very unstable and dangerous place that has provided unstable fixity for a long time, thereby giving a signal that may lead to rescue. When the signal anxiety is attached to a metaphor, it can be linked to or developed into a reconstruction of personal history that has remained in the unconscious as metaphor. This, in time, can be deciphered.

For the analysand, this metaphorical position, when explored, provides hope of rescue, of change and development, throughout the work of the analytic dyad. The metaphor of the collapsing boat reflects aspects of perceived and actual damage done in infancy and childhood to the sense of being held properly or not (another metaphor that can also be explored to reveal more early history). A realisation can emerge that the analysand, clutching the mast-top, solitary, alone, is in a relationship with another who has seen them, and can provide support to move away from such a precarious mental position. The point of exposing the fuller metaphorical emotional substrate is to develop a capacity to uncover tempestuous times in words and memories, moving away from a one-person state of mind and life towards a *new beginning*, as the analyst can be made use of by the analysand in becoming more free from his or her emotionally precarious life. There arises a sense of choice: the analysand can emerge or remain in their dead–alive life.

The psyche–soma carrying the burden of the mind

The original ego is a body ego. Early on in the development of the mind, the ego has perceptions from the body, as found in posture, hunger, pain, cold and heat. These are experiences in the body prior to and later alongside the development of a thinking–feeling mental mechanism. The mind does not exist without its body, and both structures, consciously and unconsciously, have been around for the duration of a person's life.

Later, it is the analysand's body that provides the structure and motility to bring the mind to analysis. Present-day analysis can often downgrade the value and importance of the body as part of the totality of analytic experience. At its most extreme, for some analysts, the mind becomes overvalued as their target organ. The analytic understanding of psyche–soma can become an ordinary but also fundamental way of understanding and approaching the roots of an individual's character or self.

The mind may need protection from the impact of massive affect: such that defensively there is a move from psyche to soma. In this case the body can take over in providing the contours of associations, although detached from a mental capacity to free-associate and emotionally feel. Thus, one finds a patient who might adopt particular positions on the couch—a certain rigidity of limbs, perhaps, or never moving, as a means of concealing and revealing earlier traumatic states and keeping a distance from what threatens as some terrible knowing. Such positional structures when noticed and recognised can allow for the possibility of movement away from the somatic register and towards mental curiosity. Putting the "it" into words moves psychic energy from the thing (body) presentation to word presentation, enabling affect to move from body attachment to potentially that of the clinical dyad.

As with the rest of an analysis, doing this requires time to work through the new-found memories in terms of past relationships. The patient in his/her psychosomatic place is alone and does not expect, nor often even wish for, the intervention of the other. The unconscious expectation is that the other is not there to help, and often there is a historical truth to this, as sometimes adults had not protected the infant from trauma and may even have caused it. Very often the traumatised analysand has not had an early history of being held, cuddled and loved by the mother, such that in adult life being touched becomes an ego-alien idea, and perceived as the harbinger of further assault. This leads to the possibility that only self-holding is possible (rocking, masturbating, disturbances of eating, etc.).

Sometimes, instead of feeling anxiety in the mind as a state of anxiousness, the body can take over. For instance, it is common to see children, and also some young adults, sitting with a leg or foot continuously tapping away, dissociated to the rest of the body, which is sitting quietly. The leg is experiencing rapid repetitive movement, containing what can be seen as excitement. It can be thought of as a manic somatic state concealing its depressive opposite—the physical equivalent of manic depression in a limb—whilst at the same time, the person is talking apparently normally about something or other, split off from their rapid leg movements.

Repetitive anxiety leading to phantasies about the imminence of a heart attack is also quite common, especially if a parent died too young from a myocardial infarction (heart attack). Rather than examining the processes of mourning of the death that has already happened, the patient claims the heart condition for the self. The sense of impending doom about oneself is then a projection into the future of a past that has already happened, and like the tapping leg, continues a vibration of twinges in the body that are experienced as alerts for the approaching heart attack. This can continue for years, without any cognisance that these many alerts about dying are a stream of false alarms. As such, the somatic phantasy provides cover for not mourning, perhaps chiding the patient with survivor's guilt, together with an overarching expectation that one cannot, must not, surpass one's parents.

When such somatic containers of anxiety, excitement and depression can be noticed, and insight allows conversation from the soma to the psyche, analysis opens up a new possibility in the telling, a possibility that the listener, who may be experienced after a while as benign, can hear, and that the patient registers, perhaps for the first time, being heard. The patient may begin to know that the other is listening and can also listen to themselves beyond the mindless vibrating body.

Metaphor in music

No one can truly know himself
Detach himself from his innermost being
Yet still he must test, each day
What he clearly sees from without
What he is, what he was
What he can do, and what he stands for.

Goethe, "Zahme Xenien"

I once heard a performance of Richard Strauss' *Metamorphosen* under the baton of Antonio Pappano at Covent Garden. On 2 October 1943, an Allied bombing raid destroyed the Munich National Theatre.

Richard Strauss, born in Munich described the desecration as "the greatest catastrophe which has ever been brought into my life, for which there can be no consolation" (quoted by Richard Bratby, Royal Opera House programme notes, 2018).

Worse, on 2 March 1945, after hearing of the firebombing of Dresden he wrote, "I am in despair! The Goethaus, the world's greatest sanctuary destroyed! My beautiful Dresden, Weimar, Munich—all gone" (ibid.). Ten days later, the Vienna State Opera burned to the ground. This fired him to write *Metamorphosen* as a great lament for the destruction of a civilisation. As Richard Bratby describes,

> A final, impassioned, climax totters into an equally final collapse, and the music of the opening returns, destined this time to lead only downwards into C minor darkness, where the source of the transformation becomes clear, and a fragment of the funeral march from Beethoven's *Eroica* symphony stands blackened in the basses. Strauss wrote the words "IN MEMORIAM" over its broken remains.

The world totters and links with the real and metaphorical forlorn pile of bricks, which was all that had been left of the castle that once towered over the old square in Warsaw, destroyed in the Second World War.

Strauss was offering the world a requiem, such that the listener might feel, in the music, the devastation of the destruction of war against a centuries-old culture. He knew that beyond the burning buildings stood the Nazi persecution of the Jews, including his daughter-in-law and family. The music is themed with darkness, which, despite attempting uplift, returns to a deeply sombre and terrible ending. It is too much to mourn the full enormity of what has happened. And the lines from Goethe are for all of us, as-yet untested, unknowing of how we will manage to realise that we will each decide "What he can do and what he stands for".

I wrote this as part of the epilogue to my 2019 book *Dark Times: Psychoanalytic Perspectives on Politics, History and Mourning*, to illustrate an attack on culture that came in a time of war. The attack was both physical and metaphorical; the usual holding capacities of concert halls, theatres, opera, ballet, jazz, poetry readings, libraries, museums—the places well established for how culture is perceived in society—expected to just continue. My theme of that epilogue is here carried across to this chapter, six years on, as events that we have experienced since have shown that, as in war, in times of Covid and of the severe disruption to Mother Earth (vast forest fires, rising waters overwhelming flood defences, dangerous winds and storms, heatwaves) we find that, suddenly, cultural activities diminish or completely close down. And we are bereft, at a loss, miserable, and feel less alive. The good-enough holding of the mother's arms, the transitional phenomena that Winnicott described from the creativity of me–not-me, is, in dealing with reality, further transformed to his third area of creativity: that of culture in society. If the infant has not achieved transitional phenomena, then the acceptance of the symbolic is deficient and cultural life is poverty stricken.

As Winnicott states:

> Put rather crudely: we go to a concert and I hear in a late Beethoven string quartet the firebombing of great Dresden and the Goethaus (you see I'm highbrow). This quartet is not just an external fact produced by Beethoven and played by the musicians; and it is not my dream, which as a matter of fact would not have been so good. The experience, coupled with my preparation of myself for it, enables me to create a glorious fact. I enjoy it because I say I created it, I hallucinated it, and it is real and would have been there even if I had been neither conceived or not conceived.
>
> This is mad. But in our cultural life we accept the madness, exactly as we accept the madness of the infant who claims (though in unutterable muttering) "I hallucinated that and it is part of mother who was there before I came along." (Winnicott, 1989, pp. 57–58)

In a similar way paintings on the walls of galleries at night disappear from our gaze but when we visit them, re-find the missing object, become alive because we are viewing them. Our vision of the painter's creative life put into a painting is captured by our gaze and we muse, imagine, trace our own patterns on the thing we try and see as it momentarily is possessed by us.

And when the culture–breast, a profound reason to continue to be alive in the world, disappears or shuts down, or worse still, is destroyed forever, like great Dresden and its special buildings and memories through generations, we become listless, empty and depressed. It is part of Covid symptomatology, which attacks our mental equilibrium and causes us great suffering, which then reverts back to an unconscious questioning about whether we were really held in our mother's arms all that time before.

Metaphor in literature: *Austerlitz* on the edge of impossibility

There are some times when some things are too painful and terrible, the impact of description too bald as the words slip away from their meanings, so that the ability of metaphor "to carry" meaning fails. How is the Holocaust able to be examined? A straightforward history of the concentration camps, Wannsee, details of train schedules, the routes of the trains, composition of carriages, how the round-up of Jews occurred, the clothes, tattoos, camp buildings, lists of everything, cannot do justice to how the Jews, long dead in their millions, thought about their living–dead incarcerations. In *Austerlitz*, W. G. Sebald instead evokes this impossibility of description by bypassing where his tale goes to, and instead the reader hears about the construction of train waiting rooms, the defences of impregnable castles that always fail, photographs of strange architecture, a sense of the photo as the frozen capture of a "then" moment. Photos of people live in the moment of the shutter release, and as such are indicative of a deadness, the then-ness of place and person, as displaced, meaning that very conclusion has to suffice to discombobulate the reader within the fronds of the text and photo, all long gone and not possible to bring to life in the now. It is too monumental to describe all the complex wefts and warps of the skein that is too frail to hold together an understanding that makes no sense. The extraordinary tale of *Austerlitz* does not offer an ordinary history. The narrative darts around in a way that seems to express a free-associative discourse, even one that appeals to a psychoanalytic engagement. Yet the narrative stays in the dark as the reader tries to connect the pieces. The seemingly seamless account keeps returning to what was beneath the very structures that are engaged with and we learn many things about the different uses through times such as the change of use of massive fortifications or what is beneath a church or a main train station.

And the narrative darkens as if the journey undertaken is similar to the Stations of the Cross which is, of course, the strange and yet appropriate metaphor for a travelling Jew. Yet for all the formidable knowledge offered, we do not really know Austerlitz, which perhaps captures an ever essence—a mere hint of what his mind disallows him and us to see, as it is punctuated by breakdowns and intermittent hospitalisations, the contents of which is only silence.

Austerlitz's start, and its sudden stop, renders him essentially unknowable. Austerlitz tells a story to the narrator who then tells it to the reader, a device used by Proust in *À la recherche du temps perdu*, where, as much as we might desire it, Proust is *not* the narrator. Instead he writes as if the narrator has some characteristics of himself. This means that knowing the author can only be vaguely surmised, if at all. Yet we are kept away from "the heart of the matter"—the architecture of Austerlitz, as he invites the reader closer to ghosts, monsters and madness. For instance, the dread of Liverpool station can be derived from it having been, when he was able to remember it, the place where he arrived in London off the Kindertransport from Prague. It was the place where he lost his parents to the new foster-parents. "I felt at this time as if the dead were returning from exile and filling the twilight around me with their strangely slow but incessant to-ing and fro-ing". In time, Austerlitz reveals the layer beneath of the living dead walking around or carried in the deaths carts of Terezin.

To face the Medusa's gaze is to face death as well as trying to bring back the dead. The same is true of looking at any photograph which is always about *then*. The dead cannot return, and hence the paradox of looking for what can never be found in order to allow missing bits to be placed into the absence at his core, that Austerlitz feels is his right and duty. Yet the long dead can neither be saved nor buried, leaving only the option of mourning as the replacement for madness.

And the narrative moves progressively and intensely to a photograph of young Jacques Austerlitz reproduced on the book's cover. Austerlitz narrates looking now at his self-image then, when he still had parents.

The horror now of Sebald's narratory device is to allow the reader to believe that this is a real and authentic moment as we can even infer the image of the eyes of his mother reflected in his own. Jacques Austerlitz is but a fictional character and that photograph cannot be him or anything to do with his mother's gaze. It exists only, power-fully, as a metaphor, as actually the whole narrative and narration of Austerlitz is but a story. In Sebald's literary archive in Marbach, outside Stuttgart, the reader can find an ordinary photographic card of this boy with, on the reverse, "Stockport: 30p" written in ink. Little Austerlitz is but the image of a boy who probably lived in Stockport, England.

Now identities slide away as Agatha is shown the picture. We are now taken to a very dark place indeed where the sense of the possibility of a salvatory atmosphere crystallises for Austerlitz. Yet all is but meta-phor. It is but a story.

And what has this to do with severe trauma? I think the idea that such analytic treatment is about gathering the pieces of the unconscious psychosomatic fragments so that the mosaic can, in some way, be under-stood, felt mourned, and recovered from is an all too emotional kind of countertransference reaction to the severity of the emptiness that some analysands bring to analysis. For me, the task of re-finding lost frag-ments may include finding out secrets that some elderly relatives had not thought necessary to reveal or had protected both themselves and the next generation from their impact.

Perhaps the place analysis can take the dyad to is close to the *black hole* of profound devastation, to weep, to mourn. And to realise that phantasies going into the future do not address the blackness of the his-tory which has cruelly wiped out grandparents, parents, siblings, leav-ing a black hole inside the survivor (and hence guilt). Now the analytic task is to visit that hard-found horrid knowledge and to digest the then-ness and its future as a missingness inside the analysand. And so the enormous value of metaphor becomes clearer, as within the digestion is the possibility for stories. It is stories that we tell and teach children early on and it is what many adults continue to learn from by reading storybooks. This is the final task that the analysis can help solve if the analysand is brave enough to be beside the brave-enough analyst look-ing into the dark irrecoverable empty space. This, I think, is the profun-dity of Sebald, who instead of writing his memoir of the little German boy born in 1944 and growing up detached from a father who served in the Wehrmacht and was a prisoner of war until 1947, learnt about the Holocaust at school, and recalled that no one knew how to explain what they had just seen. His novel is about just that.

As a coda, Sebald, near the end of the narrative, describes Austerlitz as looking for traces of his father at the new Bibliothèque nationale de France in Paris. This was built on the site of a huge warehouse at Austerlitz-Tolbiac that in 1943 to 1944 collected all the objects and loot stolen from thousands of Parisian Jews, their houses systematically emptied as they were gathered to Drancy en route to Auschwitz. As Walter Benjamin wrote: "There is no document of civilisation which is not at the same time a document of barbarianism". And this was undoubtedly the destination when Agatha Austerlitz was almost certainly "sent East" in 1944, and the place that Maximilian Aychenwald was almost certainly sent to from the French camp in Gurs in 1942, to Auschwitz the place never mentioned in the book but which is by metaphoricity implicit on every page of the book.

Conclusion

I have taken you on a walk around seemingly different themes, yet all of them contain a sense of alienation. It is the sense of being in a state of alienation that is so difficult, at times, for the human subject, necessitating special measures on the part of the individual to manage, and even, sometimes, to bear to stay alive. St Christopher has been paired with the Erl-King—the Divine and the Perverse are also a pair, often each being a stranger to the other.

The body bearing to carry the weight that the mind cannot bear is also a stranger to its master. Can we feel what has happened?

The self enjoying the city of today, unable to see the subtle traces of the past violence covered over in its reconstruction is another form of *xenos*. Can we see what has happened?

Who carries the heavy load and who does it belong to through the generations?

Metamorphosen was Strauss' form of metaphor as his music carries the immense loss of European culture to the ear of the listener … can we hear what has happened when it has been lost?

Analysis is always about the finding and re-finding of lost objects in the unconscious. More than anything is the importance of the analyst being in communication as the *flâneur* of his own unconscious as the best guide to analytic process and far deeper than our theories.

CHAPTER 2

Velázquez and the transmission of psychoanalysis*

> *In attempting to uncover the deepest strata of Western culture, I am restoring to our silent and apparently immobile soil its rifts, its instability, its flaws; and it is the same ground that is once more stirring under our feet.*
>
> Foucault, *The Order of Things*, p. xxvi

In this chapter I will examine some problems of transmission of power using two main examples. The first is from seventeenth-century Spain, when King Philip IV had the problem of his succession following the early death of Crown Prince Balthazar. The relationship between Philip and his court painter Velázquez is examined through Velázquez's painting *Las Meninas*. The second example is from 1936, when the Nazis annexed the Berlin Psychoanalytic Society, substituting a Nazi, Matthias Göring (Reichsmarschall Hermann Göring's cousin), as leader, who then deliberately wiped out psychoanalysis, seeing it as a Jewish, Freudian science. Germany invaded Austria on 12 March 1938, and the

---

* This chapter was first presented as a paper at a memorial conference at University College London, 2019.

Viennese Psychoanalytic Society chose a different route on the following day, when Freud and its members voted to close itself down. After the Second World War, the DPG (German Psychoanalytic Society) was de-legitimised and closed by the International Psychoanalytic Association.

Some artists have a capacity to have profound resonances and even offer incisive commentaries about society that carry a creative trans-mission over centuries. Art can provide a focus for "speaking out", which we are very much in need of, as much of today's world returns to old totalitarian habits.

Velázquez's *Las Meninas* was painted in 1656 in his studio at the Alcazar, formerly the rooms of Balthazar, the crown prince and only son of King Philip IV of Spain and his first wife Elisabeth of France. Balthazar died of smallpox aged fourteen in 1646. Five years later the Infanta Margarita Theresa was born, and five years after that was to fea-ture in the centre of *Las Meninas*. From 1653 to 1659 a series of portraits of the Infanta were painted, and three were sent to the Imperial court in Vienna, as without a male heir the court of Spain needed to make an alliance. Ten years later Margarita was married to Leopold Emperor of Austria. It was stipulated that she should maintain her position in the line of succession to the Spanish throne and would pass her rights to her descendants. *Las Meninas*, the most famous picture of the series, con-tains much to do with the concerns and even the underlying anxieties of the court for the future transmission of power of kingship.

By examining some of the elements of this painting I want to frame a particular and important element in Anne-Marie Sandler's psychoana-lytic life, namely her determination to return to her neglected German mother tongue in order to transmit psychoanalysis to the Nazified DPG after the Second World War. It needs to be admitted that this was not a strategic plan of hers. Rather, it came to her slowly, alongside a dawning realisation that her cessation of speaking and understanding German (which all along she perceived as a self-deception, as she could speak it to her German grandparents) was perched alongside her wish to be of use to the neglect of depth psychoanalysis within those colleagues and friends in the DPG whose analytic roots had been torn up. And for this she was required to reattach her command of the German tongue.

* * *

Figure 5. *Las Meninas*, Diego Velázquez, 1656

His king honoured Velázquez by allowing him to occupy Balthazar's apartment as his studio. This is the locus of *Las Meninas*. The infanta in the centre of the painting is psychologically placed where the prince would have been located, making the picture a remembrance, in his former room, of what was not to be. Mourning concealed is central to the meaning of *Las Meninas*, with the implicit potential crisis of what will happen to Spain without a future leadership. After her marriage, Margarita kept her Spanish language and customs and did not speak German, leading to anti-Spanish sentiment among the imperial court.

After her death the rights of inheritance were disputed both by Emperor Leopold I and King Louis XIV of France, son-in-law of King Philip IV, leading to the War of Spanish Succession. Uniting France and Spain under one monarch would upset the balance of power, such that other European powers would take steps to prevent it. Its outcome was the creation of the Spanish branch of the House of Bourbon in the person of King Philip V, Margarita's great nephew.

Las Meninas is complex, and the centre of the painting seems unclear, with Velázquez present in a self-portrait while painting on the canvas, which is concealed from view, a court scene to his left with the infanta as well as the king and queen who, represented in the mirror, are standing in the position of the onlooker, gazing at the scene. Evidence against the royal couple being the subject of the hidden canvas is that a courtier is opening a door at the back as their Majesties are about to pass through the scene. As in analysis, at times eyes gaze on the parents, even though for most of the time the scenes do not seem to contain their physical presence. The room is rather dark, with the only other light source coming through an opened shutter to the right of the picture, the rest being closed. Later Picasso will open all the shutters, throwing light on his homage.

Velázquez paints himself larger than all other figures and is Gulliver to the Lilliputian king—a somewhat dangerous statement. This is made worse, in a court that was particularly concerned with pecking order and strict dress code, by exposing the bare canvas-back to the king as if the painter exposes his backside without breeches to the royals. The canvas-back, rough and unconcealed without its frame, certainly is a fracture of the courtly setting, letting in a different sort of light against the dark forms. It is a radical idea within the heart of the painting. And, realising the deep relationship and friendship between Philip and Velázquez, the painter can express truth to power. Foucault writes that "The knowledge in the picture is no longer self-referential but invites the participation of the spectator in an endless process of representation" (1966, p. xxii). This makes the picture dynamic, with us the spectators as part of its emotional fabric—the audience is not just a passive observer of those times. Standing in front of the picture in the Prado, the visitor stands in the place of the royals, which gives an eerie, heady affect of being in the present moment with this old object. Again Foucault: "Thus, in every culture, between the use of what one might call the ordering codes and reflections upon order itself, there is the pure experience of order and of its modes of being" (ibid., p. xxiii).

The modernity of *Las Meninas* has been captured at various times, both by other painters as well as commentators who take Velázquez's masterpiece into their own times. Picasso, also Spanish, painted his "Velázquez" in the last five months of 1957, with a series of fifty-eight works, of which forty-five are interpretations of *Las Meninas*, from his studio of La Californie in Cannes. Picasso, too, is commentating on contemporary events in Spain, from his exile in France, away from Franco. The reverberations of the Spanish Civil War had not abated and *Guernica*, Picasso's iconic homage, still hung away from its designated home in Madrid. Picasso was now involved in campaigning for amnesty for the release of Spanish Republicans still imprisoned by Spain eighteen years beyond the end of the civil war.

Picasso dedicated the whole series to his secretary, Jamie Sabartes, and said to him in 1950:

> If someone wanted to copy *Las Meninas* entirely in good faith, for example and if that one was me, I would say. what if you put them a little more to the right or left? I'll try it my way, forgetting about Velázquez. The test would surely bring me to modify or change the light because of having changed the position of a character. So, little by little, that would be a detestable Meninas for a traditional painter, but it would be my Meninas.[1]

And Picasso's *Las Meninas* has the moustache of Franco mockingly painted on the female dwarf's face. The point is that great art is not about looking at the then of when it was painted, as a form of looking backwards in time, but to have a resonance for today's audiences that can oscillate a social–political presence now.

Later still, in 1973, Richard Hamilton would make an extraordinary print, *Picasso's Meninas* in honour of his ninetieth birthday. Hamilton, the inventor of Pop Art, paid homage by evincing every graphic style of Picasso's inventions (Blue, Harlequin, Analytical Cubism, Primitive to Neo-Classical). Velázquez's figure is exchanged for Picasso, who has

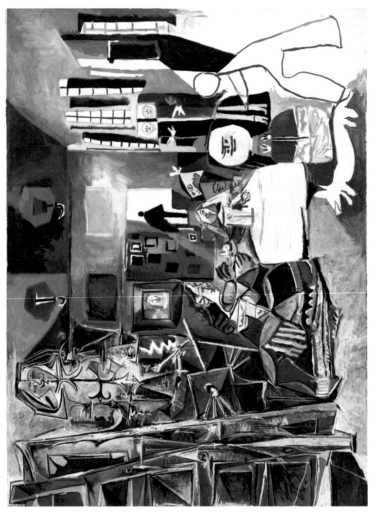

Figure 6. Pablo Picasso, *Las Meninas*, Cannes, 17 August 1957 © Succession Picasso/DACS, London 2024. Oil on canvas, 194 × 260 cm, Museu Picasso, Barcelona. Gift of Pablo Picasso, 1968. MPB 70.433. Museu Picasso, Barcelona. Photo: Fotogasull. Reproduced under licence

a hammer and sickle replacing the red cross of Santiago on his chest. A dying bull replaces the mastiff. Hamilton replaces the king and queen with himself and his wife-to-be. In this way he points out that we are standing in the centre of the space in the picture, as if, momentarily, we have become rulers of Spain, preoccupied with the future and the transmission of power. We, the people, continue to be empowered by Velázquez's masterpiece, in relation to the order of things.

Figure 7. Richard Hamilton, *Picasso's Meninas*, 1973 © R. Hamilton. All rights reserved, DACS 2024. Photo: Tate. Reproduced under licence

Anne-Marie Sandler

I first met and was befriended by Anne-Marie when I was an analytic candidate in 1982. Her stepdaughter Trudy had invited my family and me to go to stay with the Sandlers at Cipières in the south of France. Like so many who met her, I took to her, initially I suspect because she showed an interest in me as myself, rather than my lowly position as candidate of the British Psychoanalytical Society. Much later we would meet regularly for a Sunday morning whisky when I was vice president of the European Psychoanalytic Federation, of which she had been president and more recently when I was on the board of the IPA. She always revealed new ways of seeing complex objects, together with some charm at how to speak about near impossible political paradoxes. Later in her life she had discovered a certain natural politic, which, combined with that charm, her capacity to see the concerns of different clinical and political positions, and her readiness to effect a coming together, taught me much of the art of the possible.

Although born in Geneva, where she lived until moving to London in her twenties, both the maternal and paternal sides of her family were German Jews: her father from Berlin and mother from Hamburg. Her family survived the Holocaust due to the perspicacity of her paternal grandfather, leaving Germany in 1907 for Lausanne as he refused to stay in a land that prevented Jews from becoming civil servants. Every single one of her maternal grandmother's relatives who remained in Germany died in the Holocaust.

> By the time I was a young school child I was most impressed, when coming home in the afternoons having been out with my parents or at school, to be greeted by two very smart policemen. One policeman stood guard for the British Embassy, which happened to be on one side of the apartment building in which I lived. The other stood guard for the German Embassy, which was on the other side of our building. I remember thinking that we must be very important people to have our house guarded on both sides by policemen! At the time I could not, of course, appreciate the irony of these circumstances. (Sandler, private biography[2])

Perhaps this is an early picture of her being able to differentiate two separate and antagonistic positions, which were both on guard. Anne-Marie was brought up bilingual in French and German. In 1933, her father told the children that Hitler had become the leader of Germany, and that he was a bully, persecuting Jews. The German nanny, deciding that she was unable to work for Jews, suddenly left because "the wonderful Führer needed her help". Soon after, Anne-Marie lost her ability to speak and understand German. Yet when, in 1938, her maternal grandparents arrived in Geneva following *Kristallnacht*, she and her brother would only speak German with them.

> This would mean that as soon as I stepped through their door on Thursday afternoons, I could speak German but from six o'clock, when we left, I could not! I would open their door and German would tumble from my mouth, but as soon as the door closed, my brother and I spoke exclusively in French. I have no idea how I managed this split. (ibid.)

Yet the Jew in Anne-Marie found fertile ways to come to terms with her "split" of loving German culture and hating and fearing German anti-Semitism. Later, living in London, she was quick to feel British forms of anti-Semitism, particularly when investigating public schools for her children. Despite the hidden Jewish quotas, she would identify herself as Jewish in a take-it-or-leave-it way with headmistresses and masters, often leaving her husband Joe to rescue the situations in some "crafty way". But the recognition of the German part of her mother tongue was linked to shame of Jewishness.

The Jerusalem Congress of 1977

At the 1977 IPA Congress in Jerusalem the President of the German Society (DPG) Dr de Boor invited the IPA to consider Berlin as the next host, informing the assembly that "the Unter den Linden was not quite as famous as before the war", but he could assure that the part under Western control was wonderful, with many restaurants and cafes. Not a word about the Nazi era was mentioned. Anne-Marie Sandler writes:

I was quite bewildered and incensed by the tone of this invitation. Was Dr de Boor not aware that he was speaking to an audience composed of many Jews for whom the fact that the IPA had chosen Jerusalem for that Congress had a special and profound meaning? Dr de Boor, whose German manner was so familiar and whom I had found so likeable, had suddenly become for me an insensitive man … Despite my shyness and my sense of still being quite a junior member of the psychoanalytic community, I felt compelled to stand up and share my feelings of dismay. I must have sounded very emotional but I said that I was quite amazed at Dr de Boor's invitation. How could he invite us to come to Germany without being aware that, for the majority of the audience in the hall, coming to Berlin would raise profound conflicts? It would not be easy for most Jewish people to visit the land of the Holocaust. The fact that the past was not mentioned in any way, only the restaurants and the charms of Berlin, felt most offensive to me. To my great surprise, I received a standing ovation. (Private autobiography)

The Mitscherlichs' thesis in their book *The Inability to Mourn* (1967) was still alive, such that a senior German analyst had "forgotten" the Nazi era and its impact on Jews and psychoanalysis. Such profound cover-up at the heart of much German psychoanalysis became the tool that eventually enabled Anne-Marie both to confront German analysis by teaching and simultaneously to begin to understand what was behind her own internal split in not understanding or speaking German.

A seminal conversation with Serge Lebovici was about her implacable hostility to visiting Germany and speaking German.

Was it not time to turn the page, especially as most of the perpetrators of the atrocities were either dead or old men by now? This conversation—with a man who had spent the war in hiding and whose father had been shot dead by the Nazis—made me think anew. (ibid.)

She became aware of her own guilt and shame at having been safe throughout those terrible war years, which fuelled her rigid refusal to cross the border to Germany. In Switzerland she had lived just 300 metres from the German border and saw the flow of children and adults seeking safety.

> It was as if I *had* to show how indignant I was in order to bury even deeper my secret but powerful *attraction* to things German. Worse than this, I had always been privately grateful and relieved that I did not appear Jewish! I realised how force-fully I had banned my secret attachment to Germany from my consciousness and how terrified I was of being discovered! I was convinced that if people knew, I would be totally discredited and regarded as a traitor and a coward. (ibid.)

Transmission of psychoanalysis? Or, what happened to the Berlin Society?

Stephen Frosch (2005) has written about "the ferocious silence" about the Nazification of the Berlin Society and its turning away from Freudian psychoanalysis. This was the legacy that Anne-Marie heard de Boor supporting. As Frosch describes:

> The controversy has been and remains one between those who see the Nazi period as an aberration in which psychoanalysis was destroyed and therefore had to be recreated anew in Germany, and those who argue about a "continuity", that however much it was constrained by its Nazi masters, psychoanalysis continued and possibly—at least as a form of psychotherapy—flourished. This controversy was part of the post-war debate between the two German institutions claiming psychoanalytic legitimacy. The Deutsche Psychoanalytische Gesellschaft (DPG), which was the "original" group, claimed that psychoanalysis had been "saved" by its members during the war. The Deutsche Psychoanalytische Vereinigung (DPV), which split from the DPG largely on issues of the "purity" of psychoanalytic practice and which was recognised by the IPA in 1951 (Bibring, 1952), with Carl Müller-Braunschweig as its leader, argued that psychoanalysis had been destroyed and that a new organisation was needed to resurrect it. (Frosch, 2005)

In 1935 Boehm and Müller-Braunschweig attempted to persuade the Nazis that psychoanalysis could be divorced from its Jewish origins and its socialist associations to try to ensure its survival in Germany. For the Nazis, the proportion of Jewish analysts in the DPG made it very likely that their organisation would be banned, and it was argued that for the sake of the survival of the DPG, the Jewish analysts had to go. Ernest Jones sent telegrams in November and December 1935 urging the Jewish analysts to resign and chaired the meeting that finally provoked them to do so. The DPG was "Aryanised" by the end of 1935, nearly three years before other Jewish professionals, such as lawyers and doctors, were excluded from their equivalent organisations. Many non-Jewish colleagues embraced the exclusion of the Jews with some enthusiasm, whether through fear of being associated with the specifically derogated marginality of the Jews, or through active anti-Semitism. An ironic outcome was most of the Jewish analysts, deprived of their livelihood, left Germany before the Holocaust (although fifteen did die in the concentration camps, as Jones confirmed at the first post-war International Congress (A. Freud, 1949)). Jones' heroic part in getting them out and relocating them also had an intentional yet failing strategy of attempting to appease the Nazis.

In February 1936, Boehm, leader of the analysts who stayed with the DPG, was told by the Ministry of Culture that psychoanalysis would be allowed to continue if the Berlin Psychoanalytic Institute would join with other branches of psychotherapy in an organisation under Matthias Göring's leadership, with a commitment to developing a "new German psychotherapy" (Goggin & Goggin, 2001, p. 104).

The DPG handed its building to the Göring Institute, combining psychoanalytic training with that of other psychotherapies. In October 1936, Göring gave his inaugural remarks on the new German psychotherapy, which was to be founded on a non-Freudian, pro-Nazi and anti-Semitic basis; the reading of *Mein Kampf* was made an obligatory part of the training and any remaining Jews were excluded. The survival of psychoanalysis in the Third Reich would be bound up with both Göring the person and his Nazi psychotherapy organisation as the DPG dissolved itself on 19 November 1938 and its former members became part of Work Group A in the Deutsche Institut fur Psychologische Forshung und Psychotherapie (Brecht et al., 1985, p. 140).

As Frosch shows,

> Göring answers the question of, "how *psychoanalysis*, a very modern branch of medicine, could once have had *so destructive an effect?*" His answer is that, "since Freud, it has been almost exclusively the domain of *Jewish doctors*". Freud, as a Jew, could not understand that the unconscious is not a domain of repressed sexual activity, but the "foundation of life", the source of creativity.
>
> It is clear that it is precisely in a field of work like that of the mind that Judaism could bring its destructive influence to bear most fruitfully. For the Jews, psychotherapy became a business, and the poisoning of mental life a necessity, so that they could then undertake to cure the poison. *Today a thoroughly German form of psychotherapy has been developed.* (Frosch, ibid.)

The "new German psychotherapy" aimed to "strengthen belief in the meaning of life and reinforce the link with the higher world of values; it was to convey to the patient the consciousness of being bound and incorporated into the common destiny of the German people" (Brecht et al., 1985, p. 152).

> It is clear from this that what was being proposed was a psychology without the critical doubt so central to Freud— without, that is, something of what might be thought of as its "Jewish" heritage. Instead, the objective of psychotherapy was to facilitate in the patient the discovery of an unconscious energy and purpose, which could be activated in the service of the German state. (Frosch, ibid.)

Here is a profound fracture in transmission of psychoanalysis.

* * *

But what was the IPA to do with the earlier Nazification of psychoanalysis in Germany? The 34th IPA Congress was held in Hamburg in 1985. I had qualified as an analyst with some eighteen months standing and had to deal with my sharp Jewish ambivalences about visiting Germany. I had grown up with a father who abhorred buying any German goods from its post-war recovery. Eventually I decided that if my own analysis could not withstand the weight of the waves of remembrances of the dead and its perpetrators, then how could I function as an analyst, without mourning and coming to terms with my unconscious mind?

In Hamburg I met a young German candidate training in the German Psychoanalytic Association (DPV), which had been founded by Müller-Braunschweig. Discussing our different trainings, she told me a very disturbing story. One of her training patients, a potter, had given her as a Christmas present a piece of pottery that she had made. Her older training analyst had communicated to her that he would sooner throw it against the wall than accept such a gift. This was a shocking revelation of something that I instantly realised was nothing to do with psychoanalysis, rather it contained an attack on the potential creativity within an analytic encounter. I asked her if she knew what that analyst had done in the war. She did not, but our conversation made her dare to think the—until-then impossible thought—that he may have been a party member or had grown up in a Nazi-supporting family during the war.

Since then, and having taught much in Eastern Europe and South Africa, I have continued to realise the importance of the imagination of what one's trainers have done in earlier conflicts, including facing reality as essential in order to deal with the internal paranoia arising from growing up in a family with such residues. And such matters will be an interpenetrating (perhaps non-harmonious) mix up, to misquote Balint, containing phantasy and what might have been the real that needs to be teased out in an analysis. The background noises of the Nazi, Stalinist, Apartheid or Maoist constructions in the unconscious really do need to be faced and determined. Otherwise, a normative paranoia will remain at the heart of the developing analyst, which may interfere with the free-floating listening of the analyst to their patient. Winnicott's profound meditation about the destruction of the analyst resonates as "yes you have killed me, and I have survived".

A diversion

I will now look at an example of a transgenerational transmission of authoritarian hatred and control.

In the summer of 1973, Marie Langer received a copy of *Vos Operaria*, a clandestine publication of the Brazilian communist party containing an article on torturers. The following paragraph was highlighted:

> Another army officer who is part of the team of torturers is lieutenant-doctor Amilcar Lobo Moreira. This officer advises the torturers concerning the physical resistance of the political prisoner. On the other hand, as a psychoanalyst, he is responsible for the "monitoring" [*acompanhamento*] of the mental health of the tortured person, and for the best way of extracting confessions from him. (Langer & Bauleo, 1973, p. 93)

At the bottom of the page, an anonymous handwritten note supplied further details on the psychoanalyst in question:

> psychoanalyst in training of the Psychoanalytic Society of Rio de Janeiro—his analyst: Leao Cabernite—his address: rua Gén. Miguel Ferreira, 97 Jacarepagua (catalogued in the register of the Brazilian Association of Psychoanalysis). (Besserman Vianna, 1994, p. 270)

Lobo was a candidate in training analysis with Dr Cabernite, who was President of the Rio de Janeiro Psychoanalytic Society, and who refused to stop the training analysis. The analyst was a silent accomplice to the torturer, as if it had nothing to do with analytic training. The story is well documented (Nobus, 2016) and eventually the candidate was removed, as in time so too was Cabernite from the Rio Psychoanalytic Society.

In 1928, Werner Kemper, a German physician, was a candidate in analysis with Müller-Braunschweig, and became a regular member of the DPG in 1933.[3] Earlier, he fought in WWI on the Western Front, at one time being buried alive in an explosion. In 1934, he was dean of the Berlin Psychoanalytic Institute and in 1936 a board member of the DPG, at the time of Göring's takeover of the analytic society. He managed the Polyclinic from 1942 to 1946. In 1947 he became director of the DPG's Institute for Psychotherapy. One year later, in 1948, with the support of Ernest Jones, he departed for Brazil and became the first training analyst in Rio de Janeiro. It is not clear why he moved so quickly, having become the director of training at the DPG. Following being a member for eleven years in the Nazi Berlin Society, he now became the training analyst of Cabernite. Is it surprising that, years later, Cabernite, now a training analyst as well as President of the Rio Psychoanalytic Society had a corrupt blind spot to the meanings and implications of a candidate in analytic training simultaneously being a state torturer? Here in all its horror is an example of transgenerational trauma, which allowed a strand of Nazi psychotherapy training with its own corrupt ethics to infect the Rio psychoanalytic training. Following the initial exposure of Lobo Amilcar and his analyst accomplice, it needs to be reported that it took the IPA twenty years to reach a position of taking responsibility and authority for appropriate sanctions, and both Amilcar and Cabernite were thrown out of the Rio Society. Ethics is an essential core of clinical psychoanalysis, and it is essential that it is included in the transmission of psychoanalysis.

A second diversion: *documenta* 1955 and its origins

From its establishment in 1955, the makers of *documenta* sought to offer insights into current trends in art and to document the spirit of the times of the Federal Republic of Germany in the second half of the twentieth century. The first art exhibition was in Kassel, still in ruins after the war. The venue was also very close to the East German border. The placement of the first post-war exhibition of German art was also a broadcast of the idea of freedom in art and beyond to East Germany nearby and communist Russia beyond: a clear and unambiguous use of art and culture as a political tool towards the East as part of the tactics of the Cold War.

It is important to note the use that the Nazis made of German modernist art. Internationally renowned artists' work, particularly by Jewish and communist artists, were removed from state museums and banned as an insult to German feelings. Those designated as degenerate artists were dismissed from teaching positions and forbidden to exhibit or sell their art. *Degenerate Art* was the title of a Nazi exhibition held in Munich in 1937. It was designed to inflame public opinion against Modernism and as a propaganda tool travelled to several cities in Germany and Austria. Establishing *documenta* was a reply to the Nazification of that art. The former West German President Theodore Huss stated: "You can't make culture with politics, but maybe you can make politics with culture".

This was recently put in doubt at the recent *documenta: Politics and Art in Berlin* (2021),[4] which examined what art was championed and what was left out. What was ignored was art by women and artists of colour. Ten of the original organisers of *documenta* were either Nazi party members in the SS or SA. The second show in 1959 involved six former Nazis; the third, in 1964, involved fifteen. "The presence of former National Socialists in positions of power had disturbing and defining effects on what art was shown" (*documenta* catalogue, 2021). Wegner Haftmann, a co-founder, was a Nazi party member and involved in the first three *documenta*. The other co-founder, Arnold Bode, likely knew that he was surrounded by Nazis, according to Juliet Voss, a co-curator in 2021. Artists who spoke of or who experienced the Holocaust were excluded, and Jewish artists murdered by the Nazis were not shown in Kassel in 1955.

So what had been created as a new transmission of art in culture carried within itself from the beginning the Nazi culture of anti-Semitism, racism and misogyny. And it took until 2021 for the present *documenta* to examine its establishment and throw a dark light on what has been regarded as a "new beginning" of the transmission of a previously perverted art culture.

Facing the fracture of transmission

Anne-Marie Sandler was invited to attend a meeting of the DPG at Bad Sonen in 1991. She had an eruption of horrific phantasies as her "anxiety gave way to irrational fear and she felt terrified at the thought of facing elderly men" (Sandler, private autobiography). In her mind, they were the young Nazis of the past who raped Jewish women and killed any Jews they came across. The elderly women she imagined as large blonde guards in the concentration camps who had tormented the inmates. "I have gradually become aware, partly as a result of writing this memoir, how much I have repressed and distorted about this first official visit" (Sandler, ibid.). This powerful realisation pulled from her unconscious is a position that we all need to dare to face—our own prejudices of the other, in all its racist, anti-Semitic, anti-immigrant alterities.

From that weekend experience in which her DPG colleagues warmly welcomed engaging with a senior analyst willing to present *her own* five-times-a-week psychoanalytic clinical work came regular visits three times a year, and a true engagement with the DPG. Her anxiety continued as she came to realise that the Kosestrasse—the venue where the seminars took place—had been the home of the Nazis' therapeutic clinic. Yet slowly she decided to face her German colleagues who wished to learn psychoanalysis from her, by facing her own prejudices against "them" and finding ways to rehabilitate the old centre of psychoanalysis—the Berlin Society.

Later came invitations from the Stuttgart Institute and groups of colleagues in Nuremberg, Bremen, Hamburg, Heligolander, Ufer and Göttingen. In 1997 she was made an honorary member of the DPG.

By 1999, a clear majority of DPG members—feeling increasingly isolated from the international psychoanalytic world—were determined to make another attempt to be accepted as an IPA Component Society. In order to take forward the DPG reapplication process, a new IPA body was formed, known as the Exploratory Committee and Anne-Marie was invited to be its chairman. Ultimately it was agreed that every DPG member who wished to be part of the IPA had to have their work evaluated by members of the Exploratory Committee. At the 2001 IPA Congress in Nice, a sizable group of DPG members attended under the leadership of Franz Wellendorf. After a prolonged and painful discussion from the floor, the DPG was accepted with twenty-seven members as a "Provisional Society of the Board".

Several obstacles to full membership remained. The most important of these was the DPG's concern to avoid at all costs a split between those of its members who wished to fulfil the requirements of IPA membership and those who did not. It took several years of further discussion and hard work before an innovative solution was reached. A two-track training model was agreed, one track preparing for membership of the IPA/DPG and the other for membership of the DPG alone. Every single would-be DPG/IPA analyst presented their credentials for approval, sharing their analytic work with a panel composed of members of the Exploration Committee and Training Analysts from the DPG. A particularly important requirement was that each analyst had seen at least one patient for a minimum of a year, four times a week.

While for some DPG members this was already standard practice, the norm for most had been to see patients on a three-times-a-week basis so this expectation represented a significant change of depth. A total of 145 DPG analysts, sixty-two of whom were Training Analysts, gained approval, and at the 2009 Chicago Congress, the DPG was finally recognised as a full Component Society of the IPA. The fracture in analytic transmission in the DPG was now restored.

Anne-Marie had found ways to put depth psychoanalysis back into the centre, heart and desire of the DPG, and with her adroit political sense steered it—almost seventy-five years after the annihilation by the Nazis of the DPG and the destruction of German psychoanalysis—so that the DPG could take its place once again within the international psychoanalytic community. For her, and for many other analysts in Germany and beyond, this was a deeply moving moment.

This was and is a very important achievement by Anne-Marie, and by discussing it here in such detail I want to do homage to her capacities to go to Germany, manage a profoundly difficult, near-destroyed analytic situation following its perversion by the Nazis, and resurrect it. And yet we need to keep vigilant in these dark times in Europe and beyond, where fascism, alterity, lying and deceit are again becoming the norm, as is shown by increases in acts of racism and anti-Semitism (Sklar, 2019). Recently a senior German psychoanalyst, a member of the DPV, has come out as being a member of the very right-wing AfD party, probably to act as a receptacle for gathering similar intolerant colleagues. I tell you this because I cannot end this chapter with the pleasurable complacency of the good, but rather a warning that, as citizens' minds can be taken over by the group, as Freud wrote so long ago, and despite the Mitscherlichs' warning to their countrymen, our analytic community needs to take stands in ways that were not understood deeply enough or were impossible to think in the 1930s.

Today we are living in a world in which it is axiomatic that Trump and other politicians lie, and daily the truth suffers, ignored by power. Scientific discourse around the real knowledge of global warming is similarly dismissed as fake news, and the Amazon and California have been burning. Those with knowledge are dismissed as "so-called experts" with the sense that real knowledge is to be disbelieved by the people. When the Berlin Psychoanalytic Society was taken over, psychoanalysis as expertise was destroyed, inculcating a perverse interior to the analytic shell that had been acquired. Anne-Marie returned to the analytic core and over many years and innumerable case presentations, particularly of intense four- and five-times-weekly analysis as a necessity to understand and analyse ill patients, returned the truth of analytic knowledge back into the minds of colleagues from the DPG. Her presentations from her own depth cases separated psychoanalysis from embedded forms of unconscious Nazi psychotherapy.

Yet as Foucault warns in the opening epigram of this chapter, "it is the same ground that is once more stirring under our feet". And in our recent times, politics in the IPA have now opened up the Eitingon training of three to five analytic sessions weekly, potentially and arguably altering the potential for depth of analytic training. This is happening alongside the wide-ranging pull towards right-wing politics and attacks on alterity in the United States and throughout Europe with the rise in racism and anti-Semitism.

Putting Freud back in the centre does not mean that psychoanalysis is a Jewish science. Psychotherapy tainted in Germany by the Göring Institute becoming a Jew-free institution had smeared therapy with an anti-Semitism that was extremely difficult to differentiate from therapeutics. The move to recreate thinking about depth analysis was the linchpin around which Anne-Marie based her revolutionary return to Germany, which required her re-finding her mother tongue in order to speak psychoanalysis, and not psychotherapy, thus returning the transmission of psychoanalysis from the point where it had been fractured. These complexities required noticing and mourning the destruction of core analytic values and ethics that led to a freedom to return to psychoanalysis and a freedom for her to return to her mother tongue.

* * *

And so back to *Las Meninas*, where Velázquez's picture invites reflections on how a particular society can begin to manage its profound anxieties about "what will become of us" without a leader, a king or an identity. The death of the heir apparent led the court of Spain to look to alliances with France and Vienna by marrying off the infanta to obtain security. The mourning in the painting is concealed in the place in which it takes place, namely the dead Bartolemeo's apartments given to Velázquez as his studio. Yet mourning does not necessarily mean that the old order need continue. Elizabeth I of England challenged the model that only men can be monarchs and became a most powerful queen-leader. And whatever else is contained in the complexity of *Las Meninas*, with a central role given to the infanta, it is also the human relationship between the largest figure, Velázquez, and his patron and friend, painted as a very small Philip, King of Spain, which articulates a silent truth about a capacity for people occupying different hierarchical positions to speak with each other about truth and power. In a world of nationalism and nostalgia there is no obligation to return to some past place as if that means an authentic renewal. An identity remaining fixed is often the problem to be understood and developed in analysis. And sometimes the issue is worse, when it emerges that the self has become psychically broken. The transmission of psychoanalysis became broken in Germany and required attachment back to its primary object— the unconscious.

Picasso, in his engagement with Velázquez's masterpiece, similarly re-articulates a profound argument with Franco and the Fascists, now about the need for freedom. This is a task that the creativity in and of art can perform. We return to such iconic paintings because within some of them we might glimpse unconscious representations that can help us human beings in our present conflicts by noticing psychic detachments, cruelties and the possibilities of "new beginnings". This is what cultural experience can do for us. And the re-finding of the lost threads can only occur in relation to mourning, in the individual, the group and society.

Reintegration: a parallel process

I will end by giving Anne-Marie the last words from her reflections on some of her life:

> In conclusion, I would like to return to where I started—the lifelong conflict caused by my painful attachment to Germany and my identity as a Jew. I have written a great deal about my work with German colleagues and particularly about my role in the re-acceptance of the DPG by the international

psychoanalytic community. In the course of helping the German Society reapply for IPA membership, I was continually confronted by the ambivalence of my feelings towards Germany. Yet, through engaging so closely with a wide range of German colleagues as they courageously went through the experience of being scrutinised and evaluated, I found myself identifying powerfully with them as human beings. They became no longer "Germans" but individual men and women who were struggling with their own complex reactions to this process, and with their own feelings about their history and identity. My involvement with and attachment to them has helped me finally to embrace my early and enduring attachment to all things German. The feelings that tormented me for so many years are now a source of pleasure and satisfaction. Through enabling a process of reconciliation in German psychoanalysis, following decades of estrangement, my own conflicting emotions have become reconciled. The feelings that, as a confused little girl I felt compelled to hide, even from myself, have been liberated and restored. For this I am deeply grateful. (Sandler, private autobiography)

CHAPTER 3

Francis Bacon and the radicality
of free association

It is a remarkable thing that the Ucs of one human being can react
upon that of another, without passing through the Cs.

Sigmund Freud, *The Unconscious* (1915e, p. 178)

The well-known train of thought in Freud's "On beginning the treatment" is "Act as though, for instance, you were a traveller sitting next to a window of a railway carriage and describing to someone inside the carriage the changing views which you see outside" (1913c, p. 135). What is still so remarkable about this description of the listening tool of free association is the banality of ordinary scenes that inexorably and inevitably lead the analytic pair to view a scene that neither analyst nor analysand could have imagined at the commencement of the session. For Freud, it is an investigation of the ordinary and of even little things. This is invariably surprising to the analysand, expecting erudition from the "wise analyst".

Psychoanalysis is formed by the Freudian Pair described by Bollas, trying or not trying to communicate beneath the surface of unconscious states of mind. For Freud, free association was not only speech, but patterns of talking and tonality, as well non-verbal expression and body movement. It does not just happen, rather the unexpected paths of free association allow for finding oneself speaking with freedom of expression as well as being in the act as a new state of freedom. The discourse is listened to by the analyst but also by the analysand, whose thinking has actually physically moved from the inside of the mind, through the vocal cords, and out of the mouth to being corporeally outside of the body. Now the thing in the mind can be heard again through the ears taking the sound patterns back inside the mind. Curiously, the free associations have been making their own journey out of the body and back again, somehow investing meaning in a more exalted way as "analytic dialogue". It can be worth trying to listen to oneself.

The words tossed out in free association invariably have different strata of meanings. We have already passed by the "train" of associations even before the actual being on a train is introduced. As if the unconscious was being prepared for the thought of associations. That last word contains the word "ass", so those who eschew the Freudian method are included, such that our simplistic method is for the asses indeed, or psychoanalysis is an ass for taking such little matters seriously. And that of course was Freud's point, that things from the unconscious are always pressing to get through to the surface but need to be noticed and decoded. Big words contain little words, and both can contain a musicality of connected feelings.

Alongside the fear of moving away from the position of aloneness, because of mistrust of the other, comes the disability of communicating. Instead, one can offer disdain, restraint or, at its most intense, being in a state of one person-ness (Rickman, 1951).[1] The state of mind of oneness, perceived when a regressed analysand does not notice the analyst as either being present or existing in the room, is a communication that insists on enacting being alone. Later it can be transformed to a state of Alone-in-the-Presence-of-the-Other, as Winnicott described, where there is the beginning of a risk of inclusion as a two-person relationship begins to come into formation.

The associations of words, thoughts and memories are invariably not being communicated if the analysand is particularly silent.

This leaves unconscious communication as a possibility. The state of oneness needs also be thought of as a representation of the baby or young child being pathologically alone from mother, through early neglect, not being desired, maternal death or something else. It can be a representation of the failure of basic trust following a psychosomatic attack by an adult on the child as described in Ferenczi's "Confusion of tongues" (1933).

Free association, affect and the body in Francis Bacon

> *Tell him that in my view Millet and Lhermitte are consequently the true painters, because they don't paint things as they are, examined drily and analytically, but as* they, *Millet, Lhermitte, Michelangelo, feel them.*
> Letter from Vincent Van Gogh to Theo Van Gogh, on or about
> 14 July 1895 (Jansen, Luitjen, & Bakker, 2009)

In my meanderings I will reflect on silent paintings that induce conscious and unconscious thoughts, free associations about how we look and think of art. I am not putting Bacon on the couch (a somewhat stupid and horrific idea), rather I am describing reactions, mine and others', to the experience of being under the gaze of his work. I am finding, in some of Bacon's paintings, not just representations of aggression, but unconscious links to desire for a violent father figure together with a female counterpart of the Furies of vengeance. Bacon's depictions can both horrify the viewer and also point to a voluptuous sexuality, and, for him, pleasure of dealing with such affect by turning it into sadism and masochism as part of a potentiality in being human. Or animal, as he liked to say, and from human being to being a piece of bacon. This in turn can be used as a lens to examine society with clarity, for instance Hitler and Nazism, as he does in a painting from *c.*1945, *Figure Getting Out of a Car*. The car is a precise, realistic image known to have been copied from a photograph of Hitler emerging from a Mercedes at a Nuremberg Rally, which is deeply disturbing and scary, with a long reaching head vomiting out filth (Sylvester, 2000, p. 18).

Figure 8. Francis Bacon, *Figure Getting Out of a Car*, *c.*1945 (First version of *Landscape with Car*, *c.*1945–46) © The Estate of Francis Bacon. All rights reserved. DACS 2024

This image predates Bacon's *Crucifixion*, which similarly shows the long-necked, frightening mouth of the Eumenides, the Furies, the goddesses of vengeance.

Beyond the frame of a painting, the violence of his living in fascistic times was well-noted by Bacon.

The 1944 triptych of *Three Studies for Figures at the Base of a Crucifixion* substituted the three Furies from Aeschylus' *Oresteia* for the Madonna and Mary Magdalene.

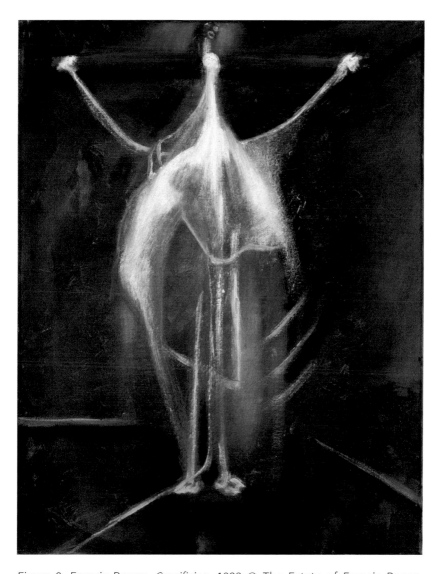

Figure 9. Francis Bacon, *Crucifixion*, 1933 © The Estate of Francis Bacon. All rights reserved, DACS/Artimage 2024. Photo: Prudence Cuming Associates Ltd.

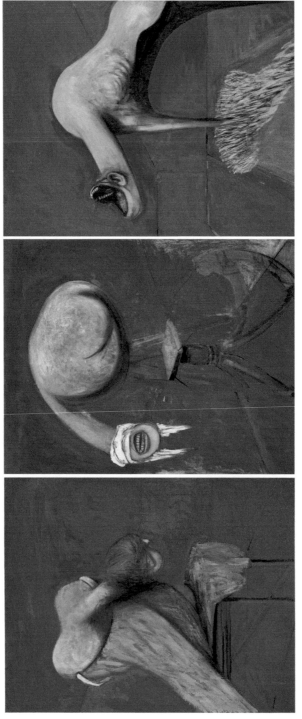

Figure 10. Francis Bacon, *Three Studies for Figures at the Base of a Crucifixion*, 1944. Photo: Tate © The Estate of Francis Bacon. All rights reserved. DACS 2024

The backgrounds are painted in a livid orange. The creature in the first panel, seated, hunched, is turned away. The central figure, long-necked, and blindfolded, perhaps cornered in the room, exposes a face that is featureless except for a grinning mouth. The right-hand panel has a mouth at the end of a long neck, with two rows of threatening teeth in a creature that seems to be free to stalk, chew up and devour the onlooker. The figure has one ear and one limb. The severe sense of violence has moved from the external, social frame of the 1941 painting to a dangerous interiority, and the reference to the Eumenides indicates the revenge of the female.

* * *

Bacon, born in Dublin in 1906, was, like many artists, interested in small, ordinary parts of life, like grass. Henry Miller described grass as follows: "Grass only exists between the great non-cultivated spaces. It fills in the voids. It grows between–among other things" (quoted in Sylvester, 2000). The idea is that we need to become interested in ordinary grass. Ordinary grass as ordinary associations to find the way into the unconscious.

Gilles Deleuze described Bacon's pictorial language as very factual. By this he meant the isolation of a character within its box as a description of fact of "what takes place" (Deleuze, 1951, pp. 5–7). The figure that Bacon places in the transparent box (Nietzsche, 1886[2]) is isolated and trapped but also visible and noticeable. It is a moment captured in order to be transmitted to the viewer/voyeur, who may feel some of the essence of the unconscious trapped affect. In particular, the pain and aloneness of the image can be transmitted, but not necessarily the mental content in the mind of the figure. It is not like William Blake's picture of Newton, who can be seen to be thinking. It is instead a picture of otherness, in which thought is far off and may be inconsequential in the moment. As Bacon said, "I never look at a painting, hardly … It's not so much the painting that excites me as that the painting unlocks all sorts of valves of sensation within me which return me to life more violently" (Sylvester, 1975).

At other times his figures are in a state of movement, which is also a representation of internal movements in the mind. This seems different to the captured moment in the box, in which the body *might* be set free in order to help one become more alive. One problem, then, is that for Bacon becoming more alive or being alive is predicated by affect, and very often with feelings of violence. Humanity usually requires broader brushwork than a singular insistent affect.

When inviting the viewer to notice the contents of a painting, there is an implicit assumption also to feel something of the affect. Otherwise, the picture stays at a far distance from the viewer, who may want to shun or even shut down the invitation to be in touch with its parts of representations of what may seem to be frank aggression to the onlooker. Bacon is not considered to be a painter universally enjoyed, rather an acquired taste with his often-bloody themes.

To quote Miguel Egana, Deleuze, like Bacon,

> believes in the work of art, considered not as a death-dealing instance, but conversely as the very expression of life as the thing that, in a way that is genuinely un-timely (escaping time, history, death) magically affirms (this is the role of sensation) a moving and irresistible eternity. (Deleuze, quoted in Ottinger, 2019)

This way of perceiving, thinking and feeling about art can be close to the analytic encounter. Subjects are thrown up into the space of the consulting room, and reappear in some unrealised linked form until analysand or analyst may see a moment that stands out. Like a figure that Bacon paints fixed in a box for a moment of clarification. In that moment, change becomes possible as a deeper fragment of knowledge may be allowed to be represented, seen and felt. One of my associations to Bacon's intense boxed figures is that, whatever else they represent, there is also an association to a return to being inside the womb, and a particular transparency that conceals mother. The maternal or the matricidal is behind the often violent and sexual aggression between the male figures. Bacon's father Eddy threw his sixteen-year-old son out of the house on discovering him dressed only in his mother's underwear. His mother gave him an allowance sufficient for living in the big city. A little later, his father, wanting to "make a man" out of his son, put him in the care of Cecil Harcourt-Smith, "a fine young man", on a trip to Berlin. The adolescent Bacon was introduced to all the raunchiest sex clubs there. Bacon confided to John Richardson that "Harcourt-Smith was an ultra-sadistic sadist who fucked absolutely anything" (Acocella, 2021). Two months later, Harcourt-Smith tired of him and took off with a woman. Bacon left for Paris alone, where he encountered Picasso.

Bacon moved to London in 1928, aged twenty-two, and his childhood nanny Jessie Lightfoot joined him. She would scan the papers for adverts on Bacon's behalf from wealthy men seeking a young companion, and later, during his illegal roulette parties, collected the fees for the use of the bathroom (Acocella, ibid.). Another time, John Richardson (2022) reported, the now-blind nanny presided in a rocking chair over the party that Bacon gave to celebrate his friend Wishart's marriage, Bacon returning to a house around the corner that his mother owned to collapse during the two-day party. Nanny Lightfoot quietly centered herself as a primary maternal witness over Bacon's life and loves until her death in 1951. They had lived together for over twenty years, and he was heartbroken by her loss.

Bacon's overriding preoccupation was what he liked to call "the brutality of fact". "I would like my pictures to look as if a human being had passed between them, like a snail, leaving a trail of the human presence and memory traces of past events, as the snail leaves its slime" (Sylvester, 2000, p. 33). Bacon often concentrates in particular on what may be felt as the violence of oppression and the violence of suffering within, say, his portrait of the scream of a pope.

Figure 11. Francis Bacon, *Head VI*, 1949 © The Estate of Francis Bacon. All rights reserved, DACS/Artimage 2024. Photo: Prudence Cuming Associates Ltd.

This painting concentrates on the mouth with its silent scream, or the soundless aggressive torrent of word-rage, or ectoplasm pouring forth. Ectoplasm coming out of the mouth was of interest to the German psychiatrist Albert von Schrenck-Notzing who investigated mediums, seances and telepathy in his book *Phenomena of Materialisation* (1920), and this volume was in Bacon's library. Arthur Conan Doyle, in good company with von Schrenck-Notzing, was also a believer in the genuineness of the medium Eva Carrière—later found to be a fraud (Houdini, 2011).[3] Bacon leaves the viewer with a double axis of both believing the portrayal of violence as horror as well as its sado-masochistic pleasures, just as in analysis the belief of the horror of the violence in early life against a child can be held onto, together with the internalised use of identifying with the perverse corruption. Realising the double register is of profound importance. The ahistorical position that now the patient is attempting to pull the analyst into some cor-rupt position as an attack on the analysis belies a potentially deeper meaning, that the analysand realises they are believed as little in their narrative as by the grown-ups in their family, potentially disavowing an actual mental and physical attack. It may not all be in the imagina-tion of either the child or of the analyst.

In discussing the mirror-role of the mother, Donald Winnicott writes about what the baby might see in her face. "I am suggesting that, ordinarily, what the baby sees is himself or herself. In other words, the mother is looking at the baby and *what she looks like is related to what she sees there*". He goes on: "Francis Bacon is seeing himself in his moth-er's face, but with some twist in him or her that maddens both him and us". Knowing nothing about the artist's life, he writes about the Bacon who forces thought about the face and the self. "Bacon's faces seem to me to be far removed from the perception of the actual; in looking at faces he seems to me to be painfully striving towards being seen, which is at the basis for creative looking" (Winnicott, 1967, p. 214). If Bacon intuited that he had not been perceived, it might account for his use of ciphers and arrows to point things out more clearly.[4]

Bacon used a medical notation to locate material that could be pinned down similar to images that emerged from radiographic plates (Clark, 1939). The pathological image is captured in particular ways, including how the patient has to lie before the machine, with arrows even being drawn on the body so that the X-ray can target the image. Some parts of Bacon's bodies are highlighted by circles, which draw specific attention to a particular part.[5]

This use of medical science highlights a ghostly presence that he sometimes plays with and to which he directions attention by use of an arrow shown on the body in the painting.

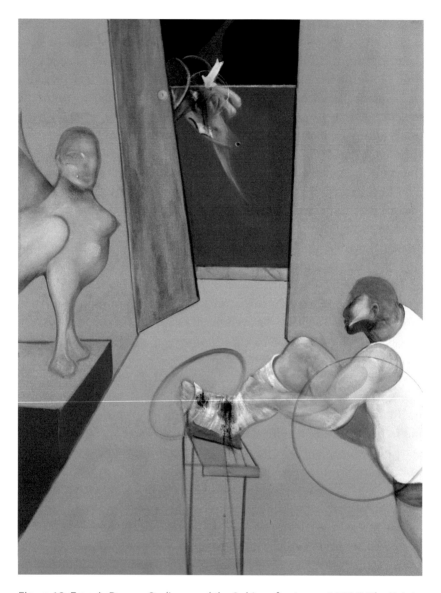

Figure 12. Francis Bacon, *Oedipus and the Sphinx after Ingres*, 1983 © The Estate of Francis Bacon. All rights reserved, DACS/Artimage 2024. Photo: Prudence Cuming Associates Ltd.

Yet he also points out a body part to be noticed as the place of a wound. This can stand in for a piece of lost history that is somatised rather than understood in the psyche. Sometimes it is a whitish X-ray swirl of the

Eumenides. Bacon, speaking of the Furies, quotes from the *Oresteia*: "The reek of human blood smiles out at me" (Sylvester, 1975, p. 21), indicating his associative pleasure at spilt blood as affect. In his life, he actually enjoyed being beaten up. Bacon was regularly found in the early hours by the Tangier police, collapsed and bloody. The chief of police, when asked to assist, said *"Pardon, Monsieur le Consul-Général, mais il n'y à rien a faire. Monsieur Bacon aime ça"* (Peppiatt, p. 172).[6]

Bacon has spoken of the image of Velázquez's *Pope Innocent X* as Il Papa as an obsession with, as well as a crush on, "the greatest painting in the world". He updates the seventeenth-century image by transforming the confident figure into a screaming victim.

Figure 13. Comparison of *Pope Innocent X*, Diego Velázquez, *c.*1650 with Francis Bacon, *Head VI*, 1949 © The Estate of Francis Bacon. All rights reserved. DACS 2024

Here the Pope is located in a spaceframe, a description provided by Bacon's friend David Sylvester. The frame concentrates an object within the painting to be viewed in a separate and particular form; similar to the patient pointing out some matter to us for more attention, while simultaneously unconsciously waiting to see if we leave the rest of the whole. Likewise, the analyst in clinical work can circle a specificity of association. After all, Il Papa is likely to represent in one formation Bacon's father Eddy, who he had a "crush on", in the negative sense of his father's cruelty. His father had been in the army, serving in Burma and

South Africa, retiring with the honorary rank of major (Acocella, 2021). He became a gentleman horse trainer, not needing to find employment, having married Winifred Firth from a wealthy Sheffield steel family with a considerable dowry. The father, hating his teenage son's effeminate manner, had him horsewhipped by the grooms, as Bacon spun his story. Velázquez's importance then represents Bacon's maturity in realising the vitality of the relationship between artist and king—one beyond the relationship that was a failure between father and son. It is plausible to think that the pope's name *Innocent* is an important word association relating to an affective state.

Bacon wrote:

> Great art is always a way of concentrating, reinventing what is called fact, what we know of our existence—a reconcentration … tearing away the veils that fact acquires through time. Ideas always appear as veils, the attitudes people acquire of their time and earlier time. Really good artists tear down those veils. (Davis & Yard, 1986, p. 110)

The scream is derived from a still from Sergei Eisenstein's 1925 film *Battleship Potemkin,* with a vivid picture of the panic and impact of an old woman who, at the moment she sees a woman shot in the belly and letting go of a baby, is herself shot in the eye by Czarist troops while descending the Odessa Steps (Eisenstein, 1925, Odessa Steps scene). The cry of the victims.

Originally, the face of the Pope began as a study of David Sylvester; then it was transformed into a laughing Teddy Roosevelt, baring his teeth, until the full screaming in the sixth and seventh transformation (Davies, 2001). In an interview with Hugh Davies, who curated the 1953 exhibition of "The Papal Portraits" at the Museum of Contemporary Art, San Diego, Bacon states: "I think about Velázquez, I think people believe that they're painting other people, but they paint their own instincts … do you want grandeur or do you want instinctive, the pulse of an instinct beating in you?" (ibid., pp. 34, 41). Here is an interesting free association, as it were, on the psychosomatic beating pulse that he is describing in his own métier. Yet the scream had perhaps had a previous form in an early work following his 1933 *Crucifixion,* a large specimen of human flesh called *Wound for a Crucifixion*, which he destroyed, ever after regretting it (Tóibín, 2021). The screaming mouth as wound.

Winnicott wrote about "The creative artist" who could obviate the need for guilt feelings and the usual associative restitutive strictures.

> The creative artist or thinker may, in fact, fail to understand, or even despise, the feelings of concern that motivate a less creative person; and of artists it may be said that some have no capacity for guilt and yet achieve socialisation through their exceptional talent. Ordinary guilt-ridden people find this bewildering; yet they have a sneaking regard for the ruthlessness that does in fact, in such circumstances, achieve more than guilt-driven labour. (Winnicott, 1958b, p. 145)

Bacon's exceptional talent in displaying ruthless aggression is available not just to be seen, but also viscerally felt in the viewing of many of his paintings, as they can exercise points of morality and mortality similar to paintings of Heaven and Hell and the flagellation of Christ. Perhaps the core being encased in a perspex box is a protection for both painter and voyeur of the horrid power of internal states of aggression with which he is in serious play. However, it did not loosen his addiction to the necessity of sadomasochistic activities in his personal life, principally because they were not forbidden, and being linked to Il Papa, were probably accompanied by mental relief. In Winnicott's terms it was a suffering from the oppressive feelings of guilt, mitigated through his attachment to the environment of his art.

The time and place of the object

From 1963, Bacon had a stormy eight-year relationship with George Dyer. In 1971, he had a retrospective at the Grand Palais in Paris, and went there to oversee the installation, staying with Dyer at the Hôtel des Saints Pères. The private view was to be opened by President Georges Pompidou, followed by a large party. The night before, Bacon and Dyer had a huge row and Bacon slept elsewhere. In the morning Dyer was found dead, sitting on the toilet. Bacon's friends asked if the discovery could be delayed by twenty-four hours and the room was duly locked.

At the opening Bacon toured the exhibition with President Pompidou, who "made a show of stopping" in front of one particular triptych, *Three Figures in a Room*, recently bought by the French state. The left panel showed George Dyer sitting on a toilet (Tóibín, 2021). Bacon returned regularly to the same hotel room over the next year or so. Curiously, Bacon's earlier sadistic lover, Peter Lacy, had died in 1962, the day of the private view of Bacon's first big retrospective at the Tate, London. Two important retrospectives preceded the day before with the death of his lover: that silent association is an unexpected finding. And Bacon's painted scream is an initiation in the arrowed direction of the death to come that had already been unconsciously anticipated.

Hunting with dogs

Recalling the words trapped, boxed, pinned down, target, and the use of arrows, all of which I have used in this chapter, I was fascinated to read a paper by the philosopher Howard Caygill on "Bacon's cynegetic visions" (2019). Cynegetic is an ancient Greek term for hunting with dogs, and Caygill writes about the violence of the hunt, developed particularly into the hunt by the Eumenides within his paintings. Michael Peppiatt, Bacon's friend and biographer, observed "An awareness of life as a perpetual hunt—the stalker and his prey, the aggressor and his victim—was fundamental to Bacon" (Sylvester, 2016, p. 21). Bacon described painting (to David Sylvester, ibid., p. 17) as "trying to trap" an image or having to "in a sense, set a trap by which you hope to trap this living fact alive" (ibid., p. 36), or "to trap the reality of the subject matter that one started from" (ibid., p. 76). Whilst psychoanalysis is neither a trap, nor analysts trappers, one can understand what he means about the really difficult task of capturing and making the unconscious conscious. And how hard Bacon finds it to capture, in paint, an authentic and violent moment that "unlocks the valves of sensation about life in general which is the way I always see painting" (ibid., p. 202).

This is also a psychoanalytic given, seen through the *Oresteia* tragedy. As Caygill writes,

> The cycle of violent death that preceded Agamemnon but continued through the sacrifice of his daughter Iphigenia,

his murder in revenge by his wife Clytemnestra and her murder by her son Orestes driven by Apollo, seems to be closed by the end of the cycle. The Erinyes pursued vengeance, hunting down those who hunted their own families before being received and exalted by Athens and the Athenians (and allowed home into the polis). (Caygill, 2019, p. 36)

Here we find a deep unconscious psychology of the violent imagination in family life through the three generations until peace follows, or may follow, in the analysand's unconscious life and times. Here the strands of the life of the unconscious are found in us, as we hear again and see the Greek myths performed through the intensity of paintings of extraordinary painters trawling their unconscious to provide us onlookers with an evocation that stirs us and our subject, the unconscious in psychoanalysis (Freud, of course, used Oedipus as a crucial myth in discerning the unconscious). I am thinking similarly of Titian's series of *Poesies* recently on show at the National Gallery.[7]

There are many ways that free associations are available to be found, captured before their fragility blows them apart and we have to hunt for them again. That which we discover from free associations, dreams and slips pulling unconscious strands into conscious also contain their antimony as we forget, and the dream fades back to its unconscious lair. Paul Klee viewed the artist's role as "to gather and pass on what comes to him from the depths. He neither serves nor rules—he transmits" (Klee, 1966, p. 15). The analyst's role is the same.

Unconscious communication, free association in a clinical session

The patient knows the way but is blindfolded;
the analyst can see, but he does not know where to go.
All that is necessary is that the patient should feel safe …
Karin Stephen, *Psychoanalysis and Medicine*, 1933

The patient began a session by saying that she was interested in two African masks, and in particular Picasso's use of them to evolve understanding between an object in another time, to help him in understanding his own art forms, linking to a past knowledge. Were they frightening, what was their power and meaning in their cultures? The patient then mused for a while about Cy Twombly, having seen his late series of four paintings of Sanaa. She liked his paintings of writings that cannot be deciphered or yet read. I said that she was describing a decipherment of "coming into the moment", relating it to particular changes that were being initiated into her own life, which, too, were linked to her past. There was a pause while this was being digested in an alive and even enjoyable way.

During this sequence I had been looking at the patient framed, as it were, by a pair of African masks on a bookcase behind where she was sitting. It seemed to me that she had never noticed them, yet the unconscious knowledge of her sitting between the two masks was inescapable. I asked if she realised that she was sat between a pair of masks behind her. She swiftly turned around, shocked, and said she had never knowingly seen them and was very curious. She thought she must have unconsciously seen them, and I added that, like the Twombly, it was a coming into the moment that had always so far been unnoticed.

She had recently met a man at a dinner who had easily spoken of his own interest in being tied up. She thought that was not of much interest as she mused on her own sexual phantasy of "being in a library". She said that at another time in her life she would have become very frightened. Now she could quickly realise that he was not to her taste, and did not need to see him again, as she feared being attacked.

She had been brought up in a very split home, a single child confined to the upper level with the nanny. She was allowed to see her parents downstairs once or twice a week for a few minutes, yet when they were away, she roamed freely. There were many books in her father's study. And, she added, in the next room was her mother's large clothes closet and many high-heeled scary shoes. We had discussed much about her great fear of her parents, like a pair of wild animals. Having not much spoken of her own sexual phantasies, she began to say how erotic a librarian in low shoes was, and more interesting than being tied up. I said maybe the man was offering himself to be tied up perhaps in order to later demand the opposite—that he wanted to tie *her* up. The similarity between him and her mother had made her not want to see him again. She was understanding why she was ambivalently interested in the controlling woman. She was thoughtful about why her mother would want to dress so powerfully and could see that it may have been in rivalry with her very powerful husband.

The session was nearing its end and she told me that she was soon going to have a colonic investigation and was uncertain how she thought of it. She didn't mind it … but could appreciate that being in my room was a deeper kind of penetration, that she had to allow me to be able to connect these things together and she was not as afraid as she used to be. She returned to thoughts of the masks and wondered why she had not seen them. I said that she had decided on her rule that she had to sit on the chair. If she took the freedom to use the couch, she could look at the other side of the consulting room. She looked back again at the masks as she left.

Discussion

The session began with the patient thinking of Picasso using another culture and form (African masks) to understand more deeply how she saw the other. She associated to Twombly's painting and scrawly writing and loops over paintings as if it was a blackboard. Twombly once wrote: "To my mind, one does not put oneself in place of the past, one only adds a new link" (Gagosian writing about the artist's gestural vocabulary (online), original quote from Cézanne[8]).

Sanaa, capital of Yemen, is one of the oldest continuously inhabited cities in the world and this establishes an unconscious idea of that which has survived for a very long time. The patient unconsciously doubly locates inside the cadence of tribal Africa then and now. She spoke of a date (who had grown up in North Africa) who suggested that he could tie her up, and she imagined that could be in a library, citing her father's library while sitting in my library/consulting room, also unconsciously linked to the writing on the paintings and her own writings, which surpassed those of her father. Someone might tie up another sexually in a library, and this resonated with the sadism and masochism of dark sexuality, and her imaginings of the dangerous intercourse between wild animals. More complex might be an imagining about intercourse between them. The couch floats into view as a very dangerous locus for analyst and analysand to work.

The unconscious mycelia reform as a mirror image, as she quickly re-frames me sitting beneath a print that she also owned—our shared taste, her competitiveness identifying with her ruthless father and mother. Is this a spatial representation of the split in the large apartment she was brought up in? The parents' living space was usually a no-go area and the child's space together with nanny. Her part of the room and mine. She had taken the couch to be her no-go area, inhibiting her from seeing other views.

The session moved into touching on dark spaces, which were, for her mother, a room for her clothes and shoes and not words or writing—a different culture. And then the analyst's space, cultural, perhaps paternal, like her father's library but as dangerous as her mother's closet, as the consulting room, because one may get tied up behind a civil mask.

How the associations weave, connect and reconnect in the differing formations, yet a primitive structure holds at the end of the session, morphing into someone examining her anus and its dark interiority. The body is central to her fear of dark places and dark matters in the mind. Her preferred position of being the victim belies her identification with the aggressors.

An alien unconscious

Freud's idea was that:

> the attitude which the analytic physician could most advantageously adopt was to surrender himself to his own unconscious mental activity, in a state of evenly suspended attention, to avoid as far as possible reflection and the construction of conscious expectations, not to try and fix anything he heard, particularly in his memory, and by these means to catch the

drift of the patient's unconscious with his own unconscious. (Freud, 1923a, p. 239)

This is still a deeply radical position. We expect to catch the unconscious drift of our patients, including what have been the primary introjections from mother. Yet for some patients such mental material can act as a foreign body, unknown to the patient and not understood by the analyst's analytic listening tools.

As Enid Balint described in a 1990 paper,

> some patients are affected by aspects of their parents' unassimilated unconscious life, which does not seem to affect their parents' activity or behaviour but does affect their own. In analysis it can be traced to the experience of grandparents, which was bypassed by the parents, instead of being introjected and identified with, and handed on to the children. The children do not introject it, but it is not identified with and cannot become conscious. I have come to see this as a *foreign body* inside the grandchild, which remains unconscious but gives rise to affect and action, which did not occur in the parent. (Balint, 1990, p. 115, my italics)

This is probably an issue over a difficulty in unconscious maternal transmission, predating the censorship of the paternal order.

Is this negation, disavowal, or is this the mechanism of the order of encryption described by Abraham and Torok? The analyst receives a gap in the unconscious, an unknown, unrecognised and unformed "phantom", already subjected to a form of "repression" before the fact.

> The buried speech of the maternal register will be perceived as a dead gap without a burial place in the child. This unknown phantom returns from the unconscious to haunt its host and may lead to phobias, obsessions and/or psychotic functioning. Its effect can persist through several generations and determine the fate of an entire family line. (Abraham & Torok, 1994, p. 140, footnote)

We are in the territory, for instance, of the grandchildren victims of the unspoken Holocaust experience of grandparents, without speech and living in an unconscious gap as the surface evinces, by its occasional disturbances, an unknown foreign body beneath. What Enid Balint draws attention to is that the gap in communication provides a signal to the analyst. The usual route of attempting to understand the associations and histories of the early life of the patient is blocked. Also blocked is the transferential and countertransferential confirmation of such reconstructions, indicative of early trauma. The analyst is not in touch because of the caesura. The disturbances of the patient do not have the freedom of associations that is the usual analytic route of analytic discovery, other than the analyst eventually realising that the clinical impasse is one of *non-transmission* prior to the patient's parent's unconscious knowledge. The patient is left more and more alone, separated and still in a state of dread, as the analyst feels more out of contact. We are back in the "area of the basic fault" (Balint, 1968). The analyst keeps finding him or herself, to utilise the earlier reference to Bacon, in a transparent box, unable to know the words for the wordless experience, nor its image or shape.

And if words are found, they can be trapped inside the near-invisible box and are not heard or perceived other than perhaps as noise from the analyst. For Enid Balint, in time, and with her intense perception, her patient "was able to create me, or to let me into her creative space. She could, that is to say, imaginatively perceive me and parts of reality that had been closed to her" (Balint, 1990, p. 118). It is as if the invisible box in the unconscious—unknown, unseen, unthought—acts also as a hidden incubator, awaiting the discovery of being found and delivering the missing piece of the unconscious puzzle. For our purposes, I can add that the capacity for free associations has been restored, as and when the analyst is freed from being inside and alone in the encrypted space of, say, the grandparent's experience.

For my patient, both her parents had grown up with very disrupted lives due to severe impacts of war, poverty and migration. One conclusion that we can draw out is that an analysis is inevitably about three generations—the grandmother, mother and patient. If the analysand is female, it will include her own capacity for pregnancy or not, in identification (or not) with the transgenerational feminine.

The radicalism of free associations

Has the term free association become a formulaic term, describing the dialogue in an analytic session as if there is no discrimination about its presence or absence? Or is the manifest text heard mainly about the importance of the surface, with no need for the analyst to discover the latent unconscious forms of thought? One can find a similar proposition when it comes to the dream in the session. The dream is always full of unconscious nodal points, with mycelial lines of ideas, thoughts, images and sounds radiating from the manifest surface. Freud's radical position, based on the exegesis of a Mishna text from the *Torah*, is to examine each sentence, and the individual words, letters and wordplays, to find hidden associations. In Freud's *Interpretation of Dreams* this is presented in all the complexities that are then revealed, and the associations open out, enriching the starting point of the manifest text and the day's residues. But is this how analysts still play with the dream? So often it seems to be the surface description that is listened to and worked with. I think it fits in with the seemingly important "here and nowness", again listening to the surface of a session, belying its unconscious underbelly. The unconscious is not some text that, once translated, is now represented in consciousness. This is an argument about the coherence of rationality overriding what paths may ensue if we dig beneath the surface. This, after all, was one of Freud's valuable metaphors about the vitality of discovering histories of who is doing what to whom in the mycelia threading their way beneath the manifest "allowed" formation that breaks through into the preconscious of the analysand.

Dreams are always difficult, as the patient realises when making clear that a capacity of talking is about to change, and "the dream" is spoken with some of its parts unremembered, with vague and dissonant themes, tonalities and complex words with their many meanings. And the dream is often presented in the last few minutes of a session, to allow it to be said and quickly left as the patient departs the consulting room, leaving it behind, the "dark behind" un-worked on, (as my patient did). The difficulty often starts with a warning of the arrival of the next dream, that it is likely to bring the impact of more complexity into the session. And even more difficult that it contains material from the unconscious that might be hot, like the hissing magma shooting out of an active volcano. The work is not just about a textual exegesis, but a free associative larval/lava interflow of words, associations, condensation and displacement beneath the manifest surface. While this might be welcome, as part of the task of making the unconscious conscious, it may be felt to be hard to follow, until one remembers that Freud helps us by telling us how to listen with evenly suspended attention, or to not remember what one is hearing, rather letting it just flow over us, so that we unconsciously get the drift—unconscious perception of the unconscious. Here it is useful to know several analytic theories or schema, but keeping them in the back of the mind, in order for the theory not to lead the analyst to arrive at the wrong place of understanding.

As Barnaby Barratt writes,

> the psychoanalyst has a particular value beyond a friendly witnessing of the patient's being-in-the-world/word and being the interlocutor who becomes the "object" of the patient's transference in at least a double sense. Being the one who listens free-associatively to the thing-presentations of the repressed differentiates psychoanalytic process from psychoanalytically "informed" psychotherapy. The psychoanalyst takes on the position of Other, receiving and holding experiences without retaliation, including that which has not yet come into consciousness, while the freedom to associate continues despite fear disrupting the equanimity of the analytic position. We are, at times, there expecting to be destroyed and to stay alive in the paradox. More than any other therapy, staying at the collecting point of the free associations means facing the potential sharp shards hidden in the unconscious, as we listen to the incomprehensible messages, enigmatic signifiers, thing-presentations, traces and proto-emotions that occur insistently and persistently within our lived experiences. (Barratt, 2016, p. 118)

I have likened such listening as to being very close to the edge of a black-hole experience, pulling the analyst into the vortex. This is far from the caring, understanding and supportive helper demanded by the patient and sometimes by the therapist utilising a conversational dialogue. The psychoanalyst is there, listening, expecting the disruptive *Unheimlich* of the daily encounter without knowing, paradoxically, what is to be expected. One could say that such a position of being in the experience of free association without retaliation is love, as Winnicott describes, without the mother paying the baby out. Free association at the core of analytic work is very different from the making sense of a narratological imperative, such as training the patient to use higher cognitive skills as in ego psychology or self psychology, and the forward arrow from paranoid–schizoid to depressive.

Analysts well versed in a particular analytic language can help the patient, despite the proliferation of theory. The humble free association has the power to find the gaps in analytic societies' conscious and unconscious grip on analytic theories, even freeing the analytic pair from a necessity of (sometimes rigid) theoretical explanation.

Analysts fear losing the threads of the associations: the analysand's and their own, especially if the dream becomes excessively lengthy. This in itself is a form of unconscious self-erasing of the dream back to its unconscious form. As Barratt describes, "it is as if each association in the concatenation simultaneously reveals and conceals something other than itself" (ibid., p. 52). The impact of the difficulty is that if something can be represented, it is not repressed. So the act of representation also contains, like so much of psychoanalysis, its opposite, its capacity to repress. It is hard to remember dreams as they can just fly away. And the word associations can fade into the thingness, which is wordless and as Freud notes, they become an "unfathomable navel" (ibid., p. 52). For Barratt, "This umbilical scar intimates a connection of which we cannot speak—the erotically embodied, life-giving connection that antedates the formation of our subjectivity" (ibid., p. 58). In addition, the navel points in the direction of the mother, and to the unconscious shapes of foetus–mother, birth, feeding and early development as part of the maternal unconscious register. This is the form of the infant body lying on mother, reformed and refound as the dream lying held in the mind of the analyst. The umbilical cord comes into formation with a cut, which the just-born infant survives.

It is valuable to remember such matters when the unconscious of the patient signifies its opposite, as the analyst, like mother, need not be opposed by such a mental cut.

Dream associations can provide a new energy as some unconscious fragments make their way to the surface to be received, remembered and become part of consciousness, forming a new way of understanding unconscious object relations, history and affect. The actuality in an analysis of the analyst silently listening *and* interpreting creates in the analysand a capacity to surrender to the free-associative process. The stirrings of *the underworld* made conscious allow a focus on new ways of being and understanding representability. The unconscious has no centre, although plenty of theories pick out and reify salient parts. It is only free association that allows access to the overarching whatever-ness of the unconscious. The energy provided allows for a maturity of realisation that it is alright to know, and that one can continue to wrestle with one's unconscious. This is true not only for the analysand, as the impact of free association enables the analyst the same continuing freedom. It is also true for the onlooker involved in experiencing culture, art and poetry in that transitional creative space described by Michael and Enid Balint and D. W. Winnicott. Here, play is enjoyed as the destroyed transitional object is unconsciously found reinvented and the mature adult functions in the area of creativity, in one's own creative life.

The term "Geometry of Fear" was coined by the art critic Herbert Read when reviewing the work of a group of young British sculptors at the 1951 Venice Biennale. These followers of Henry Moore—Kenneth Armitage, Reg Butler, Lynn Chadwick, Bernard Meadows, Eduardo Paolozzi and William Turnbull—showed spiky, alien-looking, twisted, tortured figures. They were cast in pitted bronze or welded metal, vividly expressing a range of states of mind and emotions related to anxieties and fears post-war. Read wrote:

> These new images belong to the iconography of despair, or of defiance and the more innocent the artist, the more effectively he transmits the collective guilt. Here are images of flight, or ragged claws "scuttling across the floors of silent seas"[9] of excoriated flesh, frustrated sex, the geometry of fear. (Read, 1951)

Figure 14. *Black Crab*, Bernard Meadows, 1951–1952. Photo: Tate. Reproduced with the kind permission of Julia and Anthea Meadows

The environment of World War II and its aftermath is the perspective that this young generation of British artists created out of their own psychosomatic turmoil. Bacon was of this generation too.

Freud made the unconscious conscious, and the artist Bacon made the invisible visible, particularly in the arena of violence, love and perversion. Each require an other to know and feel. Freud (1915e) felt that we seek in the world of art compensation for what has been lost in life. The horror of trauma, including for Bacon the horror of Nazism, is beyond words and images as simply signifiers and can only be conveyed (ironically through words and images) as visceral affect. Joseph Conrad knew this too, especially in *Heart of Darkness*, with its famous "The horror, the horror". The freedom that the analysand can obtain from analysis is not just about a state of an alive life. It is more about having an existential capacity to be in the process of freeing oneself, as we never find utopia, other than momentarily. I will leave this discourse with the image of Michelangelo's slave, freeing himself from the block of marble as a representation of the ongoing freedom in self-analysis from the eternal struggle of being human.[10]

Figure 15. *Awakening Slave*, Michelangelo, 1525–1530. One of the *Prisoners* series for the tomb of Pope Julius II. Galleria dell'Accademia, Florence

CHAPTER 4

William Tillyer: against nature

The art dealer Bernard Jacobson, who has long supported and championed William Tillyer, wrote in a volume titled *Willliam Tillyer: The Loneliness of the Long Distant Runner*, "In my opinion he has, within the past few years, become a giant among his peers, and quite possibly this country's greatest painter since Constable and Turner" (Jacobson, 2018, p. 7). The runner in the title referred to Tillyer's enjoyment of running across his beloved landscape of the North York Moors.

I will begin with a brief orientation to the creativity within psychic life. Freud described and developed the idea of inner psychic reality, differentiating between the conscious and the unconscious, inner experiences and the external world. Freud conceptualised the idea of sublimation; although he pointed to the meaningfulness of cultural experience he did not develop where it was located in the mind. Anna Freud classified sublimation as one of the major "defence mechanisms" of the psyche (A. Freud, 1936). Later, Winnicott describes the early concept of the me–not-me object, such that the baby imagined the mother was part of itself as well as the maternal object having her own disappearances, and developed his idea into the play space between me-and-not-me. As Winnicott wrote: "The place where cultural experience is located is in the *potential space* between the individual and the environment (originally the object). The same can be said of playing. Cultural experience begins with creative living first manifested in play" (Winnicott, 1966b, p. 433).

Tillyer was born in 1938 and began painting in the 1950s. He painted landscapes, which he brought to Jacobson's attention in 1969 when he first visited Jacobson's London gallery with a portfolio of his work. Artist and dealer have been entwined ever since. Before leaving for London, Tillyer wrote his first ever catalogue note, for the 1958 final year art exhibition at his local art school in Middlesbrough. He wrote:

> In this exhibition I have tried to put down my feelings about such elements as sea, sky, beach, moor; and relating objects, including man, to them. Such areas have appealed to me because one is always aware of one's size and of surrounding objects. Objects become more important—points of excitement, such as a single figure on an open beach; giving size-scale.
>
> Standing on a beach I find my eye travelling down the beach by progression—pebble to man or a boat, to the horizon, up to a cloud and back to a pebble ... Isolated from its surroundings, a pebble could appear to be of an immense size. But seen against the vastness of the beach or covered by the water which stretches away to become the ocean, the pebble slips into its correct scale.
>
> In this way my interests have centred around scale from a space and scale out of natural order or progression. (Tillyer, 1958, p. 10)

In this very early painting, *Beach and Sea, Seaton Carew*, we have the artist's early credo of how he saw nature and how he would tackle painting its size in an arc that ranges from vast to a mere speck. As I write this I am imagining and realising how large the shadow of mankind is over our planet. Yet the forced retaliation of the Earth by global warming is likely to return man's place to a considerably smaller imprint—perhaps as a Tillyer evocation as "civilisation" becomes more pebble-sized.[1]

Observing his paintings in their different time frames, looking in particular at how he begins to re-frame what was in front of the canvas in his later use of industrial materials, allows the arc of this early

Figure 16. *Beach and Sea, Seaton Carew*, 1956, William Tillyer, painted at age eighteen. Reproduced with permission

credo on nature, and his vision of its three-dimensionality, to be seen and felt.

While being a known British artist, Tillyer has no paintings in our national collections and despite many exhibitions is rather unknown to the general art-visiting public. It is as if he has metaphorised *himself* to being a small speck, even though his early credo understood the arc from tiny to vast and reverberating back again. It is like a game of hide and seek. Tillyer does not seek being found, as many artists do, rather he is captivated by being in the conundrum. As D. W. Winnicott wrote, "It is a sophisticated game of hide-and-seek in which *it is joy to be hidden but disaster not to be found*" (Winnicott, 1963a, p. 439).

* * *

Tillyer was an only child. He was just ten days old when Hitler's troops marched into Czechoslovakia and one year old when Germany invaded Poland. His father joined the army and Tillyer was brought up by women: his mother, grandmother and great-grandmother in north-east England. With his father returned back home, five years later, after the war had ended, the young Willi remembered their home life above the family hardware shop in Middlesbrough and fishing with him on the River Esk. That river was to become an important fixture by repetition in his paintings, hanging as a type of armature, a metaphor appropriate to his repetitive use of industrial materials in his art. Yet prior to that, the wartime child had somehow to deal with and process the long absence of his father.

Perhaps one can muse on the subject of his created arc from a speck to huge as a reversible context: a huge father object becoming a speck as his disappearance continued for years as the son grew. And "years" for a child feels forever in the long moments. Not throwing a very large artistic shadow in the environment of the world perhaps allowed him the freedom to be the monastic painter he wanted to be observing the moving arc of nature. His studio was an hour's walk from his birthplace: not too far and held onto closely as he began his artistic journey of examining nature, following the British tradition of Gainsborough, Constable, Turner and Samuel Palmer.

As previously mentioned, Tillyer grew up in the containment of three strong women: his mother, her mother and his maternal great-grandmother from Glasgow. His grandmother was pregnant when her husband went off to the First World War. The Battle of the Somme lasted from July to November 1916 and the British troops sustained 125,000 deaths, including Tillyer's grandfather. The first holiday that William was taken on, in the late 1940s, was to northern France and included visiting that battlefield. For the rest of that decade, on an annual basis, the family visited the grave of his grandmother's husband, there in Péronne, Somme.

Tillyer's mother grew up, first as a baby and then as a child, without her father. Her unconscious had to carry the emotional absence of growing up without a father. Many years on she married and then saw her husband off early into the Second World War to potentially bestow the same fate onto her son. Not hearing from her husband, and fearing the worst, she contacted the War Office. They refused to comment. Later she heard that he was still alive. He was a dispatch officer with his own jeep in North Africa. There he was, with the troops that landed in Italy, fighting all the way through Europe prior to his return to his family and his son. The imagination of the triumvirate of women was that he had had a good and even enjoyable war, as having been provided with his own jeep meant he had somewhat of an independent time. Yet the length and intensity of the fighting, which must have included seeing the horrors of war up close, and the death of his comrades over years, was a topic that he never spoke about.

His returned father developed a hardware business, which in time included two shops. The family lived over one of the premises. William was often left in the care of his maternal grandmother, including when his parents regularly went off to holiday without him. For his grandmother it seemed some sort of solution to her private loneliness. William perhaps sensed his grandmother's loss of her husband, as well as his mother's absence of having a father, and knew aloneness despite not being alone in the family.

And, although he was an artist in the world, he stayed a man alone, as a contented outsider who felt no requirement to join the group of artist colleagues of his generation (Yau, 2021).[2] These included Hockney, Nicholson, Hitchens, Spencer, Sutherland, Caulfield, Blake, Holland, Hodgkin, Hamilton, Tilson, Jones, Lanyon, Passmore, Heron, Uglow and the quartet of British greats: Auerbach, Freud, Bacon and Kossoff. Jacobson contends that so many (all) were unable to improve on their early form, archly commenting on the artist closest to Tillyer:

> Hockney recording nature is like Paul McCartney writing opera. Tillyer recording nature is like John Clare recording nature. Hockney's nature reflects back the colour supplements, Tillyer's is a Modernist mirror of nature itself.

He continued:

> William Tillyer needed to see the world through the eye of a needle and express it through a grid, seeming cerebral and even expressionless and yet a pictorial space which opens outward onto a view of landscape and the natural order. It also opens inward, creating a space behind the picture plane which evoked

past worlds of perspective and illusion. To understand the grid or lattice you need to return to Constable, via Cézanne … The grid and lattice are rational and architectonic forms which incorporate the compositional geometries of John Cage or Steve Reich. (Jacobson, 2018, pp. 101–102)

Meander

In 1966 Tillyer created a black bas-relief constructed from a wood panel and timber mouldings, suggesting that the act of painting is a maze, with no clear path or direction. As Yau suggests,

he has replaced Malevich's *Black Square* of 1915 by leaving an empty space at the centre through which we can see a wall. He reverses Malevich's idea by removing what (Tillyer) felt was an illusion, no matter how reductive and final the square might have been. This is the earliest instance in which Tillyer focuses on the idea that a painting establishes a bond with the wall it hangs on, however transitory. (Yau, 2021, p. 28)

Figure 17. *Black Square*, Kazimir Malevich, 1915

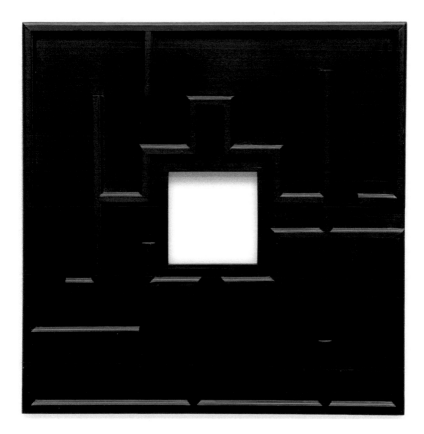

Figure 18. *Meander*, William Tillyer, 1966. Reproduced with permission

Tillyer is also claiming the position of *flâneur*, to have the freedom of artistic movement in any direction that the path takes. Walter Benjamin's hypothesis in the *Arcades Project* was that not looking up the recommended places to visit in a city allows one to meander without a particular goal or direction, and to find out that one finds oneself in a place in which one had no idea that one would be standing. This is indeed a way of discovering the city, which is of course a metaphor for obtaining knowledge. As such, it is a core principle of psychoanalysis: that of free association, "to find oneself talking about something that is totally unexpected", or as extended by Bollas as the place of the *unthought known*. Despite its simplicity, free association allows unconscious thoughts to be exposed and available for thinking about, similar to the aftermath of the dream.

In exposing the background wall at the centre of the maze, Tillyer's picture *Meander* gives importance to the reality that a painting needs to be hung on a wall or that a sculpture may need to stand on the ground. Art is grounded in reality, wherever else it also soars. Now we will see his development from wall to grid.

The grid

In the 1980s, Tillyer explored the red sandy plains and dunes of the Simpson Desert in South Australia. Later that decade he followed in the footsteps of Turner with his "First Grand Tour" through France, Italy and Switzerland, and in 1984 he traversed southern California and the Southwest. As Yau comments:

> Each of these travels inspired at least one body of work, ranging from paintings to watercolours, pastels and prints. It is during this decade that Tillyer begins to identify himself as an artist of specific places, and deepens his engagement with English landscape painters from John Constable, Samuel Palmer and J. M. W. Turner … (2021, p. 75)

Tillyer made a breakthrough by examining the relationship between nature and the man-made, specifically between the changing landscape and the painting as a layered object as it consists of canvas with stretcher placed on a wall. Now he was working three-dimensionally on a two-dimensional surface. This had been done in the seventeenth century by Dutch painters, and of course later by Braque and Picasso. Yet Tillyer was intent on finding new pathways to open up his paintings of the landscape—in order to find new and unexpected possibilities of passages in a place.

In the late 1960s he had experimented with wire meshes attached to the canvas. The lattice grid was very important in his thinking, as "any point in such a grid related to every other point on that grid. Early toys, like Meccano, were perhaps an influence. This structure remains important to me" (personal communication). By the 1980s he was thinking out the interconnectedness of the stretcher, canvas, grid and wall as a new dialogue developed with the landscape in Australia.

But what does the grid represent? Like the earlier removal of the central black square to reveal the wall behind, so the grid allows space to be regulated within a picture. Once the man-made object is fixed to the picture as an addition to the usual and usually ubiquitous canvas, space is opened out within the painting. Yes, it becomes, in a formal sense, three-dimensional, but to my mind this is not just about providing depth as well as further linking the pastoral subject with the man-made. It offers an unconscious psychological solution to his perplexing history.

Let us look at some of the features of his known history. Born of two parents and being an only child. His mother was born missing a father. Early on, his own father is missing, with no certitude of his ever returning from war. He is brought up in a triumvirate of women—a transgenerational matriarchy, which, however pleasant and even good and valuable, contained a "man-made", missing character. His father was present in the minds of the women, keeping hope in wartime, but this was the reality of his childhood, and without knowledge of what would come to pass in the future other than hope in wartime.

The spaces in the grid contain an evocation of seeing life as space. Tillyer places empty places within the painting, not by painting an empty space but by use of an ever-ready thing. The space within the grid can act as an unconscious, in and out, or being part of and separate or connected, and revealed or not revealed, allowing the availability of unconscious equivalents of not having the object within the emptiness. And experiencing the emptiness of loss such as a no-father provides can conjure up an imaginary phantasy of having the lost object returned—the empty grid space can be painted or the space can be attempted to be filled as paint is pushed through the metal grid, from its back to the front of the work. With the return of the lost object in the painting, it can have an actual place to be visualised and when the space is lost again it can return, just as eventually the "foreverness" of five years in the eyes of a child is mastered following the father's actual return to the family and to his son. Of course, the return of the disappeared father does not necessarily mean he won't go missing again.

The action of the grid is a private unconscious play of being and empty, here and gone, as Freud vividly showed in the *fort–da* game of his little grandson Ernst. Here, the missingness of the object becomes unconsciously organised as the throwing of the cotton reel out of the cot, and, when ready, pulling it back by the string to return it to the cot and himself. The loss of the object is turned into a game that allows a return of the lost object. Freud was theorising on the complexity of the baby dealing with the reality of the loss of the feeding nipple that can also be licked, snuggled into and played with, by imagining a new dialogue that the infant is imaginatively in control of mother, when in reality this is not true. In phantasy all he has to do is reel the object back by pulling on the string. This early child's game shows the compulsion to repeat to be an early unconscious process containing the potential for masochistic control by getting rid of the cotton reel, controlling the object by bringing it back to oneself with pleasure. Interestingly, the primordial violence in these sequences of *fort–da* were by Freud's account—later Ernst, then thirty months, throws aside a toy and unequivocally identifies it with his absent father, who had been *"sent to the fwont!"* (Freud, 1920g, p. 16, my italics).

As Freud further writes (ibid.):

> Throwing away the object so that it was "gone" might satisfy an impulse of the child's, which was suppressed in his actual life, to revenge himself on his mother for going away from him. In that case it would have a defiant meaning: "All right, then, go away! I don't need you. I'm sending you away myself".

A year later the boy would send the toy to the *fwont*, a word he had heard used about the location of his absent father, whatever he imagined the place was. Here we see the power of play by turning a passive position into active.

Tillyer talks, in a film made to celebrate his 80th birthday,[3] of painting a return to the landscape with a piece of architecture in it (a stone bridge over the River Esk, close to where he grew up). "I am not painting a specific landscape. I don't care about that. Everything is natural ... everything is nature". As an aside, Tillyer told me that his great-great-grandfather on his mother's side was the chief foreman to Sir William Arrol, the designer/architect of the Forth Rail Bridge. The real making of a bridge became a momento of a piece of family history, passed down the decades, and becoming unconsciously transformed into the importance for William's "own" bridge on the Esk, revisited in his paintings. The bridge is a utensil/metaphor to introduce geometry into painting and illusion as the eye passes through the picture plane into space. Pushing paint through the grid is a metaphor that moves from passive to active, as these further quotes explain:

> As well as the paint having a physical quality and coming from the support a kind of push–pull mechanism ... I am trying to invoke the surface as being active and interactive rather than passive. (*Hardware in a picture is a fixing*)—geometry and the apparent chaos of paint coming through.
>
> The beach and the moors you can get lost on the moors. All you have is sky and beach. In the painting I have delineated all the coordinates of the beach (to take in the totality). The first landscape you know gets into your DNA. It's the first landscape you know as a child. (*William Tillyer: The Golden Striker*)

Fixing things

The idea of going missing on the moor, an unconscious phantasy of what had happened to his absent father in his early years, perhaps coalesced into the continuing pressure of painting over and over as a form of fixing that which was lost. And this, as in the act of *fort–da*, needs to continue until it is no longer necessary. This artist in continually questing the seeing and finding the elusive psychological "hardware" to represent beyond the landscape that must contain humanity, is his creative drive. Geometry of the structure feels too clinical if it directs attention for the avoidance of emotions. Perhaps the phantasy about fixing things is too important if there is an idea that emotions might only interfere. Tillyer was seven years old when his father eventually returned to the family and his son. His father then developed the hardware store, which contained a multitude of metal and mechanical objects. As a boy, with his father returned, the new hardware store became an evocative playground, as he picked up and opened the boxes of wares, playing with and learning about how the screws and nails, together with the tools, could and would fix things. It is well known that many men returned from years of violent warfare refused to speak of the matters that had so delayed their return.[4] In such an absence, the motif of playing at fixing the previous loss (lost) becomes very important. Yet the constant pull to fix human activity can become a central unconscious motif, once he discovered absence–presence of the human within the paintings of nature. So, the items of hardware, screws, handles, metal armatures and grids as the equipment to fix things, and make them better and whole again, became a profound metaphor.

Play becomes formed as a way of dealing with loss by evoking the possibilities of passive or active performance, which can develop into states of paradox. And does this not presage the interconnectedness of nature and humans more than ever, in our times, revealing our hubris at the idea that we are in control of our kingdom of Earth?

As discussed earlier, the basis of my speculation of the fixing of things with hardware, which enters his painting oeuvre from 1965, is the introduction of grids onto his paintings. Later these become actual metal grids, fixed to and part of the painting, and painted over. In the 1970s, according to Yau,

> Tillyer kept returning to the conundrum of what connects the visible to the invisible and the image to the field. Between the mid and late 1970s, however, he began his relentless push into new areas. Rather than depict a vase of flowers as distinct from the space it inhabits, Tillyer focussed on the bond between figure and field. His attention to the *inseparability*

of *the thing* from the air and light around it is what led him
to become the most radical painter of his generation. (Yau,
2021, p. 44)

Tillyer, using an off-the-shelf garden product, collages the mesh to the
canvas in his first such use in *Portrait, Head and Shoulders*.

Figure 19. *Portrait, Head and Shoulders*, William Tillyer, 1978. Reproduced with
permission

Figure 20. *The House at Karl Gustav*, William Tillyer, 1979. Reproduced with permission

Hardware: variations on a theme of encounter

In 2002, Tillyer published, on an exhibition of a series of paintings with the same name, a book whose title is above. Here he describes paint as object:

> paint reacting to its support more than paint being an expressive mark or gesture, and more than paint being a surrogate or medium for some figuration or narrative. (Two Objects). (Tillyer, 2002, p. 5)

He adds

> As well as providing a space frame, a window on the world of illusion, the lattice was as real for me as the actual hardware

I had been incorporating into my work at that time, 1965–7, i.e. hinges, locks, D-handles and glass showcases. For the first time I was able to couple a found reality with an imagined illusion. To use a metaphor from my trans-American trip, I was able to couple the twentieth century to the fifteenth. (ibid., p. 30)

And by analogy, to couple the work of the adult artist to the child perplexed by the lost object of his father. A piece of psychological mourning of early absence, as something lost all that time ago in the fifteenth century and now re-found in his father's store. Hardware became his solution to the fixity of a personal history, as he constructed grids on the canvas that showed the forward movement of discovering a new platform for containing the paint simultaneously representing the empty-space potential for the ever-present lost object of childhood.

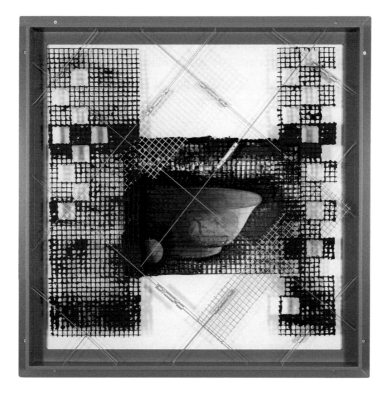

Figure 21. *The Percival David Bowl*, William Tillyer, 2022, from the "Mulgrave Tensile Wire". Reproduced with permission

The important breakthrough

Bernard Jacobson had sent a draft of this chapter to Tillyer and arranged for us to meet with his wife Judith on the last Sunday of Frieze Masters[5] 2020. Towards the end of a very interesting private discussion between the three of us, I mentioned my interest in Velázquez as well as having written an essay on *Las Meninas*. William seized on this and told me that *Las Meninas* was one of most important images he kept revisiting. He was intrigued with the spaces that Velázquez had created, the mirror image of the king and queen standing where the onlooker stands away, central to the painting. And he was intrigued by the open door near the back of the picture with a courtier standing, either at the moment of entering or leaving. This sense of the picture providing a range of possibilities for entering and leaving was very important to him.[6] And of course, the monumental space required in the picture, showing the back of Velázquez's canvas, including the wooden shafts holding the canvas in place as well as the boundary of the picture. For Tillyer, the painting contained a circularity of movement of entering and leaving or coming and going, whilst at the same time the component figures of the princess, the dwarf and her maids stayed at the centre. He then linked these thoughts to what he considered as one of his own most important canvases, painted in 1983.

In 1983, Tillyer created *Double Crossbar with Blue Vase and Arrangement*. It is an oil painting with string and canvas. Standing in front of his painting, that by happenstance was on display at the exhibition, William described to me how he realised that by cutting out pieces of the canvas he would reveal the wooden struts holding the canvas as well as the bare wall behind, signalling the imaginary of the painting now connected to reality. He also provided spaces to enter and depart the scene, like in Velázquez's masterpiece. The addition of string saved Tillyer's canvas from just flopping and gave the whole painting a real and internal tautness. Here, Velázquez's *Las Meninas* continues a journey to modern times with its innate qualities of challenging space and reality, now with Tillyer's interpretation allowing him the freedom to open the canvas and see through the picture in an arc from the painting of a vase to the wall itself. I think Tillyer translated the light from the door near the centre of *Las Meninas* to a real open space, with his counterpart of it integral to the painting itself. A moment of real and imaginary, art and artifice, to exist in the same place, encased by the still life of nature and a vase.

Figure 22. *Double Crossbar with Blue Vase and Arrangement,* William Tillyer, 1983. Reproduced with permission

À Rebours

Against Nature [*À Rebours*], a novel written by J. K. Huysmans in 1884, fascinated Tillyer from 1974 to 2017, during which time he created a portfolio of 52 etchings from the book. He came across it as an art student when a fellow student suggested he read it. The narrative centres on the mind of Jean des Esseintes, an eccentric, reclusive aesthete who is the last of the line of an aristocratic family. He detests nineteenth-century bourgeois society and builds himself a retreat where he creates his own vision of an ideal artistic world. In his preface for the 1903 publication of the novel, Huysmans wrote that he had the idea of portraying a man's "soaring upwards into dream, seeking refuge in illusions of extravagant fantasy, living alone, far from his century, among memories of more congenial times, of less base surroundings" (Huysmans, 1903, Preface). The character seems based partly on the author himself, as well as the aristocratic aesthete Robert de Montesquieu, who was the basis for Proust's Baron Charles in *À la recherche du temps perdu*.

Interestingly Huysmans' father died when he was eight. His mother quickly remarried, leaving the boy to much resent his stepfather. Another story of a lost father, albeit occurring at a slightly later time in childhood, perhaps also being the creative drive to want to return to an earlier century and recreate past reality in a protective phantasy.

The character of des Esseintes bears a terrible ennui for the reality of life that gradually envelops him, and so is determined to create, by building a private world in which he lives separately and alone. In phantasy he provides himself with mechanical tools with which he is watching the clouds and seas from within his sanctuary, despite the artifice of what he has constructed.

> There was no further point in self-analysis, nor in listening to presentiments, nor in taking protective measures; the psychology of mysticism was worthless. It was so because it was so, and there is no more to be said. "Why what a fool I am," thought des Esseintes: "if I continue like this, the dread of the illness will bring on the illness itself." And so, the character embraces a hermeneutic solitude. (Huysmans, 1903, p. 103)

> This admirable art had long fascinated him, but now he
> dreamt of planning a different kind of flora. He had tired of
> old artificial flowers mimicking the reality; now he wanted real
> flowers that mimicked artificial ones. (ibid., p. 114)
>
> The truth is these flowers are taffeta and mounted on brass-
> wire. (ibid., p. 159)

These sentences from the book seem to link with Tillyer's disavowal
of the impact that his art makes on the world such that he too lives in
a *hermeneutic solitude.* His unconscious identification with the artist
des Esseintes shows that his creation of his own artistic place/space
is separate from as well as connected to reality. Or, as written in the
text: "At bottom, the sum of human wisdom consisted in dragging
things out; in saying No and then Yes; and the most effective way
of controlling the rising generation was to keep putting them off!"
(ibid., p. 200).

As a teenager, Tillyer imagined from a choice of three what he
might do in his life. The list was: farmer, monk[7] or artist. Each
of these choices contained, for him, something of a solitary life.
The position of monk was to be alone and Tillyer agreed with my
hypothesis that the idea of des Esseintes fitted very well with his
own idea of building a complete private world. Later, he found a wife
at art school, who accepted that she would look after much of the
workings of living in the reality of life so that he could retreat to the
solitary life of his studio, an hour away. I was somewhat surprised
to find, when I assumed that with his canvasses becoming larger
and larger, he would have engaged staff for such big projects, that he
quickly rebutted such an idea. He made the structures for his paintings alone and only by himself. The artist alone, in and surrounded
by his studio.

In 1990, Tillyer created a painting that he called *The Wildenstein
Hermitage.* He told me it refers

> to the idea of a single person—a person, living in a hermitage.
> The inner world of the habitat and the outer world of the land-
> scape. It is, in a strange way, biographical. I have not lived as a
> hermit, but it has always appealed. (Personal communication)

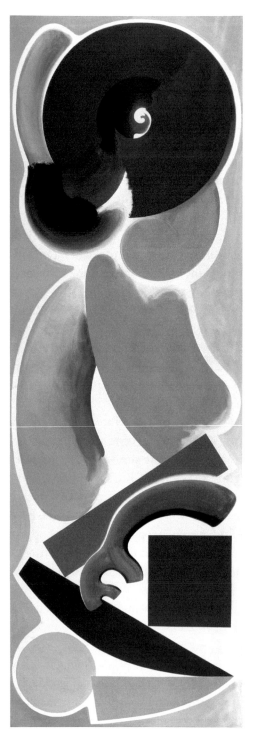

Figure 23. *The Wildenstein Hermitage*, William Tillyer, 1990. Reproduced with permission

Tillyer also spoke of the landscape and the hermitage just touching and that where they kiss is interesting. Here he evokes a meeting point of the privacy of the inside with its unconscious pull and the outside landscape. And that meeting point, described as a kiss, is perhaps the point of desire and the impact of sensuality and sexuality, and potentially violence.

Huysmans' novel tracks the obsessive character continually relocating energy in new systems, from perfumes, exotic and foul-smelling flowers, or by covering the shell of a tortoise with jewels, thus causing its early death due to the heavy weight. The lone hermit has a very rich and perverse inner life, which is written out on the canvas of the novel in many aspects of sexuality and violence. Tillyer created over many years a series of prints that now are incorporated in the new translation of the novel (Huysmans, 1903). Some of the colours are grey and delicate, incorporating a feather or piece of lace, as well as vivid, brash colours that are full-on and sometimes edgy but with a great capacity to exude energy. As a *momenta mori*, it is the moment of the kiss between nature and the human subject, beneath which is contained the unconscious well of deep anxieties within the human's capacity for perversion, aggression, and its impact on the planet as that of no other species.

And, near the end of *À Rebours*, "The result was a literary concentrate, a distilled essence, a chemical sublimate of art". Such are Tillyer's struggles with finding the most authentic ways to produce his vision of the landscape and of the waters of the sea meeting the clouds in the sky. Tillyer, like most artists, has a need to keep creating. The finished painting already creates a gap, an emptiness that the act of creating anew can temporarily deflect. Perhaps the impossibility of mourning the gap, overcoming it such that the space heals, is an impertinent metaphor, as the empty space obsessively returns as the platform for another creative gesture. Whilst he, like des Esseintes in the novel, continues to strive to find that authenticity of creative life, Tillyer shows a much more alive and livelier singular pathway for our pleasure, and for the enjoyment of his deep philosophical connectedness with man and his history in the landscape of life.

Painters are very often imbued with the idea that they just have to keep on creating paintings. The process of knowing when a painting is complete is somewhat imprecise and even mystical. And it is entwined with a necessity to keep on, together with a fear of what will happen next without the creative space in front of the artist. Often their solution is to set up a fresh canvas and just make a rudimentary mark on it before retiring to bed. This, to my mind, means that the creative act is a necessity for their life; or it prevents a falling apart by holding the frame—their psychic frame—from fracture. What is the compulsion for Tillyer? He carries the traumas of dead soldiers—his unknown grandfather dead at the Somme, together with his grandmother's loss of her husband. And attached to that is his mother's loss of her father, who she never knew, as she had yet to be born—a state that is particularly hard to mourn as the lost object never had representation as an object.

In addition, as a little boy he was often taken "on holiday" to the British war graves of the Somme: a massive object, too large to under-stand for all of us. The empty space is a way of facing the impossibility of mourning the psychic emptiness of his grandfather, especially in the mind of his mother, generating even more layers of anxiety in case she would have to face the replication of the loss of a husband, which for-tunately did not happen. Tillyer then would be the unconscious carrier of the empty death space of two women—for that, he found a creative solution in the repetition of his creative endeavours.

Bernard Jacobson summarises Tillyers' works as "the adventures of modernism and romanticism—bringing these two together in a piece of art".[8] And for Tillyer, "Art is short for artifice in my book!"[9]

I will leave to last this wonderful picture of Tillyer, an exuberant little boy standing in front of a trellis garden fence that years later he will re-create into his art. The creative act was there already waiting to be released.

Figure 24. Photograph of William Tillyer. Reproduced with permission

CHAPTER 5

Psychosomatic reflections in the analysis of a heroin addict

Prologue

This chapter is based on the first paper I wrote relatively soon after qualifying as an analyst. I was learning the craft, and I was surprised at how the patient took me on a psychosomatic journey as he laid out a developmental line from feeding to urinating to defecating, and to his sexuality as he protected his mind through his strange uses of his body. At that time, I had not read Ferenczi's paper "Psychoanalysis of sexual habits" (1925a), and it was somewhat a relief later to find that he had been writing about similar phenomena as early as 1925.

I have written a chapter that is particularly slanted towards the specific manner in which the analysand shaped his narrative around his perplexities in relation to his physicality and in particular his constant streams of phantasies about how he imagined the inside of his body worked. If you find his associations mechanical, that is surely how he was self-preoccupied, as he was attempting to answer questions of life through the narrow prism of his bodily functions as a safer option to think—an analysis of his body ego.

Introduction

An undergraduate heroin addict was referred for psychoanalysis. His father, himself in psychoanalysis at the time, had thought that this was the only treatment for his son. At the consultation, I met a happy-looking young man of twenty-three, with shoulder-length blond hair. He wore patched old jeans, a cowboy shirt, carried a large bunch of keys attached to his belt and was wearing a pair of ancient shoes that were falling apart. He had an unwashed smell. His uncared for, neglected state elicited an image in me of someone very ill and fragmented, yet just contained and held together.

He had been taking drugs since the age of sixteen. He first tried heroin soon after taking A-level exams, when he was eighteen, injected by a male school friend. His university studies had deteriorated, and he was sent down for a year. Instead of obtaining treatment for what the college felt was his *ennui*, he immersed himself in further drug addiction, becoming the sidekick to a dealer near to his home. At this time, he was apparently taking one eighth of a gram of heroin daily, injected by the dealer, and was spending some £70 a week on his habit (the equivalent of £220 today). He was awaiting prosecution for possessing and distributing the drug: being the subject of criminal proceedings precipitated his referral. Up to this point, his parents had little idea of their son's shadowy life.

Mr X's father was in his mid-fifties. I was given the impression of his being a successful businessman. In time, however, this view was to change, as the patient began to realise how his father was always awaiting the "big deal" that never really happened. His father was emotionally distant, preferring to be in contact with his son by inveterate letter writing. Mr X viewed his father as being very possessive of his wife, preferring her to be indoors, unseen by other men. The patient also viewed his father as being an honourable man, unlike his father's brothers, who were "rogues", financially cheating the taxman as well as each other.

His mother was interested in amateur dramatics and escaped the tedium of her life by going out for weekly play readings. Mr X could otherwise barely describe his relationship to his mother, except for her overfeeding him. He remarked that he found it impossible to refuse her. Generally, Mr X was emotionally distant from both his parents and siblings.

A most important family member, who cast a long shadow, was the paternal grandfather. He was very wealthy, having built several factories, but he had also been financially devious. All his sons had been in the business, except Mr X's father, who left to find his own path in life. Just prior to the grandfather's death, he was under investigation for fraud and tax evasion. The rest of his shadow was his apparent paedophilic interests. There was a family concern not to leave the children with him, based on the patient's father's fears. Mr X had already deduced that his father's distance from him was due to his fear that he had inherited his own father's interests in young boys' genitals.

Mr X had a brother three years older who worked for his father. He was very shut off and seemed to manage life by drinking excessively. Mr X was concerned for his brother's health. He also had a younger sister, about whom he had nothing to say.

During his early life Mr X was anxious that nothing should ever change, and he was often in a state of fear about this. When he was two years old, the family moved house, which upset him greatly. It is likely that the house move occurred in relation to the birth of his sister. On his first day at school, he had, apparently, to be forcibly separated from his mother, leading to much anxiety. He presented a picture of growing up a loner, without friends, living in his own private world.

His medical history seemed relevant, as he had a congenital bone abnormality in both his feet. Walking was painful for him. For years, both his parents thought that he was just being lazy ("lazy bones") and making a fuss about walking. They did not believe that he was actually in physical pain. When he was eleven years old, a schoolteacher was concerned enough to seek a medical opinion, which confirmed his congenital disability. He was subsequently allowed off playing sport at school and later was permitted, unusually for an undergraduate, to have a car at university due to his locomotion difficulties.

The commencement of analysis

Mr X began attending analysis four times a week, initially commuting from quite far away. The court had made it a condition of bail that he was required to live at home. He received a suspended sentence for possessing heroin, and the charge for supplying drugs was dismissed. However, his colleague received a hefty prison sentence.

A few months later, Mr X was attending five sessions of weekly analysis, and continued for several years.

During the first few weeks of analysis, he spilled out his preoccupation with his sexual life. With embarrassment mixed with bravado, he told me that he had lost his virginity two weeks prior to his initial consultation with me. A flatmate, on hearing his difficulties, had invited him to sleep with her just once. He had felt even more perplexed and continued to avoid women for the next three years.

What began to emerge was a man who attempted to exercise great control in order to maintain his passive position in relation to the world. When he was twelve he found, to his horror, that he could not retract his foreskin. He investigated his condition in medical textbooks and for months secretly manipulated his foreskin until he broke the adhesions himself. He was too embarrassed to discuss the matter with his parents or his general practitioner. His fear of telling what he had done to himself was greater than his anxiety around the damage he felt he had done to his penis. I said that, by telling me, he was releasing a psychological adhesion for the first time. He replied that he had felt he had triumphed over his brother, who had had to have a circumcision operation when he had been about eight years old.

Two other incidents were to compound his passive position in relation to sexuality as he was growing up. When he was six years old, the boy next door, who shared the same birthday as his brother, was in the patient's sister's Wendy house. As he spied on them through the window, the boy was examining his naked sister. He went at once and told on her.

The second incident involved a male cousin, one year older, who had entered puberty much earlier. Aged eleven, he was held down by his cousin, who displayed an erection and ejaculated. He felt paralysed and erotic, but mainly disgusted, and had hardly seen his cousin since. These stories involving voyeurism began to reveal his unconscious passive position in relation to the other.

During the first five months of analysis, he had been preoccupied by thoughts of his sexual inadequacy. He had a dream reminiscent of the primal scene:

he was in a dark cinema resting his head on the balcony and feeling its vibrations. There was some new equipment possibly with 3D lighting. There was a psychedelic show on the screen. On the other side of him, was the projection hut. It had three windows and he could see inside. A girl went in with her clothes on. She belonged to the projectionist. He saw them together and she had her legs outspread, but the equipment obscured his view. A man looking like the pop singer Boy George, with yellow hair ribbons, leered.

His associations were to the two earlier childhood memories already mentioned, as well as to the man called Dick who used to inject him with heroin, who invited him onto the bed. He felt afraid. He said he would have liked to have been the projectionist!

The 3D lighting and the three windows may have signified his being three years of age in the dream. The balcony could be a representation of the cot that was at the foot of his parent's bed when he was that age. In the dream, he was perhaps the voyeur of parental intercourse; lighting illuminated the darkness, enabling him to see better, but also to be more easily noticed. He could feel the vibrations in the dream, perhaps of parental intercourse, maybe of his own bodily excitement. His fear of lighting and mechanical devices had been mastered by his studying such mechanisms. His sexual identity, like that of the singer Boy George, was uncertain. Mr X, too, had long yellow hair, until just prior to analysis when he had had it cut, and he was the leering voyeur in the dark. An escape from such a scenario was towards the psychedelic drugs show, but even there he was the passive body being penetrated by a needle wielded by a man.

In the transference, the new equipment referred to the analysis, which was seen to obscure things. He showed anxiety at being on the couch, at my mercy, expecting me to leer at him. He would rather have been the projectionist putting the projections onto me.

He began the next session by telling me that he had always had the thought of wishing to suck his own penis. He was very embarrassed at this disclosure. He told me that he had read somewhere that one in a thousand men could do this, and he wanted to be able to perform such an act. He said it would be like disappearing into nothing, an atom, and this would be so as to stop people seeing what he was doing. I interpreted the opposite of this phantasy; it was that he, far from becoming a minute speck, could become very large, so he could show off his penis, as his cousin had once done (Ferenczi, 1926, p. 41). He then remembered that when he was sixteen he had stayed the night with the same boy who years before had been observed examining his sister. This boy woke him and enticed him into his bed. They ended up sucking each other's penis, but he felt that the boy did not exist. He then said, "It was like his mouth was mine, as was his penis—I was one body and he fitted into me". I interpreted that heroin was completing such a circle of injecting himself. He had created a solipsistic world with no need for another person, such as his analyst, and especially not a woman with no penis. In such a circle, he could be a man, a woman and a man–woman. He then told a dream in which his penis moved in his anus as it had somehow, passively, found its way there, so that he did not know where his legs had gone. He linked this to a masturbatory phantasy of being a woman being penetrated, adding ruefully "I suppose by myself".

He discovered that the real basis for his interest in engineering was a phantasy that he desired to design a mechanism to link his lips and his penis, so that he could complete the circle and suck himself. He did not require people to fill the gap, because they did not seem to exist. Instead, other people had qualities that he would have liked to possess, in order to complete his own narcissistic circle.

At this point, he was describing a life in which, by not knowing about the inside of a woman, he constructed his own circle of knowing. He wished to get away from anxiety both of the unknown and of the woman. He imagined changing his body size, manifestly by shrinking, and this connected with his disparaging term for his psychoanalyst: "such a shrink was a pleasure". He felt it was necessary to get away from other people. Being alone was pleasurable (and protected him from his fear of castration). Yet, at university, he had difficulty keeping the imaginary circle going and then used heroin to ward off reality, as well as to keep his solipsistic system intact. The heroin(e), which, linguistically, is the female hero with whom he identified, was an effect of his sexual world, and not its cause. It was seemingly used to conceal the knowledge that the circle that he made was to avoid knowing that two parents have sex to make a baby—something that was unbearable to him and in all likelihood followed the birth of his sister. This can be seen in the first dream, where he was alone outside the projection box, apart from the two people inside. Yet some part of his mind was curious.

Aspects of anality

Some months into treatment, he entered into an anal phase of analysis, which lasted about eighteen months. He brought a daydream of feeling that he was in a tunnel, which was blocked off at one end. His associations were about his fear of monsters, a concentration camp, electricity, and machines. With the tunnel closed at one end, he felt a little safer, though it would have been safer still if both ends were blocked off, he told me. However, if the tunnel were open-ended, he would have been very scared and feared not being able to escape or hide. Monsters passing by would be able to see him. Even a lamp was dangerous, as it meant he could be seen. He felt paralysed, "unable to move forwards or backwards". He seemed to be construing how he might keep his true self safe from anything to do with reality. I interpreted that it sounded as if he was describing being inside the bowel, or the anus, nearer to one end. He was very shocked by this, and after a pause, said that he did not think that his description fitted any other part of his body, especially as it had no branch lines in the tunnel.

He went on to say that he used to have difficulty in defecating. He thought it strange to talk of it, but he described how he knowingly used to store up his faeces and be constipated as a child, to the point of even staining his underpants. I interpreted that his faeces would then be a barrier for him to hide behind, and that included hiding from our work and understanding in analysis. He agreed, remarking that he feared the open toilet bowl, and used to stand on the seat. I interpreted that he felt his faeces to be dangerous when outside of him, in the same way that he kept his distance from me once material was outside of him (i.e. his resistance beyond his utterances and from session to session).

What I have not yet described was his great obsessionality. He was slow, often boring, and silent, as a means of enacting what he was now describing, storing his associations rather than letting them out, as analysis was, unconsciously, a dangerous toilet for him. These associations could, in phantasy, be placed inside his anus, lodged and imprisoned there, even though it appeared that work was going on.

Later in the analysis, the position of the analyst moved in the patient's mind, beyond his anus, and the attack on thinking changed to a urinary attack. He had a dream of a machine full of water with a laser beam shining on it. The bottom of the machine had a pipe issuing streams of bubbles; it reminded him of a urinal, and he was interested in how the laser light was reflected by the bubbles. I said that perhaps he experienced my interpretations as laser beams, and he deflected them by passing a stream of urine onto my ideas about his mind. The attack on thinking was still present but was moving along the developmental path from anal to urinary at this point in the analysis.

As a boy at school, he was fascinated with the subject of sewage. He imagined fresh food going inside his body, gradually decomposing through layers inside himself and then, at the bottom, being faeces. In this scheme, urination was a form of water purification. He marvelled at the idea of a sewage plant, which invited one to drink purified water. In my countertransference I felt I was the sewage plant, with him giving me his feculent material and my returning "a purified interpretation". Yet he blocked himself. A girl at his university, when asked what she wanted from people, replied that she preferred being understood by others. Mr X was beginning to feel more understanding of himself, but more importantly, understood by me: another person was being allowed to enter his solipsistic world (and a person rather than a mechanism). He commented that he wanted to be me with my knowledge. I replied that then he would lose out on having the other person to understand him. He replied "Oh, I see that now. If I am you, I can't have that".

In this material, he was beginning to have a surface transference identification with his older brother, with whom he shared scatological conversations. Yet he was allowing a deeper relationship to grow, in which he could communicate his sense of isolation to me, and rather than just being the "projectionist", he was becoming aware of his feeling a state of loneliness. The beginnings of a dialogue with a separate other were now becoming possible. In John Rickman's terms (1951), he was engaging from a one-person body to a two-person relationship.

Another daily enactment of his anal psychology was his love of old clothes. He said, "I hate to let go of any piece of clothing". His mother was greatly irritated by his filthy, threadbare, smelly clothes and shoes. He dismissed her reaction by saying that he was really very comfortable.

This was true also of his resistance to analysis. I interpreted how comfortable he felt inside the anus, adding that another way of blocking the tunnel was to bend his body round, in order to put his penis in his bottom, such as when he, apparently, said he could not remember a dream. He reacted to this by saying how fundamental a concept this was for him, and that he really had to find his way out. To my surprise, he brought a deeper interpretation himself, right at the end of that session: "Oh, I forgot to tell you about the birth of my sister. Well, I'll start with that tomorrow."

Here, he was making an unconscious equation of faeces and baby. Next session he was able to continue his associations. He remembered his sister's birth at home when he was three (linking to earlier material of the primal scene, the 3D dream, with the three also representing the three siblings). The midwife had closed the door to his mother's bedroom. This was also another aspect of the apparatus in the earlier dream that got in the way of his view of the screen. The first thing he noticed about his newborn sister was her feet. He thought they were a piano. He then commented that he was turning her from a person into a thing.

Theoretically, this was of great interest as he had a deformity of the bones in his feet—apparently unknown until he was eleven years old. Perhaps he had an unconscious somatic knowledge of this defect and was at once drawn to compare it with the new baby. Were her feet similarly changed inside mother as he felt his had been?

He turned now to his childhood theory of where babies came from. He thought it was something to do with marriage, and a contraceptive pill, and although denying that boys had babies, he still twitched his bottom muscles at night, in case a baby fell out like faeces into the toilet bowl. Part of the ubiquity of the symptom of the heroin could now also be seen as being an unconscious contraceptive device to prevent him having babies.

Oedipal development

In time he brought more overt oedipal material into the free associations of his sessions. He began a session by thinking about his bunch of keys. As a child, at school, he hated the idea of "not being able to get in".

That session he complained that I had begun by letting him into the consulting room some ten seconds later than usual, after he had rung the bell. I interpreted that he wished to control being in and out, especially feeling locked out in the cold by me.

With evident pleasure, he told me how only he could now lock his college room at university. He had taken the lock out, changed the tumblers and cut his own key. Only he had a key; the college key was of no use now. He felt much safer. I interpreted that he was talking as if he was once left out and never wanted to have such an experience repeated. After a lengthy pause, I added that the key, of course, could represent his penis and he might want to get inside a locked vagina. He at once associated to a play his mother had acted in called *Gas Light*. He told me that he had cleared out the attic above his bedroom, as he hated the idea of what was inside it attacking him. He had wired the attic with lots of lights and even cleaned it compulsively. I interpreted that the attic's dark space may have represented for him the dark space inside a woman, which he was both exploring and fearful of. "Oh yes, Pandora's box." He then described the play. A husband attempting to drive his wife mad in order to obtain her hidden jewels had entered their attic to frighten his wife. Her lover realised and rescued her.

I interpreted that Pandora's box was full of danger for him, such as his fear that his penis would be damaged inside a woman as he himself imagined that his feet had been damaged inside his mother's womb. Also, he considered that the space belonged to his father, and that if he returned there, he feared that his father would attack him. This idea connected with his observation of his father's possessiveness of his mother.

Earlier he had spoken of how he had been shown the top floor of the professor's lab and that the next week he would be shown his latest laser. I interpreted that it could be a laser to see in the dark but also a laser to be used as a weapon. He agreed, adding that it was benign and that he really did want to find out about women.

This material showed his great sexual confusion. He had the key, but it was chained to him. His paranoia was now able to emerge in relation to the primal scene. However much as he defended himself from attack, with electrical circuits and with locked doors, by possessing the only key, there was still the monster there waiting to castrate him. The monster's character was bisexual. Father was in the space, wanting to castrate the son as rival for possession of mother; but mother was also the monstrous attacker of the vulnerable baby in her womb, deforming his feet–penis.

His defensive direction was to leave two- and three-person relationships and to be within a narcissistic circle of one—himself living in a narcissistic omnipotent world. The analyst was perceived in the space above him trying to drive him mad, as in the play.

Two weeks later Mr X had a vivid womb dream, which he almost forgot to tell.

> He was in a large room like a corridor, yet bigger or perhaps he felt he was smaller. There was an incline running from floor to ceiling taking up space and there were cobblestones. He wondered where to put himself, either on the floor or near the ceiling light. He thought that two people were absent.

He associated his father's favourite poem about Kubla Khan's pleasure dome. He thought that the two absent people in the dream were his parents. He then vaguely remembered the second part of the dream.

> He was put into enemy territory to meet up with the "goodies". He was an undercover agent disguised in a Nazi uniform. The "goodies" did not know who he was and shot him. He thought he was on the "wrong" side, although he was not.

I interpreted that in the first part of the dream he was inside his mother in her pleasure dome observing his father's penis as the incline taking up the space as something in the way (the same way as there was obstruction in the first dream): the cobblestones were painful for his feet, made in the womb to walk upon. The gap between the two parts of the dream represented his problem of going from an uncomfortable space shared with his parents, to moving out into the second part to find his own space, which was felt as being dangerous. He thought he was upset that his father was shooting him. I interpreted the opposite: that he might be shooting his father (connecting it to a word play on his surname). He ended the session saying how fed up he was at having such long hair.

This complicated session showed how hard it was to understand which side he was on—with the "goodies", pretending to be a Nazi, or really being a Nazi. It was the same confusion as to whether he was the victim of heroin (a heroine needing rescue from evil) or the sadist attacking and penetrating his psyche-soma with cruelty. Such dynamics were displayed in both directions in the transference, with both needing to be worked through.

Treating Mr X as a victim only enhanced his passive feminine longings. Silent resistance through many sessions was an example of his not telling the "Nazi analyst" information about the system. The opposite, his subversive sadistic attacks on the analyst, will be shown in more detail later. Yet this session did elucidate the womb fantasy of his perception of watching his father's penis inside his mother and the subsequent split-off menace involving somebody shooting somebody. It had a resonance to *shooting* heroin.

In the subsequent session he expressed his fury at how he felt I was treating him like a naive child. He was horrified to think of Nazi concentration camp experiments. He watched a television programme about a medical intern who had been in a concentration camp; did the doctor actually do the Nazi experiments or make them better? He was reminded of having thoughts as a child of wanting to cut his sister into little pieces.

Relation to the breast

Following his parents' house move, he discovered that a plaster ceiling rose had been placed in his cupboard. He stacked some possessions on top of it and the pile tipped over. In a fury, he tried to throw the rose into a wastepaper bin, missed and found that he had thrown it through the window.

He then said that the plaster rose was incomplete as it had no centre. One implication was an idea that he had experienced being breastfed with a central hole rather than a nipple, and it was this idea that had enraged him. It was as if he had needed to construct a nipple over an absence, in order to imagine that all was well, such as an injection of heroin—a destructive filling of a hole that ultimately did not give him a satisfying feed. As a little boy he remarked that he must not make any fuss, especially about his feet, and be a good boy, no matter his suffering. His mother even provided a sleeping bag for him by her side of the bed. He had a long-standing phantasy that his mother was Sleeping Beauty, always around, waiting to be kissed by the Prince.

He needed to continually construct a nipple over an internal gap, as he developed a false self. Yet beneath such a structure lurked, within the hole, a murderous rage. This construction connected his ambivalence towards women and his fear of entering their hole sexually. It also related back to a primary experience with his mother, who, like the rose, was in the cupboard. Further evidence was furnished by the patient, who said that his mother's maiden name was a flower like a rose. It looked as if there were a whole breast from which to have a good feed. Yet, he was left with one with a hole. His feeds from Dick had been injections of heroin—a destructive hole rather than a proper satisfying feed. In the negative transference, he could experience me as a breast with no nipple as such but instead a hole where he felt I misunderstood or treated him naively.

Winnicott has written about a special example of the environmental factor.

> Either the mother has a breast that *is*, so that the baby can also *be* when the baby and mother are not yet separated out in the infant's rudimentary mind; or else the mother is incapable of making this contribution, in which case the baby has to develop without the capacity to be, or with a crippled capacity to be. (Winnicott, 1966a, p. 326)

The mother's breast from this material was a plaster rose with a hole instead of a nipple—so he had to make do within his own resources and was doubly crippled if his damaged feet are included.

Only once had the door been shut to him—at his sister's birth. He felt himself to be "the apple of his mother's eye" and he imagined he was able to twist her to make her do what he wanted. He experienced a blissful union with her, assuming that just by being with her, both of them together, he could do whatever he liked. Such a nirvana precluded the need to separate, to work, and face reality. This was comparable to the passive state of bliss with heroin inside him, equivalent to him and his mother being side by side—yet both positions were of pathological states. In fact, during his years of addiction, all his peculiar behaviour was totally accepted by his parents without too much anxiety or worry about what was happening to their son. This changed after his arrest by the police, as reality cut through the states of false self-bliss. This is further evidence that he had constructed a false self-defensive organisation, implying that his relation to his mother was blissful, while denying the reality of her lack of concern for and with him.

Death

In Freud's essay on "The theme of the three caskets" (1913f), the number three represented three mythic representations of woman: the mother who carries one inside her, the mother that one oedipally desires and, thirdly, mother death when one is returned to the earth.

Just before the end of the summer term and some eight months after discussing the special key he had made for himself, Mr X spoke directly about a colleague who had tried to kill himself with an overdose. Mr X was very concerned, but he was also the "projectionist" of the first dream. I pointed out to him that one use of the special key would be to enable him to kill himself in his room with nobody being able to reach him.

He was angry that I spoke such a thought. I interpreted that now, for the first time, he was openly bringing his suicidal thoughts into the sessions, and that my interpretation had been able to reach him emotionally. This was especially so as he was beginning to have a clearer view of his projections onto his parents and myself. He was due to have his own flat with a double bed, having just qualified with his degree. By this time his work life consisted mainly of psychoanalysis, and he realised that he needed to look for a job. He was sombre, but also relieved that his wish for suicide was something that could be discussed. He was gaining understanding about his destructive impulses, including his addictive behaviour, which was also in the realms of having been in a state of chronic suicide. The construction of a false self contained a defence against having affect too painful to bear. He did not have depressive feelings, more a feeling of deadness rather than wishing to die. In a sense he obsessively/addictively returned to a constant state of falling apart, which is part of an unconscious sense of maternal non-holding. Beneath the surface he was always on guard, anxious and alone.

Sexual theories

One Friday session he returned to the theme of his childhood theories about his body. He had recently been struck by an old idea that when he defecated he had no need to urinate. He thought that defecation was like the ramming of food through a press, and that urine was some of the exudate that went through a porous piston. Thus, the two processes, in his mechanistic theory, would occur concurrently. Now he was beginning to discriminate between different bodily functions. I wondered if he might be developing a capacity for erection, independent from his gastro-intestinal machinery.

He used to have a theory that erection worked by some hard internal object, probably, as he imagined it, a bone inside his body moving forward filling a space and erecting his penis. He was shocked when he read that it was blood that was the physiological transmission. He remarked that he never understood or even believed in hydraulics, especially the incompressibility of fluid. He agreed that such thinking was not in the past, but still actively present in his mind. I interpreted that if he thought there was an internal solid penis inside him, he may have thought that women were similarly endowed. He replied that "the vagina would then be a strange place to discover a penis!"

He had read many medical textbooks when young in order to attempt to understand what was under his skin. He had been unable to relate it to himself and thought that he was different. I interpreted one aspect of injecting heroin as putting a probe inside his body to discover what was inside. He said that he had always been relieved at seeing blood in the syringe, as he expected there to be nothing inside himself. He had no idea that he had an inside, until he had been injected! Implicit was the analytic probe that, by discovering the phantasy content of his mind, enabled him to develop an idea of the content of his psyche–soma.

The next Monday session, following the weekend break, had a very different atmosphere. It felt a dull, dreary session and I felt drained, attacked and unable to think. Despite the progress of the previous session in discriminating one thing from another, I felt we were both back in a confusional state, or at least, I was.

Some time into the session I heard him tell me a dream:

> He met a man he used to meet, two years senior to himself, when he was an undergraduate. He was a peculiar man who left medicine for philosophy, dropped out and had a breakdown because of drug addiction. This man was offering him morphine. The patient had no money and tried to obtain some from a cash machine. Despite inserting his card several times, he was unable to get money out because the machine kept asking him questions.
>
> He was sure the machine was recording various transactions that he was trying to cheat on, and he tried to break that part of the recording machine so he could withdraw money without anyone knowing. From time to time, an attendant came out and he was unable to attack the machine.

I still found it very hard to think in his presence, which was unlike my experience with other patients that day. He gave associations that were difficult for me to remember. Eventually, I made an interpretation following his association about feeling imprisoned on that Monday session, that "the dream was his desire to break up the machine from thinking and recording, and that the machine was me". He was mounting an attack on my capacity to think. The attendant in the dream was the daily analytic session protecting the capacity to think, but neither the analyst nor the thoughtful patient had been in attendance at the weekend. The patient was surprised and agreed that he found the weekend particularly difficult. He felt he had to constantly be on guard. He described an obsessional ritual in which he asked himself questions and questioned the answers in an attack designed to slowly wear down his resistance, especially why he should not take drugs. He was supposed eventually to say to himself that he might as well take heroin or get drunk. He accepted the attack on his own capacity to think because he knew that when he was not attacking "the machine" such internal dialogue was crazy.

In the session my perplexity and realisation that I was under intense attack was a communication by him to enable me to experience what it was like, by reverse transference: I being, like him, shut out from me at the weekend. He had by this time been in analysis for two years and I was the peculiar man in the dream who left medicine for psychoanalysis and to whom he was giving a breakdown. Only by my experiencing the breakdown could his breakdown come into focus for himself. My feeling was that it was a prelude to his connecting with his own affect within his true self.

He was trying to cheat on me by inserting his card (projections) into me and pretending to do analysis while craving drugs. To my knowledge, since I had begun treating him he had not taken heroin. However, he took cough linctus on a couple of occasions, and got drunk on several evenings prior to ceasing. It seemed that my retention of a capacity to think through this session enabled much analytic working through to occur over the next few months.

He remembered that, following the realisation by his teacher that there was something physically wrong with his feet, his father took him to his own acupuncturist. Mr X was fascinated by the needles and thought of stealing one but did not. It was clear that prior to an injection of heroin from a man, there had been an earlier situation where a man put a needle in him, and that this was linked to his father. This led to thoughts in him about the word "parenteral"[1] injection and his thinking about mental injections given by his parents. He had thought of Dick, the man who injected him, as a father figure.

He began to be freer to experience his cruel mental constructions towards his internal objects.

He remembered a record by the rock group The Doors called "The End". In the song, a son walked down a corridor, went past his sister's room and entered his parents' room, killing his father and having incest with his mother. He felt a chill in recounting the words of the song to me. He knew he had violent thoughts towards his father and mother.

When having phantasies about girls, an iconic image of his mother would at once come to his mind, dispelling an erotic image. Thus, he kept faith with his mother and all thoughts of other women were destroyed.

Yet, he was terrified that any movement would lead to incest. He could not bear to touch his mother and sister. He too was the untouchable icon as he identified with his mother as the untouchable virgin. The insignia for Virgin Records was a semi-circle with the word "Virgin" written above a guardian snake. He had the letters blown up and put over his bed as an unconscious picture of the Virgin Madonna looking down on him alone in his bed. He was embarrassed at even being naked in front of his insignia.

He also felt he could not have a girl in bed in case his dead grandparents would look down and see. I interpreted that he was deflecting from his parents watching and its reverse of him watching his parents as a sexual couple. If he could allow his parents the freedom to have sex with each other he might have some mental space free of the image of killing his father and having sex with his mother, so that he could own his own body with greater imaginative sexual freedom.

He began to remember warm feelings of closeness to his father, such as rubbing his tobacco for him when he was a little boy. He thought he had moved away from such closeness from his father at the birth of his sister.

I interpreted how he could not have warm memories of his father until he had appreciated his wish to kill him (and me), and that his desire to keep away from women was in one sense because his anger at how women, in particular his sister, came between him and his father.

Aspects of homosexuality

Just before his third year in analysis, he brought the following dream.

> He was driving towards my consulting room, on the motorway. He suddenly realised there a slightly overgrown slip road. He decided to go down it, having for three years never explored the small country roads leading off it. In the dream, it became a little-used road between Britain and the rest of Europe. He found himself in Norway; the connection that interested him was his idea that my surname was Scandinavian. He went through passport control, putting on the form, with some pride, his new profession that he had just qualified in from university. People were interested in him.

>He then seemed to enter another country. Then the piece of
>paper, which was the passport, blew away, and he tried to chase after
>it. The atmosphere had turned very menacing.

The motorway in the dream seemed to represent his single-minded homosexual path as in the idea of the bowel with no branchways. Then, he found a slip road. The new land (as in cuntry) that he had not explored, was a woman. Despite his pleasure there, and his professional pride, he became frightened and took to drugs in his unconscious phantasy (chasing the dragon—heroin inhalation), in order to remove himself from incest with his mother. All this was a defensive posturing to protect him from another woman who was not his mother.

He had been thinking recently that he himself had a vagina. I interpreted that this would be an attempt to allow himself to be penetrated by his monster father–analyst, as a way of being closer to his father, but also to protect him from incest with his mother and sister. He was also indicating that he thought of himself as female. An idea was emerging now that if he did not have a good-enough mother he could be his own mother for himself. Either way he did not need to *have* the object if he could *be* the object.

At the end of the session, he mentioned buying a bottle of wine to drink all alone the previous night. After one glass, he realised he did not want to drink the whole bottle as he would be ill, so he poured it down the toilet.

Some three years into analysis, he did then manage to go to abroad for a holiday. He was excited both by seeing girls in the coffee bar, and prostitutes in the town. To cope with and neutralise his masculinity, he got drunk, destroying an erotic imaginative experience. He returned to the next session with an exciting, but as he thought, disgusting sexual phantasy that he had had that night. He imagined himself as a woman being penetrated by his own penis, which was detached from him. I interpreted that this was a defence to keep himself away from having sex with a woman and was equivalent to his being penetrated by alcohol or a heroin injection. He then associated that he had a phantasy of what his grandfather did to his children and grandchildren. He remembered how his grandfather had held the genitals of his cousin, asking him how long it took to go hard. He was shaken by the destructiveness in his system of thinking, which so quickly allowed the good moments of his holiday to disappear.

Towards genitality

I was told a nightmare.

> He was the archaeologist in charge of a site and in the pit there were some bones, but something was out of place. The bones moved. This made him realise that there was something quite horrific that was still happening on the site. He could not bear to look at it, and then he remembered another part of a dream where there was a woman full of concern and loving feelings towards him, and she touched him gently on the arm.

He could at once see the anxiety about his violence and retaliation towards me. He had feared getting up to go to the toilet in case he was attacked and linked it with his fear of the attack from the high roof space in the consulting room. The displaced bone was interpreted as the bone between he and I, his apparent penile bone that contained his violent phantasies. He did not want to see what damage he feared he had done to me, and equally feared my retaliation. Yet, beyond the violence, he was also in touch with his sense of concern and love.

The bone also represented the bones in his feet, as if when he was excavating the site, he could realise that it was not all dead, damaged bones and genitals, but that something was moving. He could now be in touch with a psychic realisation that in fact his genitals were intact and that a few days before this session he actually proved it by having had successful, enjoyable and erotic sexual intercourse with a woman. This was very different from his defensive manoeuvre of losing his virginity a few days before the commencement of his analysis.

Ending

At the end of his analysis he had a complex dream in which

> he was in a large manor house where a fair was taking place. He went to the toilet and found that it was some dispensary for rucksacks.

Later he found himself naked, with his toes and hair and penis touching the ground, but there was also a faceless woman who he found very attractive. He found himself walking around with her being carried on his erection.

The reference to the fair was some years before, when he would stand aloof at a midsummer fair watching everybody else enjoy themselves and he would be just alone. He thought that the toilet dispensing rucksacks was his old home, where there used to be such an outbuilding filled with games kit and he realised that his father was very sporty. This was in antagonism to the patient, who was never good at games because of the defect in his feet. The interpretation was that he could show in a dream that, whilst not a sporty person, he did have a sexual life, which prior to analysis he thought would be as irrevocably damaged as the rest of his life.

During the analysis, various themes were examined, in particular, Mr X's anality, his desire to be feminine, his sadomasochistic phantasy life and his cruelty in his relationships. He had been able to move beyond his anality, towards genitality and from a solipsistic addictive state of mind to a more benign state of sharing, and most importantly, being able to feel. He was able to examine these in connection to his unconscious relationships with his nuclear family and the severe early trauma in his life.

The influencing machine

Victor Tausk, originally a lawyer, was one of Freud's first pupils in 1909. He studied medicine and became a psychiatrist. He wrote an extraordinary and seminal paper titled "On the origin of the influencing machine". It was published in 1919, the year of his early death, aged forty-two, in which he describes psychoanalytical concepts in regard to clinical psychosis. Tausk's influencing machine is a schizophrenic machine

of mystical nature. It consists of boxes, cranks, levers, wheels, buttons, wires, batteries, and the like. Patients endeavour to discover the construction of the apparatus by means of technical knowledge, and it appears that with the progressive popularisation of the sciences, all the forces known to technology are utilised to explain the functioning of the apparatus. (Tausk, 1919, p. 31)

Tausk is describing a machine that serves to persecute the patient, operated by enemies—paranoid features of a schizophrenic state. Yet Tausk also describes "The same complaints without influencing machine". These he classes

> as a group of patients that dispenses completely with any gratification of the need for causality, and complains simply of emotional changes and strange apparitions within the physical and psychic personality, without the intervention of a foreign or hostile power. (ibid., pp. 34–35)

He also thinks that such symptomatology begins with feelings of alienation and estrangement. Tausk even writes: "I have no hesitation in maintaining that under especially favourable circumstances it may be possible to observe the entire series of developmental stages in a single patient" (ibid., p. 35).[2] My patient went through such body ego developmental stages, which, whilst at times were bizarre, were not so profoundly paranoid.

Another way of understanding the machine is that complicated machines appearing in dreams stand for the patient's genitalia and are linked to sexual excitement, masturbation and can contain unconscious defensive structures to defend against massive anxiety. His decision to manipulate his foreskin until he broke the adhesions preventing its retraction is a case in point, as his anxiety around someone else knowing (even a doctor) and treating him was too humiliating and frightening (although later he allowed another doctor to analyse him). Losing his virginity just prior to starting analysis was another way of controlling his sexual anxieties about being a virgin. The idea of his being able to give himself oral gratification by sucking his own penis reflected his fear of another person being part of a sexual dyad and a symptom of his paranoia. Similarly, reconstructing the lock of his college rooms protected anybody else from entering him, an example of homosexual paranoia. So, although he had considerable bodily phantasies, which were towards a direction of paranoia, together with his fear of my "influencing him", he was amenable to the analytic process such that treatment was a developmental process in developing his ego towards the reality and possibility of relationships rather than frank paranoia emerging of himself as the "projectionist". Let me leave Tausk with a last thoughtful word on the entire body being perceived as a genital, and for my patient one not damaged:

> the phantasy originates in the intrauterine (mother's body) complex and usually has the content of a man's desire to creep completely into the genital from which he came, refusing to content himself with any lesser satisfaction. The entire individual is in this case a penis. (ibid., p. 62)

Womb–Tomb from intrauterine, birth, development and returning back to mother (Earth) at death.

Discussion

If a mother has no sense of adapting herself to her infant, then it is left to the self to manage.

For such a mother it may be that unspeakable anxiety leaves her no choice but to keep at a distance, escaping to go to play readings. It is likely that the patient was not held or touched much, so that a large part of his understanding of his insides was a creative development by himself, using a theory of hydraulics to make sense of, for instance, digestion and excretion. In all his ideas in this area he is patently alone, with no sense of another involved in his somatic processes. So a capacity for love has had to be contained, developed and imagined as a one-person experience, which was his false self. Under the surface of my patient's ability to cope and manage alone, it is likely that he had unthinkable anxiety, such that he developed various ego distortions, including developing a schizoid character. He had a specific defence of self-holding, which grew in his sexual imagination to thinking that he could feed himself from himself as well as have intercourse with himself later on. Thus, the problem of an emotionally absent mother was creatively solved in the pathological register of his false self.

Later he added heroin to his self support. On the surface it was a man who helped introduce him to his habit, but I think it soon become just a relationship with the drug rather than a person. Metaphorically he had discovered a heroine as substitute for his mother, one that he fed off by injecting himself as a heroic female. Analysis, when he began to have a degree of trusting its environment, allowed him to share his singular, anxious, private world for the first time and this led to his capacity to begin to experience and feel his affect for the first time.

In his "Fear of breakdown" paper (1963b) Winnicott cites a group of primitive agonies: anxieties that the baby has to deal with if the ego cannot organise against environmental failure. There is a return to an unintegrated state, assuming that there was some ordinary healthy maternal environment. Self-holding is the defensive response to fear of falling forever. There is a loss of psychosomatic collusion if the mother is absent, physically and psychically, from the environment. Ideas of how the body is constructed and how the model works is his construction of a mechanistic self that is necessarily psychotic in its creativity, as it reveals that there is nobody else there. He has created it himself. This in time becomes a discovery in analysis as the private material is revealed to another person such that the analysand begins to have a sense that he is no longer alone.

Prior to this there had been no sense of the real, as the infant was dealing with the world alone with an inability to relate to objects. This leads to autistic states, and in my patient's case to relating only to self phenomena. The work of the analysis burst into extraordinary details of his somatic and sexual psychosis trying to work out the meanings of life in a one-person state. He imagines he has a sexual prowess to inseminate himself through his mouth. There is no need to postulate the necessity for a mother or father as he exploits his primary narcissism. Yet, as he explores in analysis, by examining the private secret details he comes to experience that privation and loneliness, which until then had not been emotionally felt or experienced. As Winnicott states,

> Unless the therapist can work successfully on the basis that this detail is already a fact, the patient must go on fearing to find out what is being compulsively looked for in the future.

He continues:

> if the patient is ready for some kind of acceptance of this queer kind of truth, that what is not yet experienced did nonetheless

happen in the past, then the way is open for the agony to be experienced in the transference, in reaction to the analyst's failures and mistakes ... Gradually the patient gathers the original failure of the facilitating environment into the area of his or her omnipotence and the experience of omnipotence which belongs to the state of dependence (transference fact). (Winnicott, 1963b, p. 527)

For my patient, his psychotic self-centred theory was a defence against being empty. He needed to be empty in analysis as a negative representation of a full environment that had been denied him. As he matured, it became possible for him to experience the emptiness leading to a realisation that he was alone—paradoxically alone in the presence of the analyst. He also moved to realise that his heroin addiction was drawing him surreptitiously towards death. The clinical material of his changing the lock to his door such that only he had the "master" key meant he could not be rescued from suicide. Feeling his affect led to change, as he realised that he wanted to live an alive life.

The roots of his addiction to heroin were examined in depth during the development of his analysis, from the vengeful, addicted state of mind to one in which he had a capacity for concern both for himself and others. He was able to achieve a capacity for non-perverse genitality. He completed analysis not only having given up taking heroin and other drugs of addiction, but more importantly, the addictive and perverse types of relationships both in the external world and in regard to his internal object relationships had become more benign. He had been able to move beyond his anality, towards genitality and, from a solipsistic, addictive state of mind to a more benign state of sharing. A woman could be carried on his erection, without either of them being damaged.

Looking back on this case, which began nearly forty years ago, I am struck at the developmental unfolding of the material. The patient arrived at analysis in a state of being alone and it took much time for the realisation to accrue that his solipsistic state meant that the analyst did not exist. For a long time, such a one-person psychological state needed to be accepted. What seems to have been continually missing was any anxiety. Instead, he applied a distorted sense of "knowing" how the body worked, defined in terms of a primitive set of hydraulics, in order to wipe out feeling in himself and in any relationship. As Winnicott puts it:

> There is a state of affairs in which the fear is of madness, that is to say a fear of a *lack of anxiety at regression* to an unintegrated state, to absence of a sense of living in the body, etc. The fear is that there will be no anxiety, that is to say, that there will be a regression, from which there may be no return. (Winnicott, 1952, p. 58)

Certainly, there was much oedipal material that could have been interpreted, but that is analytic work available only later, when the other comes into focus. Arguably this is the cause of much failure in analytic technique when the analyst makes what seems on the surface a valid interpretation, as if two persons are present, or worse, that the analysand is capable at that moment of understanding and processing oedipal material. Such times invariably lead to an empty response to an oedipal interpretation and in the long run, despair in the analyst, who finds themself stuck with their good interpretations, as alone as their patient. Of course, such a countertransference position can lead the analyst to a better realisation of the state of aloneness, and in time help the patient move from the defensiveness of that state of mind to having a capacity for aloneness, as Winnicott discovered, as being in the presence of the other. As he writes:

> Gradually the ego-supportive environment is introjected and built into the individual's personality, so that there comes about a capacity actually to be alone. (Winnicott, 1958a, p. 36)

If this has either not developed in infancy or had to be regressed from, then it can be (re)established through the analytic process.

My patient had, from very early on, an arrested developmental process, which, once there was an unconscious establishment that he was in the presence of another who may be benign, could then associate through his idiosyncratic ideas of oral, anal and genital phantasy life rather than to enact a tear to the adhesions to his foreskin by himself and unknown to anyone else.

CHAPTER 6

Revisiting "A child is being beaten": reflections on maternal sadism

Not clearly sexual, not in itself sadistic, but yet the stuff from which both will later come.
Freud, recalling the Three Witches to Banquo in *Macbeth*.
"A child is being beaten", 1919e, p. 187

Miss A had a long and successful analysis. She was able to know about and understand being an unwanted and somewhat lost child. Later she was able to marry and have the family that she always feared was an impossibility. After a few years, the patient returned a couple of times annually to discuss specific issues. Some years on I realised that a habit had been formed, which required my hearing about her regular states of regression. Something had been missed or had only been unconsciously unavailable in the work over the years. Further ongoing analysis revealed a deeper psychic layer containing beating phantasies and the consequences of overt maternal cruelty and its unconscious representations, which this chapter explores.

Beating theory

Freud's 1919 paper has been and still remains controversial. Jones, in his biography, seemed not to give the paper much importance in the evolution of theory. Yet the paper is full of ideas, inferences and a sense of sitting on the fence of what may have been actually experienced in early life, memories of actual events, memory distortions as part of the forward and back time movements of *Nachträglichkeit*, as well as phantasies that have their own developmental process. Freud describes a very complex web of memory and desire, which can be an underpinning of character development, whether or not something happened to evoke a highly sexually excited scene.

From six clinical cases of beating phantasies in boys and girls, surfacing up to the age of five or six, Freud describes three phases in girls:

1. *My father is beating the child I hate*
   This can be a phantasy or the emergence of feelings towards the unwanted birth of the next sibling. Freud is unconvinced of the sexuality of this phase, preferring the meaning "My father does not love the other child, he loves only me".
2. *I am being beaten by my father*
   Here the child producing the phantasy has transformed the earlier phase into an "unmistakable masochistic character". Debased genital love for the father and punishment for incestuous wishes are both parts of this second formation. This is never remembered and for Freud "in a certain sense … has never had a real existence" (p. 185).
3. *A teacher beats children*
   This phase is consciously remembered. The teacher is a representation of the father. The second and third phases have a strong sexual excitement.

In the ensuing clinical material, we will find that my patient does not really remember being beaten by her father and, as Freud describes in phase two, such a thought "has never had a real existence".

Masochism is a central theme of Freud's paper, yet he is equivocal about its genesis and evolution, stating "little light is thrown upon the genesis of masochism by our discussion of the beating phantasy". Yet he describes the reconstructed phantasy of being beaten by the father "as a convergence of the sense of guilt and sexual love", adding, "Here for the first time we have the essence of masochism" (p. 193). What Freud is describing is the shifts in the phantasy as developments of inner unconscious constructions balance external reality at any given period of growing up. As the Novicks explain it (1997), the beating phantasy implies a particular type of relationship—one of power and submission. Freud delineates how it emerges out of the child's rage and humiliation at being dethroned from the position of sole recipient of parental love: from internal feelings of helplessness, hurt and rage, the child constructs the wish that the father should beat and so humiliate the despised rival. The transformation of the "sadistic" wish to the "masochistic" wish to be beaten by the father are spurred by the internal changes of the oedipal phase, which lead the child into the wish to be the recipient of the father's love and to have his baby. Thus the 1919 paper contains a clear model for the object-relational component of sadomasochism.

Directing attention to the object-relatedness of sadomasochism can perhaps be taken further by suggesting that sadomasochism is part of the substrate of all object relationships, from mild to pathological and perverse. We are all, as characters, unconsciously masochistic and sadistic to our objects and expect, in tandem or in talion, that our objects are so with us. The point is, rather, the degree to which helplessness, hurt and rage are refracted through a sadomasochistic relational screen as to whether the impact on our character and how we relate to the other is benign or malignant. This, in turn, is affected by the impact of any trauma in the child and what its impact is within unconscious phantasy.

Freud notes that those who harbour beating phantasies develop a special sensitivity and irritability towards father figures. Or in a wider sweep, such "sensitivity" can lead to a myriad diffusion of identifying with the victim and/or the perpetrator, which means, for some people, a complex pattern of oscillating between the two. In addition, such sadomasochistic mechanisms can also be enacted within and against the self in psychosomatic formations. From such a perspective, beating phantasies are ubiquitous and always part of the matrix of the formation of object relations and an indispensable arena for the formation of character.

The writing of the paper followed the end of the Great War, which rather than bringing just relief, led to continuing difficulty in finding work and food shortages. This led Freud to describe the "death and destruction drive", as he became attuned by the impact of the war to the question of psychic violence. The 1919 paper can be viewed in a wider societal frame of the abuses of power and the sense and impact of feelings of being beaten and suffering. In particular, political and historic forms offer some deeper analysis of identification with the father–leader who beats by projective mechanisms whilst looking after his people.

Yet where is the mother, in the beating paper that continuously returns in every developmental position to the father? As has been pointed out by the Novicks, this is Freud's "glaring omission" (1997, p. 40): "Freud does not mention the mother at all in relation to his female patients and refers to the Oedipal mother only with the males" (ibid.). Even in the oral phase, it is the masochistic fear of being eaten by the father that is described, wiping out the mother's primary and feeding role in reality and in the early constructions of the part object relational beginnings of "Me–Not-Me" as the object relationship between self and mother emerge.

Leaving aside the primary importance of the maternal register leads to the assumption of the equation of femininity, passivity and the masochistic position. As Winnicott stated in "Hate in the counter-transference" (1949), "normative feminine masochism" is false. If the mother can be the power-refracting object, then all the arguments about the supreme importance of the paternal object as the development of phantasies around sadomasochism at once fall, shifting the developmental terrain into even more complex webs of two- and three-person psychology. This becomes the terrain of Klein in the shift from paternal to maternal and, in particular, the infant's relation to the maternal body. Yet for Freud, the rethinking of the social theories of the primal horde and the murder of the father are not recast in the light of his discovery of pre-oedipality and the importance of the mother.

In my clinical example it is the mother and not the father who is specifically the early signifier in the perverse frame.

Miss A entered analysis because she felt alone, perplexed and unable to know how to have a relationship that might lead to having a family life. She was the eldest of three children in a family from abroad. Her parents emotionally neglected her, although it was difficult to ascertain much of the detail. She could, however, sketch an atmosphere of both parents being regularly enraged with the children and each other. The parents would hit each other, occasionally even drawing blood. The implication was that the children lived in constant expectation of violence towards them or someone else.

Her sister, born three years later, was probably a relief to the patient, as she was then not the only recipient of rageful neglect. In fact, the position quickly crystallised out in a particular way when it became clear that the desired son was just another girl. Their mother never stopped referring to the younger sister as "the devil's spawn", and she became the centre of the mother's disdain and contempt. The family moved between different countries over the years. Despite being highly intelligent, Miss A was unable to devote herself to getting lost, as she desired, in reading, as books were difficult to find, as well as being discouraged. Later, quickly dispensing with any schoolwork that needed to be done, her many spare hours were spent lying in the sun reading and re-reading romantic novels. She developed a capacity for living in a bubble in which she was easily able to retreat from the daily dull, and at times caustic, reality of life. During this time, she developed a debilitating skin condition of widespread eczema, particularly on her face, which repeatedly became infected, forming facial pustules. This became a somatic defence developed from puberty about anyone coming too close to her. It also represented on her skin the problem she had in life of not having been touched, held and desired.

When she was fourteen, the two children were sent to a weekly boarding school abroad, close to her father's roots and near her grandparents. Living with their grandparents at weekends became a source of some pleasure, and together with boarding, provided some relief from the profound difficulties and uncertainty of predicting the next mental and physical assault by their parents. Her father provided no money and expected that his parents would just pay for everything other than the school fees.

Shortly after the children's departure for England, their mother became pregnant, and the desired son was born. Ever after, he was treated in a "royal" way, receiving privileges and love in abundance, in sharp contrast to his older sisters.

Revising for her exams for only a few days, Miss A gained a scholarship at an Oxbridge college. Most of her time as an undergraduate was lived in a cocoon in which she over-ate, hardly worked, continued with her diet of junk books, and rarely connected with college life. Masturbation was valued, alongside daydreams of going out with a handsome young man. She gained a reasonable degree, again in the absence of much study, and began a professional career.

Some time later she had a boyfriend. He became very controlling and emotionally abusive in the relationship. Yet her enjoyment of now having a sexual life with a partner was more important to her than his disdain and her uncertainty about when he would next see her. This relationship continued for a few years, during which he periodically left her for other women, and due to her developing masochism, she always allowed him to return. Some time after that, she came for a consultation, as she was concerned that she was emotionally stuck. Later the sado-masochism of her late adolescence would return in the transference.

She entered five-times-weekly analysis and quickly felt very comfortable and held by being on the couch. As the work progressed and she developed the various threads of her story, several themes emerged. She had felt that she needed to look after her younger sister in order to try to protect her from being hated by her parents. While she was unable to alter the venom and disdain directed at her sister, she felt that she could recognise what was happening and tried hard to mitigate it. More than anything, she developed a kindness towards her sister. Nonetheless, her sister developed a thick carapace of not feeling what was being done to her, either emotionally or physically. Miss A had to realise that her kindness also contained an element of self-serving, as she was protected from the direct impingement of being beaten. Miss A valued this insight, although it covered over much of the hatred that spilled over onto herself as a girl who, culturally, was inferior to men. Moreover, her mother made it transparently clear that education was wasted on girls, as their only value was to care for their parents as they grew old. The idea that one might reap the harvest that one had sown was quite lost on the parents, as well as my patient who, despite all, managed apparently to retain a kind cheerfulness of purpose.

Another important thread was to expose her passive acceptance of her lover's sadism and constant disappearances. Realising that he was impeding her desire for a stable family of her own, she was able to let go of him, to his surprise. This early positive movement made her feel even more secure in her analysis. While she was pleased with such insights, it meant that she had to move away from a surface understanding about her family life that it had not really been so bad. She had developed an obsessional mind that inhibited her having a freedom of choice. For instance, it was hard for her to purchase new possessions unless she did a huge amount of research to ensure she was buying the best product.

Her father's meanness, concealment of funds to avoid paying taxes and his haughty disdain for her, as well as his nasty teasing of her skin condition led Miss A to realise that she was hated by him without mitigation. Gradually she was able to live a life more at a distance from his demands on her and developed more of a capacity to ignore him. This creative movement was slowly won, during which time she became considerably anxious that any resistance towards him from her would only "make matters worse". In tandem with this, her young brother was sent to an American college at considerable cost, after having been bought an expensive sports car on his seventeenth birthday. While she understood that such favouritism had been a motif in the family from his birth, she was now able to feel anger at the continuation of injustice in her family life.

Enamoured with analysis, she decided that she wanted to identify with her analyst and considered changing her career to train. Realising that her parents had hardly had to pay for her university course as she had won a full scholarship, she decided to ask her father for some financial help to pay towards analytic training. As well as being aghast at being invited to spend some of his now considerable wealth, he thought that analysis was nonsense. She persisted in letting him know her desire and with firmness and resolve declined to back down. Eventually she negotiated a sum of money from him, which he regarded as an early sum from what she might inherit. Over the next several months she received various amounts of cash. Being now more financially secure and realising that she had secured the cost of analysis, she was able to eventually let go of the idea of training and concentrated on her more urgent desire to find a husband. Years of being regarded as an object of contempt, and accepting herself as such, became an essential theme in beginning to overcome her deeply felt masochism.

In time she met a professional man who was very intelligent but had come from, let us say, a broken home. His own living space was primitive and messy, and both he and his accommodation were unkempt. She had some unconscious recognition of his private madness, and she devoted her kindness and love to effecting a rescue. They fell in love and married while being able to withstand her parents' contempt about their relationship.

For instance, her parents' wedding gift of an extremely cheap, nasty vase was returned, and her parents did not replace it by giving a good-enough celebratory gift. Together they were able to purchase a house, which the now-*Mrs* A enjoyed furnishing, although her husband had very limited ideas or capacity to understand this, other than being very pleased.

Mrs A was pleased with her analytic trajectory over many years, and she had met her external goals. Her parents still expected to have the right to intrude into her life, but now this could be regularly contained without retaliation. Her masochistic character became a much smaller part of herself as her pleasure in her own family life grew. In time she made a decision to leave analysis, and after a year of working through the ending this happened. Her life was now considerably more creative and alive than when she had first arrived to begin analysis. In particular, the obsessional doubt that required her to wait to be sure had receded immensely.

Interim period

For six years the patient only contacted me by sending me Christmas greetings containing a newsletter of the year's activity. Later she requested to see me perhaps twice a year to discuss some particular issue that had preoccupied her. Once it was to discuss the serious illness and then death of her father. Her mother seemed to be behind the continuation of her father's rejection of her. Yet before his death she was able to visit him and appeared to have some sense of rapprochement prior to his death. Her brother by this time had quickly secured a fortune from selling his own company and had been made the executor of his father's will. Their mother and her brother received everything and the two sisters were left astonished at the meanness of their father, as well as how their brother declined to consider even sharing his own portion, despite his own wealth. She returned for a few weeks to digest this turn of fate, although it had not really been unexpected. Meanwhile, although not being rich she had a well-paid job, which together with her husband's salary allowed them to be financially comfortable.

She came for a limited number of sessions to discuss the failure of pregnancy and to think about the possibility of adopting. At such times I felt that, whatever else, she was attached to her analyst by a "good parental" transference, which she readily agreed with.

In time I found myself continuing to respond to seeing her for a few sessions a year, now often about the difficulties she had in her professional life. During this time, she was made redundant on a couple of occasions, yet it seemed to be more in relation to the nation's economic decline. At some point I realised that the intermittent but continuing drip-feed of a few sessions seemingly about some "difficult" issue actually belied the fact that I was missing the return of some repression that I did not understand. She had developed an intermittent neurosis that involved cocooning herself from some present difficult problem in reality, and within a few sessions would recover from the regression. She made it clear that seeing me was so very helpful and was very pleased to return to lie on the couch in order to quickly recover.

I began to feel irritated that I was being used for some sort of ongoing "housekeeping" that I was responding to in a mirror image to the overt sense of kindness that my patient invariably brought. I began to realise that something kept being brought to me that I was misunderstanding, and that the apparent helpful function of seeing her for a few sessions was becoming a life commitment without much depth. It seemed that treatment was arrested in a phase of her having to be seen as well as seeing me, and that enactment was an essential element to the usually quick fix to her pressing concerns. Later I came to realise that she had unconsciously taken the role of her intermittent boyfriend, with me enacting her accepting, masochistic position.

Some twelve years after the end of her analysis Mrs A asked to return yet again. This time she was very worried that she was not going to be certain of finding new employment following a six-month interregnum living on redundancy money. Mainly she was desperate to throw herself back on the couch. She had realised that she had had many jobs in her professional career and that while she could always account for the difficulties with her various bosses as well as problems in the companies themselves, she felt that it was becoming a pattern of her own enacted disdain and feared never working again. I said that I did not want to keep seeing her occasionally, even though she felt it was always so very helpful. Rather I offered her to return thrice-weekly in ongoing work, with her sitting in the chair to examine that which we were not understanding. I was concerned that her throwing herself pleasurably on the couch had become a hysterical formation that was counterproductive at this moment. Her sitting on the chair was an attempt to oppose her wish to instantly regress in her use of the couch, aiding her unconscious desire to remain unknown in the analysis.

We now began to go in-depth about her contempt for each boss as well as the company rules in all of her jobs. She was able to liken this to an ongoing hatred of her father, whom she felt compelled to beat or leave. This work began to be helpful in relation to her succeeding in obtaining an extremely good new position with the realisation that she was fed up with her pattern of then making the job untenable. She kept desiring to return to an empty regressive state where, left alone, she could feed herself biscuits and use romantic novels for masturbatory phantasy, in a singular bubble for as long as she wished. This position was devoid of affect and was just a place for her to reside in, separate from any impingements in her life.

I began to hear a hitherto concealed story about her mother. While we had both understood that her mother had never wanted daughters and in particular had a specific hatred for her sister, much more emphasis in her earlier analysis had been placed by the patient on the meanness and lack of support from her father. While she had spoken of her mother's tough regime, it was mainly just a sketch, devoid of specific detail. It became clear that I had accepted an implicit understanding, perhaps as a surreptitious defence from the pain of remembering but perhaps also as a form of bubble in the transference, as if it did not need to be further known.

Looking back, I had construed various possibilities that "she did not understand", "she misunderstood", and that she "needed not to be known". Each of these states contributed to the complexity of the unthought known (Bollas). On their own, each threw just partial light on the patient's psychic economy, allowing much of her unconscious life to remain at a distance from the analysis.

Session

The patient arrived looking white-faced, collapsed and ill. She had just returned the previous afternoon from a business trip to the Far East, undertaken as part of her senior position in a new company. The work had gone, to her surprise, very well. She described her boss, who mainly ignored her, as schizoid, yet she had managed her tasks despite the difficulties in communicating with him. However, during the stopover she had arranged to meet her relatives for a meal. They all came, and it had gone rather well, other than with her mother, who perhaps knowing she was there, had not attended. In fact, there had been no contact with her mother for several years. Her mother totally ignored her granddaughter. Unconsciously she had hoped to meet her mother, and the meal for her relatives was mainly a cover for such a possibility. The realisation of a "no mother" had had a great impact on her. She felt an ongoing pain in her belly for a few days and had only managed by regressing again to overeating biscuits and reading romance novels in her hotel room.

The issue that had made her so very collapsed was returning home to an extremely messy home and an ill ten-year-old daughter who had severe urticaria over her face and body. This instantly reminded her of her own skin at a similar age. Her husband had told her the urticaria had only emerged the day before, but judging by the mess in the house and particularly her daughter's room with many soiled knickers and an unflushed toilet, Mrs A was horrified about the neglect. She said that her husband had told her he had been proud to have managed the laundry, yet had left out the state of his daughter. She told me that she had known her daughter had been neglected during her absence. She wept, fell to the floor and knelt by the couch, supporting her head, in a foetal pose.

With this painful revelation of neglect for a child, I interpreted that she might be in touch, by way of the ongoing pain in her own belly, with an unconscious idea that her mother had tried and failed to abort her. After a silence she struggled up, sat on the chair, and rummaged in her handbag. She withdrew a small package and gave it to me. I opened it and found myself looking at a large Aboriginal-carved seed from an Australian baobab tree.

Figure 25. Two photographs of a large Aboriginal-carved seed. Reproduced with permission

I thought that she had brought an image of herself as the seed, the baby alone outside the womb as an "enactment" towards my interpretation. The seed had a face carved on it with a wide-eyed and astonished look that seemed to also contain a knowing look. As if the object simultaneously contained a look of innocence and knowingness. Perhaps the face on the seed represented both not being noticed and noticing. It was a description of the problem of often being in the analytic womb space and the difficulty of taking it with her when she was on her own. She then told me that, when she had recently been in Australia, she realised she had been conceived during her parents' honeymoon.

She began to say that she would have to give up her work and become a full-time mother to stop the neglect. Her husband needed to know now about how neglectful he was with their daughter. And she needed to face her own neglect by her mother.

She was now much more settled. She told me that she had visited an old friend whilst abroad who had been adopted. Her friend lived in a house that was very neglected, and she feared for her friend's daughter. Now we were back to the theme of her great concern for her own daughter, behind which was her own neglect, as well as that of her sister by her mother.

In this powerful session, the theme of neglect emerged: of her mother neglecting her, her neglecting her own daughter, as well as her husband unable to notice the daughter. Her boss ignored her as her father had done. The deterioration of her friend's family life after she found her birth parents seemed to presage her own sense of the futility of knowledge of her past. Yet there was now a somatic imperative that led directly from her own "bad" skin to seeing a similar reaction in her daughter as a somatisation of absence, neglect and not being perceived.

Over the following sessions a new perspective emerged about her history in relation to her mother. I heard for the first time the details of her mother's continuous assaults on her younger sister. She now remembered that from when her sister was about three or four until they both boarded in school in England some seven years later, her mother would beat her sister daily with a special flogging stick. Either there would be some minor misdemeanour or the look on her sister's face would be sufficient for body blows. Her sister learned to accept these punishments by becoming tougher and staying silent. Very occasionally her father would also beat her sister at the mother's demand. Miss A, however, would usually see the beatings, either by being in the room or seeing through the open doorway. Whilst her heart went out to her sister and she tried as much as a little girl could to comfort her, she began to realise that she was also gratified that it was not her being beaten.

Now we could understand a missing piece of her history from the impact of beating on her character structure. At different times she had etched into her character structure as well as a fear of being beaten, a pleasure in being the observer, developing an unconscious sadomasochistic polarity in her life. She could escape the problem of reality of her life by going into a cocoon of aloneness in which she was cruel to herself, overfeeding herself with junk food and ignoring her mind with repetitious romantic novels. The cocoon was also brought to a reality, as now the patient would go and sit in a large airing cupboard, shutting the door and shutting out the world while she regressed to a return to being looked after in a "womb" space.

In this state she was more narcissistically preoccupied in identification with her mother than having a capacity to care for her daughter. She ignored the thought that her daughter would notice her mother's absences. Similarly in her work, she knew that she could overturn the father–boss and return herself into an empty space away from reality. The issue of neglect and of not being seen were now central motifs. This now explained how well her initial analysis had gone, as long as the underlying sadomasochistic beating system was suppressed from view. Rather than being helpful in seeing her intermittently, it was much more the opposite: that she kept bringing herself to be seen by me and I neglected to see her absence. Now I could see my neglect of this aspect of her, and see that her cruelty in identification with her mother was beneath the invariably kindly self that was on the surface of her character. Analysis had become alive within the cruel play space of a child who is being beaten.

The patient missed the next two sessions, leaving a message that she had had an accident and was unwell. When she appeared for the following session, she had difficulty walking and sitting. I was informed that she had been to hospital and needed an exploratory operation following a fall. Although she had only had to stay one night in hospital, she was still severely bruised. She then told the details of what had happened. The day following the last session that she had attended, the family went off on their bikes to the local park. She had complained to her husband that the tyres were flat on her bike. One of his jobs was to maintain the bikes. He disagreed with her that anything was wrong. She insisted otherwise and he offered his (masculine) bike with a crossbar for her to ride. To enter the park, one had to navigate a complicated metal gate. While manoeuvring with the bike between her legs she stumbled and half fell off, landing forcefully with her crotch on the bar of the bike. She cried out in severe pain, realising she had done damage to herself. With hurt and rage she left the bike and limped off to catch a bus home with her daughter following. Her husband was left to deal with the three bicycles.

At home she felt faint and was in immense pain; she rang the emergency line. An ambulance arrived to take her to hospital. Having fallen very heavily on her external genitalia, she was diagnosed as having internal bleeding, necessitating a minor operation.

I said I was impressed with the specificity of the attack as a performed beating in which she was both the attacker and the attacked (which pointed to a level of psychic danger). She was very thoughtful and associated to a recent occurrence whilst abroad. Seeing a place that offered foot massage she went in. The female masseuse began her foot massage. After a while the patient slipped into a daydream of a strong man massaging her whole body. She phantasied that he was adding the insides of her thighs and the edges of her breasts to his wanderings over her body. Despite an edge of concern, she imagined a great masturbatory pleasure. Later, at the hotel she felt a mixture of guilt at her imaginings as well as lingering pleasure.

Rather than verbal associations of her sense of guilt, she had unconsciously enacted the "accident", causing a blow to the same anatomical parts. From the safety of masturbatory enactment, she had moved far away to the rage against her absent mother and disorganised husband, as well as seeing herself as victim in her daughter's urticarial response: all this demanded punishment. In beating herself, all three objects—mother, father and sister—were unconsciously dealt with, together with her own masturbatory guilt. To attain this she has become, in the beating enactment, the victim and the victimiser—the sadist and the masochist. To achieve this, she had to give up her voyeuristic position and be watched by father and daughter/sister. Another chain of association is the precision of the psychosomatic attack on the genitals of her mother who did not want, I surmised, to be pregnant with her, a move in which mother is beaten, as well as her own identification with her mother as the beater.

We were now far away from her describing, albeit with much concern about daring to speak, her isolated sexual pleasure when abroad, which seemed to be an example of the safety of the phantasy bubble that, regularly and intermittently, she had found herself pulled to placing herself in. By this I mean her usual performance of going to bed or feeding herself biscuits and reading romantic novels. This pleasurable space had always existed as a one-person environment. It had functioned as a safe environment of her re-found womb space, away from her knowledge of the overt cruelty of watching her mother beating her younger sister, whilst simultaneously unconsciously pushing her own cruelty to beyond the space. This perverse phantasy balanced her object relational disharmony.

One can wonder where the father is in such an enactment. Her husband had become a discredited paternal object, unable to look after the child, not even noticing the development of her daughter's reaction. This too would be a re-finding of her childhood, her father unable to stand up to her mother's fierce phallic aggression, with no need to rely on the returning father to beat the child. In the phantasy of masturbatory massage her father becomes her sexual subject as she has found a benign father who gave her pleasure. Later, on her return, the guilty orgasmic relief re-explodes into an aggressive self-beating. Now she is placed at the centre of the beating, witnessed by her husband and daughter. She had become the child who is beaten and damaged. Her husband and her daughter became the witnesses, displacing her from being in the position of being the voyeur to her mother's beating of her sister.

And yet, in a curious way, the aggressive explosion brings with it great insight into her sadomasochistic beating character. Arguably the analytic work had achieved, by enabling the aggressive drive to be so overt and visible, rather than concealed, in the hideaway spaces that Mrs A had long and often returned to. Rather than generally functioning as a smiling, kind person, she was able to grasp a profound subterranean rage and make available an aggressive drive, in identification with her aggressive mother, which may make her more able to have a benign strength to stand up to the other. In her work life this would include speaking up to the imagos of the boss who is always the aggressive father containing the phallic mother.

There is the possibility for the baobab-seed baby to be born and to be able to emerge beyond the perversely constructed womb space alone, now to be desired by the other. A different formation of sexuality was necessary to help her avoid the phantasy of the safety of being alone, albeit with a primal scene that was more secure in the beating. Perhaps the imaginary introduction of a pair of hands belonging to the masseur and not her husband was, paradoxically, a forward move in her development.

Discussion

Ferenczi pointed out the importance and impact on the baby of not being seen by the object. Mrs A had long created a separate and hidden space to nourish and feed herself. It was an adaptation and defence to that of not being seen or desired by her mother. What she had to see was her mother desiring her sister, as beating her meant she was more loved, leaving Mrs A to be outside the door looking into the room containing the dyad of her mother and younger sister. Nobody was noticing her. It seems that this situation continued until her father noticed her severe facial acne in a critical and cruel way. This seems a point of reference of how she was seen. So too in the transference of this long case, as she returned briefly and periodically to show me further eruptions. Whilst each time the matter brought was resolved, the work really consisted of her desire to be seen by her father. Beneath this layer her voyeurism continued, especially by her finding out facts online about my life that she would "kindly" triumph by letting me know her discoveries. And beneath such desire lay the unspeakable beating phantasies based on a long-standing trauma of watching her sister being beaten by her mother.

Analytically it had been very difficult to reach beyond the paternal transference, much of it idealising the analyst, as the husband had been treated together with his "competent" work, in order to reach the maternal drumbeat of aggression. The gift of the seed from the country where she had been conceived began a chain of associations leading from one-person (Rickman, 1951, p. 218) masturbation to orgasm with a man to enacting phallic aggression on her external genitalia by herself in identification with the beating mother for the analyst to be the witness to the complete cycle of sadomasochism (as also in the sexual-aggressive enactment with the bicycle).

Cruelty by the mother is in a worse psychic register than that by the father as it can occur earlier in development. Also, the attack comes from the parent who gives birth and is the formal representative of womb space, where the baby used to reside. Nonetheless Mrs A had to manage the two forms of parental cruelty, and arguably her defence to retreat and make herself absent from life, and, in particular, family life, on entering her bubble was a defensive symptom against both parental attacks. Yet with the defence is the shadow of a representation of the attack. The patient identified with the cruel mother by attacking her body by overeating as well as looking after her body with masturbation and sexual phantasies from her reading. She also isolated herself from her family in the magical belief that they did not notice, just as she experienced her parents as not noticing their neglect towards their daughters.

The masturbatory phantasy involving another pair of hands was a new development. Mrs A often began sessions by saying that she wanted to talk about the difficulty in having sexual pleasure with her husband when they had intercourse. However, she would invariably fill up the session space with thoughts on work and any other subject, returning to what she wanted to discuss in the last minute of the session. Instead, she repeated and enacted the absence, indicative of her avoiding her vagina as a creative and receiving inner space. In her most exciting pleasure she was feeding herself, alone in her bubble. This was a reflection on the impact of her husband saying conciliatory sentences but at the same time keeping away from intimacy. Her marriage was not even beginning to contain the aggressive storm within herself. Finding a good imaginary sexual phantasy opened up a potential sexual direction that could be homoerotic, a direction that would follow along the line that her sister and mother were close together, albeit in the sadomasochistic register.

We found ourselves back at the problem of a form of addiction to a defensive and solitary psychic position. Ferenczi was always trying to find the possibility of new techniques to overcome such states of fixity and psychic inertia. For Freud, the dictum of analysis making the unconscious conscious was in the service of being more able to make decisions about having to face reality. The patient knew considerably more through her enactments in life and in analysis to well understand herself, but had, for so many years, constructed an alternative devouring mouth space away from a potentially creative womb space. While this provided much relief and pleasure, it became a problem to "reckon" on renunciation of "cupboard love" in order to aid psychic development. After so long, sadomasochistic defensive structures can have fixity of their own, often beyond new understandings.

As previously mentioned, when the second tranche of analysis began, I decided to invite her to work from the chair. This is because over the previous few years of intermittent sessions, she had immediately thrown herself on the couch on each visit and lovingly hugged a cushion. This was clinically unusual. Other patients returning for a small piece of work invariably did this from the chair. It seemed that Mrs A's regression was immediate and essential. Moreover, I felt it contained a sense of triumph of re-finding her state of regression, as in the bubble. I felt that she was expressing a misalliance of the couch, with intent to hold the analysis in a perverse state.

My decision to raise the temperature, rather than her accepting too much pleasure, which might dampen enthusiasm for depth exploration, was a Ferenczian leap. I anticipated that such a raising of the clinical temperature might lead to the finding of new, repressed, material and this did occur, as the picture of the phallic mother beating her younger daughter, often with my patient watching from the doorway began to be perceived, remembered and thought about in her analysis. Mrs A was very angry but accepted this condition of working from the chair, which in time was interpreted and understood. However, rethinking this restriction at this moment in the treatment might provide a new developmental journey. If the use of the couch could be loosened from the pleasure principle, it might provide a way to frame her present state of knowing about her perverse addiction from one-person masturbatory pleasure and be able to move developmentally to being able to have more sexual pleasure in relation to the object; in other words, to move from being alone to living a life within an object relationship. This was not in the script of her one-person bubble and perhaps she can make the journey from narcissism to Oedipus.

This is where I propose we leave the material. The present analytic problem is one well-known to Freud, who, on discussing the function of an analysis, thought that by making the unconscious conscious, the analysand would have more knowledge to decide his fate in relation to the reality principle. Yet for some patients, severe early traumas, repeated many times during childhood and continuing through adolescence, can lead to a structural fixity akin to addiction. Despite analytic knowledge on causation, realising that the perverse phallic mother had her own transgenerational trauma, the addiction was well fixated. Returning to find the re-expression of hate in the transference and countertransference may be the piece of clinical work available to undertake in what Ferenczi described as authenticity. If the analysand can overthrow her solitary and pleasurable regime and realise that the analyst has been a vital component, then hatred can be mitigated with movement from solipsism to pleasure in the world of object relations and well beyond the mother's beating in all of its vicissitudes and defences.

CHAPTER 7

Psychosis and the true self

The linen hanging out to dry in the yard
Is my linen, I know it well. Looking closer I see
Darns in it and extra patches. It seems
I have moved out. Someone else
Is living here now and
Doing so in
My linen.

Bertoldt Brecht[1]

I will begin by examining developments from Freud's observation of his grandson Ernst uttering the words *fort–da* (gone–there) when playing the cotton reel game. Freud saw the satisfaction derived from the play of disappearing the object and it became the foundation for developing his ideas around repetition compulsion in early childhood and the pleasure principle. The childhood game of hide-and-seek bears some affinity as there is pleasure in hiding from others with an ambivalence about being found. The child may not want to be found at that moment and this connects with Winnicott's view stated in "Communicating and not communicating" about the importance of the child not having to always communicate.

> I … came … to staking a claim to my surprise to the right not to communicate. This was a protest from the core of me to the frightening fantasy of being infinitely exploited. In another language this would be the fantasy of being eaten or swallowed up … . it is *the fantasy of being found*. (Winnicott, 1963a, p. 433)[2]

This idea developed into issues of core identity and that of the true and false self. In Winnicott's theory, the not good-enough mother

> is not able to implement the infant's omnipotence, and so she repeatedly fails to meet the infant gesture; instead, she substitutes her own gesture … which is to be given sense by the compliance of the infant. This compliance on the part of the infant is the earliest stage of the False Self, and belongs to the mother's inability to sense her infant's needs. (Winnicott, 1960b, p. 164)

There is a worse possibility beyond a mother's inability, and that might be her own severe mental dysfunction, in which projections are put into the baby/infant and disavowed, unwanted other than as her possession. In the realm of psychosis, the infant has more psychic reason to falsely comply to protect and guard the true self. The clinical material to be discussed in this chapter is about the hidden creation of a *folie à deux*. In time, the emergence of psychotic function in the son in analysis allowed the emergence of his ability to reject his ill mother's psychotic projections by cutting the psychic umbilical cord.

Winnicott was also interested in traumatic experiences in his patients and in theory. Again in "Communicating and not communicating", he suggests that in ordinary human development there can be a splitting of the personality that is benign (as opposed to that of severe psychopathology). There is a paradox about the world of me and not-me around how to isolate the core of oneself without being too insulated. His imagery of the core is the central casing of a fruit containing the seeds. Primitive defences arise and are mobilised to protect the threat to the isolated core, to its being found, altered, communicated with. The defence consists of the further hiding of the secret self.

Adam Phillips in his book on Winnicott (1988) says that

> Each psychoanalytic theorist, it could be said, organises his or her theory around what might be called a core catastrophe; for Freud it was castration, for Klein, the triumph of the Death instinct, and for Winnicott it was the annihilation of the core self by intrusion, a failure of the holding environment. (Phillips, 1988, p. 149)

Winnicott has two forms of non-communication—a simple one, a no, that can reconnect after a period of rest. The other is when the maternal provision fails, as it must; then "in the matter of object relating the infant develops a split" (Phillips, ibid., p. 183). The split can be benign or gradually widen from a *Reiss* to an *Enreiss*,[3] which is more severe. Angela Joyce writes in her introduction to Winnicott's *Collected Works*,

> in the aetiology of the false self, in pathology indicating a severe split, (there is) a schism in the personality whose function is to protect the true self. At its most severe, it indicates psychotic fragmentation held together by a carapace. (Joyce, quoting Winnicott, 2016, p. 10)

For Winnicott, despite the impoverishment that the split can create, it can lead to a more active carrying of a sense of the real within the isolation of the child. This is the terrain of the split between the true and the false self. Healthy persons communicate *and* have secret selves and he puts forward and stresses "the importance of the idea of the *permanent isolation of the individual*" and claims "that at the core of the individual there is no communication with the not-me world either way … This preservation of personal isolation is part of the search for identity" (1963a, p. 443). We find ourselves back in the world of hide-and-seek, with the benign end being the pleasure of concealment and being found, and the more isolated position of not wanting to be found, existing in the power of the singularity of the one-person state of mind.

The transitional object

Winnicott wrote of the transitional me–not-me object leading to an attachment to a teddy, a doll, a soft toy or a hard toy as a thing invested with power existing in the gap between the mouth and breast. I would add also its potential to begin an imaginative journey between the interiority of the self and the environment of the maternal. Psychic movement along such an axis provides an elasticity (Ferenczi, 1919) as the developments of the unconscious object relationships begin to find their shapes. The newborn baby's fist in the mouth as a function of the orality of a developmental spurt to imaginatively feed has to break down, as unconscious phantasy begins to come into existence. At the time of maximum dependence, "with the mother supplying an auxiliary ego-function, it has to be remembered that the infant had not yet separated out the 'not-me' from the 'me'—this cannot happen apart from the establishment of 'me'" (Winnicott, 1963b, p. 525). In the clinical material that I will be discussing, the young adult had not yet been able to establish a "me", leading to a continuation of an unconscious absolute dependence on his mother.

Winnicott knew that he and Balint were both interested in early environmental disposition but worked from different angles from each other about early failure. He wrote in a letter to Balint:

> I personally wonder very much if an infant is aware when the environment is satisfactory, and I have actually stated in positive terms that I think that the infant is not aware of the early environmental provision but is affected when it fails. For this reason I do not use primary love here because I cannot see that there is a relationship. The infant has not yet established the capacity to make relationships and in fact is not there to be related except in an unintegrated way. (Winnicott, 1960a, p. 44)

Of the pair, Winnicott is more trenchant about the negative, while Balint accepts a positive loving envelopment. Yet as Freud had showed in "Formulations on the two principles of mental functioning" (1911b), in a discussion of how the infant's hallucination of a feed breaks down in the face of actual hunger.

A new function was now allotted to motor discharge, which, under the dominance of the pleasure principle, had served as a means of unburdening the mental apparatus of accretions of stimuli … Motor discharge was now employed in the appropriate alteration of reality; it was converted into *action*. (Freud, 1911b, p. 221)

Without privation there is no need for the infant to acquire a mental apparatus, which in time will develop capacities to think.[4]

This is powerful evidence that psychic development can, when necessary, occur at the behest of the individual alone in states of privation. If the not-me developmental line is impinged upon too much, then the infant will side more with the views and demands of the mother for sustenance and an affectionate type of object relationship will come more under the sway of a control system that could include the development of sadomasochism in identification of the other. The internal phantasy structures become more permeated by negativistic phantasy, as a defence from projections from the mother. Placing the object at the border leads to a rigidity rather than developing, with a sense of fluidity, along three places: outside, inside, at the border. This can lead to a fixed relational system, as the infant accepts the particularities of maternal reality.

I am thinking of the maternal object with a desire to not let go of her baby, who continues to operate an unconscious umbilical connection into adulthood and daily life for the mother's own necessary sanity, as I referred earlier with regard to the origin of a *folie à deux*. I suggest that the function of the transitional object can become taken over by the child experiencing a psychotic inner world as his or her phantasy structures must fit in with those of the dominant character: mother. Again in "Fear of breakdown", Winnicott writes "there is collusion between the individual and the maternal inner psychic realities" (1963b, p. 527).

In addition, the infant can protect the true self by developing an unconscious internal negation. Arguably the true self, in its privacy, lies on a continuum of necessity. The more maternal impingement and projection onto the infant of the mother's core hatred and psychosis, the lonelier is the development of the infant into a private internal world. Such a way of thinking about the defensive necessity of a psychosis in the individual will require understanding its object relational roots, which essentially are bound in a sadomasochism, which can move in two directions. Either the child develops a masochism to the other in order to fit in, or identifies with the sadism of the other, or can operate a more complex movement to and fro, in what Ferenczi (1924) called an *amphimixis*, which sets the stage for later development into manic depression and perverse object relationships.

One key idea is Searles' notion of "who is crazy", developed in "The patient as therapist to his analyst" (1975). The transference and countertransference can hold the key to a particular type of early object relations in which the adult impedes the free development of the transitional space, such that the development of the "me" state is discouraged. Searles describes "the evolution of the patient's transference reaction from the analyst as being a harshly dominating father to his coming to perceive the analyst as a much gentler but threateningly devouring mother-figure". The clinical move from a threatening father to a primitive dangerous mother who, if not complied with, then devours, is defended against by the split of a faraway true self, hidden behind a forest of schizophrenic fragmentation. During normal transitional development, the healthy path for the infant is to "assume rights over the object", to cuddle as well as mutilate the object, and it never changes unless changed by the infant (1953, p. 164).

Here Winnicott gives rights to the developing mind of the infant to have the power in the use of the object. Arguably this requires a renunciating mother who knows when to leave the infant alone with his or her play in her presence. As Winnicott describes, "A schizoid patient asked me, after Christmas, had I enjoyed eating her at the feast? And then, *had I really eaten her or only in phantasy?* I knew she could not be satisfied with either alternative. Her split needed the double answer" (ibid., p. 164). For Winnicott, the individual at his or her core is an isolate, often seen clearly during adolescence: "This preservation of personal isolation is part of the search for identity, and for the establishment of a personal technique for communicating which does not lead to violation of the central self" (1963a, p. 443). This is not communicating as well as having an unconscious expectation/hope that he or she will be found and recognised by the mother having understood the noncommunicative communication. The analyst too needs to hold onto that paradox and sparingly use the finding of the lost/hidden patient until there is sufficient trust for the patient to bear to be discovered without feeling massively invaded. This territory of lost and found, arising out of Freud's observation of *fort–da* is profound as a template of the formation and development of early object relations. It also abuts on Freud's idea (1900a, p. 525) of the umbilicus of the dream—that so much can be revealed, but no more, as the unconscious core is private.

The fetish

In relation to the development of transitional phenomena Winnicott cites Wulff (Wulff, 1946): "the transitional object may eventually develop into a fetish object and so persist as a characteristic of the adult sexual life". He goes on to state that the transitional object is not an internal object but a possession. This opens the possibility that the infant can be the mother's possession, if she herself has had her own distorted transitional phenomena unchanged from her early life—in other words, her incapacity to have the qualities of being a good-enough mother and being unable to allow her baby its omnipotence or later to assist disillusionment. This is because she has not been in an early environment to imbibe such structures as a state of neutrality in her own unconscious mind. This is the territory of transgenerational trauma down a maternal line.

Winnicott comments that Wulff is using the word fetish to "describe the object that is employed on account of a delusion of a maternal phallus". He does think that "the infant's use of the transitional object and of transitional phenomena in general may throw light on the origin of the fetish object and fetishism". He clearly states that of "transitional phenomena are healthy and universal" and does not desire his concept to contain the delusion of mother's phallus. He can allow only its illusion as maternal phallus. Nonetheless he accepted that the transitional object "may ... develop into a fetish object and so persist as a characteristic of the adult sexual life" (Winnicott, 1953, pp. 171–172).

Masud Khan, in his paper "Role of the 'collated internal object' in perversion-formations" (1979) also discusses perverse transitional objects. He describes three basic features of perversion:

1. The necessity of the presence and compliance of an external object.
2. The nature and quality of the organised phantasy system, unconscious and unknowable, in the subject (the pervert).
3. The reality of the experiential situation in which the above-mentioned factors can be actualised, utilising space motility, sight and touch.

The pervert utilises neurotic and psychotic elements compatible with normal living, as being closer to cultural artifice.

I think that transitional theory is robust enough to be examined from the perspective of not just a maternal inability to allow the illusion of control to be available for her baby, but also an ill mother who actively attacks the infant's need to grow in freedom. The task of an analysis with an adult patient with such a constricted infantile environment, unable to have the freedom to possess me–not-me phenomena in early life, is in finding the up-to-now lost object or, as my patient describes, realising that he has only lived inside Plato's (mother's) cave all his life. The analysand needs to dare move from a private, alone and lost psychic core and to cope with the pain of being found. This makes sense of Winnicott's realisation of the importance of the analysand making their own good-enough interpretations in the environment of the analyst, who can bear letting go of analytic mastery to a mere patient. At the moment of so doing, the analysand is free to put words in his or her mouth knowing that the analysis is a holding environment quite different from the original early traumas. This is a freedom from, as Khan puts it,

> in certain styles of mother–infant relationships what the infant–child internalises is his mother's idolized image of him. This idolized self of the child is the mother's "created-thing" and different from the child's total experience of himself. (Khan, 1979, p. 122)

A case study

The case I will now present shows an early fracture in empathy, with the infant left self-idolised with a great capacity to not need to communicate while, paradoxically, developing to be a very able and talented communicator.

The patient was a twenty-three-year-old from South America, who spoke good English and was undertaking further university studies. He was good-looking, thoughtful and clever, and keen to explore himself. He wanted analysis as he had issues of "light and dark themes", an early indication of the split in the self. His mother's work sounded impressive at first, though I heard later that she held a very junior position. She held on to him too much. This was paradoxical as she had worked long hours while he was looked after by carers. His father worked as a contractor.

His parents rowed incessantly until they divorced when their only son was around six years old. His father had recently retired on a small pension and often went fishing. At the consultation, the patient told an early memory of when he was around two years old, of sitting on the warmth of the patio watching a caterpillar, with his father nearby. The patient became very upset, saying, "The shadow prefers autumn to summer". Clearly there was embellishment of the memory and I understood that he was communicating that he expected warm atmospheres to fracture, and his capacity to split. On later reflection, it begged the question what was the caterpillar that the little boy watched with fascination? Lewis Carroll's caterpillar is not liked by Alice as they look at each other for some time in silence. At last, the caterpillar takes the hookah out of its mouth and says, "Who are you"?

One week he missed his first session, very concerned about a recent back spasm that led to him holding himself rigidly together in his body. Instead of his session, he decided to attend an extra class at university. He added ambiguously that one of his teachers had said she was unable to hear him! He seemed to indicate that he was holding onto, controlling, his sound and not letting it out, enacting my not hearing him due to his absence. He got lost as a need to neither speak nor listen to the missed session. After a long pause I said that instead of feeling his sense of authenticity, he was holding himself together and appeared to have gone fishing like his father.

He retorted, "Have you deliberately put the serpent pointing at me?" Here I must explain that my consulting room, like that of some analysts, contains some ancient objects, creating an atmosphere of now and the past. Patients often alight on an object that they need, as happened this time. Perhaps the serpent was a derivative of the earlier caterpillar, in the sense that the transformational object was moving towards an early sexual serpentine scene.

He then said that he was very concerned about an event when he was four years old, as the twelve-year-old boy next door may have caused his parents to separate! While playing together, the older boy exposed his penis. The patient was concerned about what else might have happened. He had told his mother that same day and the family quickly departed. She may have taken him to see a psychiatrist. He felt he had a part missing. I said, "Not knowing, you hold yourself rigid to prevent penetration." He had already spoken of his interest in anal sex with girlfriends as well as the excitement of having his anus explored. I said, "By not knowing what happened at four years old, you were experimenting with setting a scene to try and understand … like your thoughts of the pointing serpent." (The patient had thought that I was an evil snake owner, and he should not be here.) Later I said he feared his mind being penetrated in analysis. "Yes, that's helpful," he replied.

Towards the end of the session, I said:

> Perhaps your rigidity in your mind and body is a defence against your fear that you were penetrated. So at times, you hold your body too tight and you can then damage yourself, your muscles, your mind, against the psychic penetration of ideas.

Later I heard that as a child he often slept in a cupboard next to his parent's bedroom, rather than his own bedroom on the floor below. It began to sound as if he had carved out an intermediate space, akin to a me–not-me transitional space, except that he was the thing in-between.

His mother was always unsuccessfully competing against her two cleverer brothers, both of whom had very successful business careers compared to her. Her parents seemed to be always on the brothers' side, something that began to make psychic sense later in the offhand way that she treated her son. She seemed to have invested in her son a perfection of his attributes as if, in unconscious phantasy, she was covertly redressing her sibling rivalry. The son had been brought up to be his mother's good boy and to achieve always at a very high level.

Now he was becoming thoughtful about the main problems with which he believed he came to analysis: having to bear a dysfunctional marijuana-addicted father had, in its shadows, a very controlling authoritarian mother. He began to notice that his achievements were taken by her as her own, making him feel hollow and inauthentic. In addition, beginning to know such structures began to cause him much guilt.

In the next session he had an image of his life as being one of clinging to a raft floating on the sea, with much anxiety about letting go.
Now he realised that the raft was his mother, and he and she cling on
rather than him swimming free of encumbrance in the sea of reality.

Five months into thrice-weekly treatment, the patient began a session by talking about the impact of his father's daily marijuana addiction. He recounted another story of his stepfather, who following their
marriage become aggressive to the patient's mother and himself. His
mother soon divorced again. He continued to describe the paternal
series with his mother's next boyfriend, an army sergeant, whom he had
loved, but who suddenly died of a heart attack when he was thirteen.
The patient was too upset to go to the funeral, feeling humiliated and
guilty that he had loved him.

The patient became very quiet. As he sat opposite me, I noticed his
face change to a pasty white colour and sensed a storm brewing.

"I have a voice in my head." And then an unusual deep bass voice
said: "I am the son of God. I am Jesus."

I felt a huge visceral wave of shock coming at me. I felt frightened by
the impact of the arrival of the psychotic, not as a theory but as a thing
that signalled a state of power in him. I waited in the ensuing silence
and tried to process my thoughts and feelings. Eventually I said:

> Instead of feeling your feelings about the premature death of the
> man who you loved, together with the loss of esteem for your
> other two fathers, you have made yourself impermeable and spe-
> cial by having a voice that informs you that you and your mother
> are a very special couple as Jesus and the Madonna. As if you
> have no need of a father (other than God the Father).

He began to cry and cry, viscerally lachrymose in his distress, yet it
seemed that in this somatic state he had ceased listening to the psychotic voice in his head. His emotion without words continued for the
rest of the session. Just prior to the end of the session I said that he
would need to look after himself well today and that I would be here to
see him for his session tomorrow. Slowly he gathered himself together,
shook my hand and departed.

We were both very shocked by the unexpected and intense psychotic intrusion. I realised that an important, absent piece of his mind was being brought to our attention. The interpretation had touched him to enable him to move from a position of lost alien psychosis, with its visceral horror projected into me, to his beginning to find a great sadness.

The next session he was quiet, and revealed that he had never told anybody about the voice in his head. He had been looking at himself in the mirror and, as usual, had not been able to see himself in the reflection. He thought the reflection was of someone looking harshly at him. I thought he was giving a pictorial representation to his auditory hallucination. As Angela Joyce writes, "the embryonic true self nonetheless has to be seen and recognised by mother in order to thrive" (Joyce, 2016, p. 11). This is more evidence that he had not been seen or reflected on by his mother. He realised that since the age of seven years he had thought there was another person exactly like him, making the same physical movements somewhere else in the world. In view of his splitting of the ego, I interpreted, "So you sent yourself away as a protection against feeling pain and damage, but it means that you became empty of yourself." He wondered if he were schizophrenic. I said that by being the Son of God he had found a device to not need to think about his fathers' (his actual biological father and the stepfathers) or his own anger. Simultaneously, his mother was special like Mary, mother of Jesus, and the voice allowed him to cover over his feelings about her choice of men. Another father becomes God and so does he, as he covers over the collapse of all three of his mother's men.

He thought that he always put his energy into supporting the other person, at the expense of himself. He always wanted to please the other, the teacher, a girlfriend, but he always left out his own feelings. At times he could explode with rage and yet he did no harm. I said, "But you were then empty of your private self." He said that the best acting parts were criminals, psychopaths and psychotics; and at the end of the session, knowing he had studied Shakespeare for his English degree, I said "There is method in your madness", to which he slowly smiled (Polonius says of Hamlet's response "Though this be madness, yet there is method in't").[5] I was laying out a metaphorical interpretation that allowed him to realise that the emergence in speech for the first time about his psychotic state had a method that we could begin to understand about the emotional killing of fathers. The metaphor helped carry the burden and he began to release the shock and impact of the split in his mind, which I was beginning to realise was a profound move away from the poverty of what a father could manage (one addicted to weed, one to aggression and the third with sudden early death), as the object of mother came frighteningly into view.

In this session we worked together on facing some of his psychotic constructs and the consequential splitting of his mind. The impact of the psychotic voice was shocking, and in my countertransference this was visceral, unexpected and scary, even though its harbinger, his face, becoming paler in my gaze, had alerted me to something dangerous in the atmosphere. It was as if at that moment I had seen in his face the angry other that he sometimes could see when he looked in the mirror. I had not, up to then, thought of the psychopathology of my patient as psychotic. Very entwined with his mother, certainly; his identification with his mother's control systems, yes, but all this in the register of neurotic functioning in an adolescent trying to break free and grow up. After all, coming to London from far away had its common transcendence of escape.

I had to re-evaluate the analysis so far, in order to register the split-off, hidden and ego-alien character that was now emerging, but which had been there silently all along. And was this material *a priori* his own psychotic material or, more benignly for him, his identification with a harsh aggressor? If the latter, I had certainly felt the wrath of what might prove to be an aggressive and psychotic imago. Following the shock of the Thursday session was the gap prior to the Friday session. I had decided to accept that he would manage the outing of the voice over this time, although I bade him look after himself well overnight. The following session found him ready to work rather than enacting to decompensate, as he began with a thoughtful question about how to begin.

Time revealed the character behind the emptied-out men, as we learned of his mother treating her son as her possession, as he was attached to her (psychotic) umbilical cord, psychically uncut and still in place. We later discovered that he had been under her influence as the passive acceptor of her phallic control and input into his mind and body.

Such an emerging of an unconscious fragment links to the weight that can be lifted and transferred for the metaphor to carry. First the dark, secret voice in his head needed its revelation, allowing shock alongside the sudden burst of his depressive affect. Subsequently words carried their metaphoric layering beyond psychotic alienation and emptiness alone to finding understanding in the analytic dyad. Winnicott makes this clear:

> I must take for granted an understanding and acceptance of the analysis of psycho–neurosis. On the basis of this assumption I say that in cases I am discussing the analysis starts off well, the analysis goes with a swing; what is happening, however, is that the analyst and the patient are having a good time colluding in a psycho-neurotic analysis, when in fact it is psychotic … there is no end unless the bottom of the trough has been reached, *unless the thing feared has been experienced*. (1963b, p. 527)

And it had become blindingly clear that, as the flash of a psychotic black hole darkened the session, my patient needed to reclaim the familiarity of his own clothes, patches and all, as Brecht's poem makes clear, rather than splitting himself off as his own *doppelgänger*. We had both experienced it.

I now heard that he had always said to himself each bedtime the last seven words of Christ ("My God, why have thou forsaken me"), as he explicitly expected to die every night. He felt great relief at having revealed this also for the first time, realising that he did not have to continue with his childish deadly ritual. I said, "You now know that you have not died, despite having a mind insisting that every day is your last one." In his lost state he was cruelly killing himself nightly.

I deliberately did not offer a transference interpretation, as it would likely have fuelled his paranoia to analysis and myself. As Winnicott offers:

> When fear of death is a significant symptom the promise of an after-life fails to give relief, and the reason is that the patient has a compulsion to look for death. Again, it is the death that happened but was not experienced that is sought. (ibid., p. 528)

A few days later came a dream:

> I told my friends that I was the Messiah. My brain is trying to work something out. In my head my goal for the world, myself is unhealthy. I don't believe I'm the Messiah, but I put Messianic God into my life—my life shouldn't be about myself but others. I believe my job as an artist is to make people feel, see and show them what they have yet to see.

This was a grandiose plan far beyond artistic integrity. Yet at least the psychotic symptom of a few days before had found its way into dream life in analysis.

His mother had told him a dream she had when pregnant with him. She was with God who was standing alongside a spirit; she chose the spirit to be her son and he simultaneously chose her. Here we can see a raw psychotic function of the mother who dreams she has the *spiritus sancti* of God transferred to her womb. When her son states that he is the Son of God, is this his symptom or his identification with his mother's psychotic system?

A few sessions later he had a dream that

> he entered a dark house. It was a witch's coven and he saw a woman in a bath, very pregnant. He could even see the face of the baby on her belly. He rushed out, terrified. The witch said: "You know it is so hard to get in here, so why think it will be easy to get out?"

Here is his nightmare that he must get inside and must not leave her. Simultaneously the dream explains that he is either inside mother or seeing himself on her belly attached umbilically. He realises that he is in fear of really becoming free, yet if he stays, so does the guilt–shame that he feels.

Once his mother had said to him "It's you and me and I love you." He went on to say "It's stuff you write to a girlfriend. It is her pressure and more shameful, when I was eleven or twelve, she gave me a kiss goodnight and pushed me away telling me not to do that." I said, "She pulls you towards and pushes you away." He agreed, realising that she had no clear boundaries. Here we can glimpse his mother's sadomasochistic control. He continued that he had had a dream when thirteen or fourteen that he was having sex with his mother, and his therapist at the time was watching. He woke, felt guilty and told his mother.

She brushed it off, telling him to tell his therapist, leaving him with a mixture of guilt and shame.

He had recently complained that for a long time his mother had been using his personal email address for communicating. I was rather shocked that it was something that he had thought was all right rather than a symptom of how enveloping she was in his life, together with his passive acceptance, in case he upset her. He decided to confront her, and to his astonishment she accepted that it was true but had neither guilt nor desire to change it. Later that week he was able to log onto her/his email system and withdrew consent for her to use his email address. Now he was engaging with his nightmare in order to cut the linkage: an act of freedom on his part. As he was also concerned that his action would disturb and upset his mother, I reminded him she had her own analyst to discuss her feelings.

Another version of his mother's dream prompted the following. A dream of his was that his mother was looking at the souls of babies and God told him to go to her, as she was the one to be his mother. He associated by saying that God chose his mother, meaning that God was his father and that his conception had nothing to do with his dad.

> It made my mother specially chosen and so I am special of God. [He continued] It's not a dream that my mother told me, we had met before I was born. It came from her. I made sense of her myth and made it my own. But it's just the imagination of a little kid, nothing more. Because she made me feel special, I wanted to believe that. That image from long ago, is just phantasy. This specialness has worked on me most of my life. She was disappointed in the father I had. I was a kid trying to make sense of my mum saying "we don't need your father". It was very traumatic in my head that mum and I were so special—both of us. Then it doesn't matter if I don't have a dad.

The patient later said:

> How can I have a girlfriend if the only two special people are me and my mom? My last girlfriend felt excluded by how often I phoned my mom. When she broke up with me, I couldn't

fathom[6] how she could do that as I believed nobody could treat her as well as me. She was right to leave. Being the Son of God means every person will be disappointed. Life without my mother inside me makes me think of Plato's cave and of going out into the sunlight for the first time. I have been a prisoner of a phantasy.

At this point I valued, as suggested by Winnicott, the patient's own interpretation. My patient had taken his analysis inside, was able to deal with his paranoia of what negative "stuff" he expected that I might have been putting into him and was beginning to swim free with the freedom to think for himself.

The patient began talking about how he hated going to parties. He was easily bored and could not handle talking in a group. He preferred being in a one-to-one conversation with a girl. The more he continued, the less understandable were his tortuous associations, but he was very fed up.

He mentioned his forthcoming birthday in three days. He did not know how he was going to celebrate. The idea in the reference to parties became clearer—as something that did not really interest him as a celebration of his birth. His birth day as a fact was also the moment of his leaving her womb. And how were his birthdays celebrated as a child? I heard of his mother's invitations to his friends and their parents, and what he objected to most: the intermingling of kids he knew from school and kids he was not particularly friendly with.

He then said that today was his mother's birthday and laughed at his only remembering about it now. It had not been in his conscious mind. She always told him that her birthday would last for a week, while his only lasted for the day of his birthday! His birthday was always subsumed as one day in her week of celebration. His birthday had no clear borders and it now became clear to him that it only existed inside of hers. He realised that the birthday party she arranged for him as if the scene was special for the birthday boy was actually full of *her* friends. He had discovered that for his mother his birth represented his umbilical attachment to her and that to her he was not a separate person, especially on his birthday. As this had existed as a reflection on how special he was, he had not really minded realising her control system and ownership of his life. It really was the opposite, as he began to see his mother was really the special one of the pair.

Yet he had unconsciously held onto the connecting primitive attachment. In his psychotic state he was the Son of God with Mary, Mother of God as his own mother. The trail of free associations led him to work out why he did not like big parties, why he thought he preferred just talking to one girl and how that was unconsciously attached to the one-to-one special relation to his mother. And, perhaps most painful of all, my interpretation that he was the special birthday present for his mother each year. Behind this was his sense of his own hollowness, detachment and sense of not really having ownership over his life.

Discussion

In this case one can think of the mother as having been psychically destroyed herself in childhood, as it is likely that her mother only valued her sons. Living constantly in her brothers' shadow deadened her, in Freud's sense that "if I cannot have the overworld then I shall have the underworld".[7] It is arguable that in a marriage with her denigrated husband, the birth of her son was unconsciously realised as the arrival of her male self, such that the baby could not have a life of its own. He was her phallus, and he grew up under the sway of the dominating maternal unconscious order. On the one hand the infant submitted, while keeping a very private self, his own imaginative life, secret. Part of his illusion of the split in his mind was the phantasy that he was the special boy to the important mother, fashioning a secret compartment of the self in which he was the Son of God and that she was the Madonna. It also accounted for the small role that his father played in family life. Such a psychotic identification allowed him to have an alive–dead life, with his crucifixion postponed to the near future. It allowed him a modicum of a special private and alone life that nobody knew, until he was able to share his frightening secret in a session.

The revelation of the content of the secret self was the beginning of his being able to emerge from being in the shadows and always under the total control of his domineering mother. For her it was a psychic formation that kept her dead life and any concomitant depression at bay. In his "Fear of breakdown" paper, Winnicott is cogent at directing clinical attention to the idea that the breakdown has already happened, rather than the impending anxiety that any change in object relations will cause a worsening of the situation. "It is a fear of the original agony which caused the defence organisation which the patient displays as an illness syndrome" (Winnicott, 1963b, p. 526).

The discrimination of the historical origins of control functions, which in this analysis showed the capture of the patient, pre-birth and beyond, as being a projective system for his mother's hatred towards her successful brother with the complicity of the maternal grandmother, allowed the analysand's return from his own negativistic lostness. Of necessity he had to confront his mother to take what was his, and reject what belonged to her, inside his mind and now with his own secure ego boundaries. The "finding" of himself with his own boundaries was something that he had to seize from his found knowledge in his analysis. "In other words, the patient must go on looking for the past detail which is *not yet experienced*. This search takes the form of a looking for this detail in the future" (ibid., p. 527). The mass of clinical detail, and in particular his dream work, facilitated important changes in his present and future life as he acquired a detailed sense of his own "me-ness" as he at last developed a separation from his ill mother. Thus "gradually the patient gathers the original failure of the facilitating environment into the area of his or her omnipotence and the experience of omnipotence which belongs to the state of dependence" (ibid., p. 527).

For Winnicott "There is an intermediate stage in healthy development in which the patient's most important experience in relation to the good or potentially satisfying object is the refusal of it. The refusal is part of the process of creating it" (1963a, p. 436). For my patient, much of the clinical work was in the area of allowing the young man's rage about being encapsulated inside his mother to emerge from the true self, so that his "no" could come into play against the mother's domination. More than anything, in the realm of psychotic breakdown, it is necessary to experience in the analysis, and this is the equivalent of the remembering in the analysis of psychoneuroses. To be able to experience the work of moving from not-me to me must be completed, as the metaphorical umbilical cord has to be at last cut. At such a moment, he can cut through an insistence that he is his mother's heroic, mythic, dream object, functioning with his own life suspended. As Bollas describes a patient with a similar clinical background:

> He would empty himself compulsively of his true self needs in order to create an empty internal space to receive mother's dream thoughts. Each visit to the home was curiously like a mother giving her son a narrative feeding. Hence he would empty himself of personal desire and need in order to fulfil mother's desire and he would preserve himself in a state of suspension from life, waiting for the myth to call him into a transformed reality. (Bollas, 1987, p. 19)

For my patient his invention of himself as the Son of the Mother of God as an enactment in a session was a mythic telling to the analyst and not his usual allegiance to his mother's desire. In the shock of the psychotic transformation was the realisation of the solution—that he would need to break from his mother's dream world.

The continuing trickle of associations to birthdays and birth and specialness came together with a great impact. I can report that three days later, in the knowledge of these facts and in developing a New Beginning, he arranged his own birthday with a group of his friends that he wanted to be with, and separate from mother, he celebrated his best birthday celebration ever. This would also be the start of his acts of freedom to cut himself down from the cross of his Jesus psychosis, and to give up being special.

CHAPTER 8

Violence, destruction and survival regression

I will examine regression, in particular, severe states of mind, in which the analysand has no belief in trust of another person, and why and how such states come into unconscious formation. To begin with, regression functions as a profound defence, which concurrently forces that person to only rely on the self. This in turn has enormous repercussions on the life led, diminishing it in somatic and psychic ways, and developing a particular sort of private life.

In states of severe attack, the mind needs protection from the impact of massive affect: a move from psyche to soma. The body can take over in providing the contours of associations but is detached from a mental capacity to free-associate and emotionally feel. Thus, one finds a patient who adopts particular positions on the couch—a certain rigidity of limbs or never moving—as a means of potentially concealing and revealing earlier traumatic states and keeping a distance from what threatens as some terrible knowing. Such positional structures, when noticed, allow for the possibility of movement away from the somatic register and towards mental curiosity. Putting into words moves psychic energy from the thing (body) presentation to word presentation, enabling affect to move from body attachment to that of the

157

clinical dyad. As with the rest of an analysis, this requires time to work through the new-found memories in terms of past relationships and experiences. The patient in his or her psychosomatic place is alone and does not expect, nor often even wish for, the intervention of the other. The unconscious expectation is that the other is not there to help, and there is a historical truth to this, as adults had not protected the infant from trauma and may even have caused it. Very often the traumatised analysand has not had an early history of being held, cuddled and loved by the mother, such that in adult life being touched becomes an ego-alien idea and is perceived as the harbinger of further assault. This leads to the possibility that only self-holding is possible (rocking, masturbating, disturbances of feeding, etc.).

Analysis opens up a new possibility in the telling—that the listener, who may be experienced after a while as benign, can hear and the patient registers, perhaps for the first time, being heard. The patient may begin to know that the other is listening and can also listen to themself.

Masochism

A mother has to be able to tolerate hating her baby without doing anything about it. She cannot express it to him. If, for fear of what she may do, she cannot hate appropriately when hurt by her child she must fall back on masochism, and I think it is this that gives rise to the false theory of a natural masochism in women. The most remarkable thing about a mother is her ability to be hurt so much by her baby and to hate so much without paying the child out, and her ability to wait for rewards that may or may not come at a later date. Perhaps she is helped by some of the nursery rhymes she sings, which her baby enjoys but fortunately does not understand?

> Rockabye Baby, on the treetop,
> When the wind blows the cradle will rock,
> When the bough breaks the cradle will fall,
> Down will come baby, cradle and all.

(Winnicott, 1949, p. 202)

The perceived and real disruption demanded by the baby needs to meet its match in the mother or father, not enacted with blows or perversity but as an unconscious counterbalance to provide an unconscious matrix to contain the baby/child's hatred.

The rhyme is not sentimental and is probably sung with unconsciousness about its storyline. Yet as an element of the upturning of a mother's life due to the birth of her baby, it does contain an imaginary falling-out of the baby from its cradle—the mother's arms—and the crashing to the ground, in the mother's unconscious, allows space for a non-retaliatory acceptance of the, at times, impossibility of the baby's demands. This does not necessarily lead the mother into a lifetime direction of masochism towards other objects, but it may do, subject to the mother's own unconscious knowledge of how her own mother dealt with her baby's demands years before. One might call such things the transgenerational feminine pattern and always includes three generations of matriarchy.

And yet, what if a mother or father or other or absence does pay out to, project into and psychosomatically damage the baby during its developmental journey to adulthood? The uncontained adult marks the child through a penumbra of fear, leaving physical marks on the body, including sexuality, and diminishes the growth of and attainment of a good-enough sexual relationship and phantasy life. The inner life of children can be damaged in many ways, beyond an ordinary capacity to recover from too much presence or absence of the object.

The analyst may find that the analysand may not be able to hear and accept interpretation, digest and work it through. The patient may not know that another person is even in the room with them. The analyst's sentences and interpretations might be heard, not as words, but as things recalling Freud's differentiation between word presentation and thing presentation (1915e). When the analyst does speak, the patient may perceive the sentence as a device to penetrate. Immense care must be taken in trying to imagine which part of the body receives the interpretation when the patient is in a state of pathological regression. As Ernest Jones showed, words are not necessarily received into the ears, but can be felt as entering another body space, with all its concomitant imaginary dangers (1951). Words at times contain the capacity to be experienced physically in the body as seduction or aggression.

Some analysands present the near impossibility of reaching some-one who has almost given up the possibility of being found by another, playing games of hide-and-seek that are very painful. Such is the life of patients who find a way of clinging to a marginal life through psychotic mechanisms, with delusional thought, drug-induced aloneness, or retreat into somatisation. In all such clinical encounters the movement from the solipsistic world to a two-person relationship, which implies transference and the possibility of re-finding the oedipal world of three persons (infant, mother and father), becomes available only by registering an antecedent traumatic landscape. This is often deeply buried or hidden beneath the surface, possibly with all traces kicked over (Abraham & Torok, 1994).

Winnicott postulates a process in which something awful that was actually seen by the child leads to a de-hallucination in which it was covered over. Subsequently a hallucination fills up the hole produced by the scotomisation. He described watching a child paint a picture using bright colours to portray a lively scene. This was quickly followed by the child finding black paint and carefully and completely covering the first scene, wiping out the earlier representation. If one had not observed the begin-ning, one would be left to speculate only about the blackness. He described such a process as compulsive in that it had to be repeated again and again.

This slight example also reveals the importance of keeping the mind open to a historical line of enquiry, for without such a capacity it is easy to promote the idea that the child's black picture is a representation of the death instinct. Clearly these representations, layered one on top of the other, convey a much more complex picture. Some patients need to be psychotic in order to arrive at memories of a very disturbed and distress-ing kind belonging to an earlier time. Like the black paint of the child, psychosis is a representation of the dark landscape concealing and point-ing towards early severe trauma. Hallucinations are a form of creative life.

Winnicott's observation also contains the idea that it is the patient who now has the desire and capacity to "black" something out. Now the past and the present reach a fusion that requires analysis to untangle the original "black" that assaulted the child and their own identification with a blackening/blanking out that is both self-protective and an attack on the object. Any affect is projected onto the surface of the picture, in the flatness of the colour, black covering the other pigments and far from the internal feelings of affect. By becoming an artist, the damaged child is unconsciously attempting to find a new location for a description of the trauma on paper as a picture or poem, which can thus be externalised. We should not be misled, however, into thinking that such transcription can be consciously understood by the patient as an important retrieval of early life. As with painting, the process is more tentative. Good-enough art has the capacity to allow the viewer to be unconsciously in touch with something of the poignancy of this early unconscious human situation.

In such cases, something unbearable is struggling for representation. Ferenczi was particularly interested in finding the balance between fantasy and trauma. "In all cases in which I have penetrated deeply enough," he wrote to Freud on 25 December 1929,

> I found the traumatic-hysterical basis for the illness [...] The critical view that gradually formed in me in the process was that psychoanalysis engages too much one-sidedly in obsessional neurosis and character analysis i.e. ego psychology, neglecting the organic hysterical basis for the analysis; the cause lies in the over estimation of fantasy and the under estimation of traumatic reality in pathogenesis. (Brabant, Falzeder & Giampieri-Deutsch, 1993, p. 376)

Similarly, in my clinical work it is the gradual or, in some cases, sudden and unexpected tripping over traumatic memories that can bring the analysis to life. The difficulty in this area is that the return of the repressed trauma can become diffused into the transference–countertransference. It is likely that a sudden violent aggression can erupt, such as the patient coming close to attacking themselves (not for the first time) and/or perceiving the analyst as perpetrator, and hence repeater, of the original sense of trauma that they experienced. Of course, such moments can signal an imminent assault on the analyst.

For Ferenczi, at times this was unavoidable. "I have come to realize," he wrote in his diary on 8 March 1932,

> that it is an unavoidable task for the analyst: although he may behave as he will, he may take kindness and relaxation as far as he possibly can, the time will come when he will have to repeat

with his own hands the act of murder previously perpetrated against the patient. (Ferenczi, 1988, p. 52)

Ferenczi found this state of his own mind in relation to some clinical material in his countertransference to his patient. In analysing patients with severe environmental failure, the analyst thus has to bear being perceived as the attacker, even the murderer, in the transference. The material intermingles present and past, without the patient or analyst necessarily being too overwhelmed by paranoia. The capacity to work in such a clinically restricted area, to both understand and to survive, is the prelude to Michael Balint's concept of "new beginning" (1968). It is a matter of finding a way of getting beneath the blackness, which may appear as emptiness or an evacuated state of the patient. Otherwise, it is all too easy for the analyst to assume that blackness is bedrock and to make the case for negative therapeutic reaction—essentially blaming the patient (again). This may trigger the sudden departure of the patient, leaving intact the analyst's unassailable sense that the patient was unanalysable! Unfortunately, such a position can simply allow a non-understanding of what suddenly happened, and protect the analyst from criticism—his own as well as others. What is lost is the analyst's capacity to notice his enactment at play as the traumatic scene returns from its usual habitat of being repressed. It is not a surprise to postulate that the unconscious of some analysts, being fearful about the deep waters they may have stumbled into, offers a dullness of response that indicates to the patient that they are not really wanted—so such a patient may well be right to depart the battle.

In the area of object relating, Winnicott later theorised in a similar way: "After 'subject relates to object' comes 'subject destroys object' … and then may come 'object survives destruction by the subject'" (1971, p. 90). Sometimes after this, he continued, the object can be loved. Winnicott does not quote Ferenczi, but the two share a belief in the importance of surviving being killed in the transference, which implies that the analyst must be available for such death. Once he survives, the patient, invariably astonished, can begin to know about the usefulness of being able to love. It is the capacity to love that is so strikingly absent when such ill patients first arrive in the consulting room, not that it is even something to be considered or even complained about.

This capacity to love also needs to include loving with ambivalence, allowing hatred of the object.

With such ill patients, interpretation is of use later in the analytic work when the analysand has dared, as it were (we could also call this "developed"), to notice the other in the room. The very regressed patient may need to deal with life by having very little of it. One way of dealing with profound early traumas is to close down much of oneself in order to provide as small a target as possible for the expectation of further mental and physical assault. The depth of trauma can be registered by the amount of empty time required for such a character to dare to seek an object again. This can be an act of considerable bravery for the analysand, who has to re-find traumatic moments that have been effectively repressed, split off or somatised. Prior to such a return to hope, the analysand has first to find a creative part of themselves as a form of becoming alive. Such matters may go on separately to the analysis, which might seem empty and sterile for long periods of time. The analyst needs to be patient and not misread such moments of stasis as negative transference or resistance of the analytic process.

Patients can only find their way to the analyst in their own time, and often with their own interpretation. For some analysands, everything that had been offered from the early carers was so tainted with self-serving that they have developed a form of primitive knowledge or impulse to accept nothing from the other. Technically, one needs to wait without despair. External reason is felt as an attack. The patient is in an unreachable place; yet knowing, despite all else, that the patient daily attends their analysis, is a hopeful sign. That is a great deal and can be a form of silent participation by just being there rather than resistance.

This can be a most unusual experience for the very ill patient, who has been filled with an earlier knowledge of what the other wants for himself. Michael Balint described the "area of the basic fault" (1968) where the patient is silent, lifeless and hopeless. Such a phase, Enid Balint later elaborated,

> is only overcome when this phase is worked through, that is, when the patient is no longer regressed to a stage where he has no mutual experience with his analyst but becomes silently hostile, disillusioned and desperate and eventually appears to

give up hope. He sometimes does this without reproaching the analyst, who may wonder what he is doing wrong. […] This state is overcome only when the patient painfully allows himself to feel alone, in the analyst's presence but with no person being there. He may then begin to perceive for himself and to enter the Area of Creativity. The patient is alone with no other person present, but the space is not empty. There is no experience of a void and the analytic hour is in fact a relief from the previous experience of compliance. (E. Balint, 1993, pp. 104–105)

For Enid Balint, entering a creativeness alone in the presence of the other is the direction of the analytic journey and must occur prior to the patient recognising the meaning of the two-person relationship. This does not mean that the relationship has not been noticed, rather that it is not perceived as important. It only becomes so when it matures into a two-person relationship, which must include, at times, the painful realisation of absence. At such a time, creative play, like thumb-sucking, is recognised as not providing the real thing. Realising the loss of the other becomes a later and nonetheless crucial experience on the developmental path. It includes the desire for the lost object, no longer in the realms of a return to a damaging sadomasochistic experience, but in the form of a new experience gradually built on trust and concern. That this is not a falsely positive vision is clear from Winnicott's insistence on destruction and survival as an inherent part of the process. Such states of mind contain paradoxes: "At the start is an essential aloneness. At the same time this aloneness can only take place under maximum conditions of dependence" (Winnicott, 1988b, p. 132).

Likewise, Christopher Bollas eloquently describes the mutuality, at times, of the destructive process as an essential component to being alive: "The analyst destroys the patient's manifest texts in order to reveal unconscious meanings and the patient destroys the analyst through that particular object usage we call transference" (Bollas, 1989, p. 36). "I suggest," he continues,

that for a good destruction of the analyst to take place, one that is not constituted out of the death instinct but is part of the life instinct, the analyst must indicate to the patient, at the right moment, that he is ready for destruction. The "to be destroyed" analyst has a different function—indeed is a different object—from that analyst who deconstructs the material. (ibid., p. 36)

If this seems somewhat formalised as something known that will occur during a moment in a session, in my experience it is rather some place or atmosphere that one unwittingly finds oneself in—a cold, horrible, unfriendly and frankly dangerous dark landscape.

When working with severely damaged patients, such moments are far more than a countertransferential invitation for the analyst to enter the experience of the analysand, all those years ago, in order to have some emotional being-in-the-moment of what it may have felt like then. Rather, or in addition to this, it feels as if the analyst's capacity to imagine that he or she can do analytic work is being destroyed. In fact, the patient is directing unconscious attention to a rock bottom to see if, in the midst of such experience, the analyst is still alive.

The idea of enactment can be viewed as an activity to draw the analyst into acting out, and therefore strengthening the patient's defences. It is as if the patient desires only to wrong-foot the analyst and attack analysis. This is very different to the idea that enactment might be a way, or even sometimes the only way, of retrieving past object states. Even if the analyst does allow that a certain degree of his own acting out may be inevitable, such a recognition serves to secure the analyst at a distance, trying to be aware, as an external and rational observer. This is far from the analyst described by Michael Balint, caught in an interpenetrating mix up, who needs to be experienced as malignant before being found as "harmonious" with the patient (Balint, 1968).

In the Independent tradition, the negative is used and is perceived less as antagonistic to the direction of therapeutics and without necessarily indicating an attack on analysis. The demand on the analyst is profound, as approaching the pull of a black hole can invoke his or her own past negative and traumatic experiences. Balint gave no clinical vignettes of malignant regression, nor how to technically develop an analysis to make such transition in object relations. I hope the following description of clinical work will add to the development of his ideas on moving from understanding the basic fault to the realisation of an interpenetrating harmonious mix-up and the formation of more mature unconscious object relationships.

The treatment of a schizophrenic analysand

I am returning to a case first discussed in my book *Landscapes of the Dark* (2011), to further examine what took place in that analysis, and in particular to examine its ending.

Mrs B wanted analysis as she felt desperate at her worsening sense of not being able to care for herself. She was anorexic, and cut and excoriated her body in secret, keeping this separate from her high-functioning and demanding job. She had been diagnosed as schizophrenic during several periods of psychiatric hospitalisation some years before. Declining medication and feeling that her treatment had been slight, she made clear that she wanted an analysis to understand herself and the content of her mind. Initially attending six sessions weekly, she began our work in a regressed silence, eschewing the couch and opting to sit on the wooden floor in a far corner of the room, abject with her head hung low. Presenting an indifference to being in the session, she observed acutely, despite giving an appearance to the contrary. Perhaps surprisingly, outside the consulting room, her ideas and concern for others' care was well-known in the community and she seemed much respected. Yet this carapace was instantly shed on entering the analytic space.

In between sessions she continued to deliberately slice her upper arms, sometimes her breasts and explored her vagina and anus with the knifepoint. After such attacks, the way she sat on the floor was a silent indication of the soreness of her body. It is such violent activity that I want to particularly discuss here rather than other perspectives.

Usually, if Mrs B told of such activity, it was in an affectless manner, and she remained surprised that I was affected by the horror of that activity. She had banished all feeling and projected herself as nothing and worthless. Thus, cutting was of no consequence to or for her. It was a piece of enacted sadomasochism separated from herself.

In time, she was able to recognise the internal battle of her internal voice demanding a cut, implying that she would obtain relief. She once brought to the session this cruel night-time demand by thinking about analysis, her analyst and the room we worked in, as well as by holding pieces of gravel she had taken from my driveway. The nightly fight was won or lost. If she failed to draw blood, the battle for survival the next night was heightened, seemingly to demand a blood sacrifice.

The analyst is placed on a tightrope in relation to such material: if I am silent, the patient is left to think that I, too, do not mind the cutting of flesh, and may even ignore it, like her. Also, the silent analyst may be perceived as being silent like the mother who did not speak up against what her husband was doing to their child, as I was beginning to hear about at that time and thus being hated by the patient for not helping. If I interpreted her cruelty in relation to the patient–analyst couple, it was understood in a surface, intellectual way, but the patient would still be left with the great problem of repetition. Yet what really mattered was whether transferentially the analyst was indifferent to what was going on. As were her parents.

It seemed essential she could begin to see the pain she was able to emotionally inflict onto the other. Hence, the slow surreptitious looks and glances at the analyst to see his face and posture. The clinical work often seemed to be in the following arenas of unconscious object relationships. Was the patient in a room with a primary loved father in the transference? Is the transference about a sadistic bully, attacker and rapist, who the patient has to be very careful of inciting? Is the patient, in the transference, the child, who, in identification with the cruel father, she is also tormenting? This would require the analyst to be in the position of voyeur. Furthermore, it is possible, within the complexity of ideas, to think all this from the opposite psychic position that the analyst is at the behest of a bullying mental assault: both require to be thought about and, in time, interpreted. And to add to the complexity—where is the maternal object? Was the mother ignored, wiped out, or beneath that layer was she part of the sadism and perversity of the parental couple?

Constantly watching the analyst at the same time as disavowing doing so, using slight glances, was Mrs B's way of avoiding contact whilst simultaneously looking out for the next attack.

The patient's wish to murder the analyst

One day Mrs B had secretly brought a carving knife into the session, and acting with stealth, attempted to stab me to death, as the voice that she could hear demanded it. It is with interest that I can report that, on the occasion that this happened, I had a sixth sense of some impending assault. In my countertransference, I felt an ambivalence of intense tiredness at the task of analysis and an alertness to minute details of my patient's physicality in the room. Even before the knife was made manifest, wrapped inside a towel, itself inside a large handbag, I had interpreted, following ten minutes of anxious painful silence, that there seemed to be a massive attack going on in the room, causing her a great deal of anxiety. This led to the patient slowly exposing the knife, saying that she wanted to plunge it into me as a way of appeasing the voices. I offered to look after the knife. Her relief was intense when she carefully gave the knife to me to look after. She was hugely grateful of the care given to her at being able to share her cruel hatred towards the other, which also contained, fused together, her desire for revenge against her parents.

There are many ways to think about such material—the meaning of the knife as a phallic object, whose phallus—father's, mother's, her own sexual confusion? Was it a representation of a sexual pairing and is this state close to murder, or soul murder as Schreber (Freud, 1911b) described it? It clearly represented an enactment of a severe sadomasochism led by the psychotic split-off voice encouraging the patient to violence, as an indication of her unconscious identification with the aggressor as well as a moment of revelation of her victimhood that she wanted me to know about. Yet by "doing it" to me, she was relying on my not retaliating.

The capacity for differentiation between her internal cruel parental objects and her analyst, and the establishment of solid boundaries, allowed her to know her wish to kill the analyst and to know that he was also alive enough to the problem to be able to survive murder. The nightly cutting of the body as an attack on the self was re-found in the transference. Her body was the analyst's body, in the same dynamic way that his dog's excrement was food for her mouth: an interpenetrating psychotic muddle, to paraphrase Balint, that in its understanding returns the vicious paranoia to a mutual understanding. Aggression against the self moves to the other. This enables the activity to be understood and interpreted, in later time, both in the transference of the here and now and in reference to past parental assaults. The difficult task of disentangling phantasy from reality needs to be attempted in the examination of the violence in the transference and countertransference. However, this can only really happen once the threat of a real, sharp knife in the consulting room has been acknowledged and neutralised.

Gradually, I heard about her early childhood in which she and her younger brother were the sexual objects of her paedophilic parents and their friends. Her mother was totally involved in her husband's perversion. The children were regularly cruelly and painfully sexually degraded.

The analyst's murder of a session

My interest in this pair of ideas on murder was set off by the statement in Ferenczi's *Diary* quoted earlier in this chapter:

> I have finally come to realise that it is an unavoidable task for the analyst: although he may behave as he will, he may take kindness and relaxation as far as he possibly can, the time will come when he will have to repeat with his own hands the act of murder previously perpetrated against the patient. (Ferenczi, 1988, p. 52)

In such a psychotic–perverse context, enactment can have a dangerous and severe momentum. Some months later I destroyed a session by terminating it early, as at that moment I could no longer bear the massive daily cutting of my patient's body. This attack had continued for several weeks, and despite all my interpretative attempts, her destructiveness just increased against her arms, anus and vagina. The patient had arrived for the last session of the week with even more bandages dangling, commencing the session as if it was utterly separate from her bodily attack. Within a couple of minutes, I "found myself" asking her to leave. She rightly confirmed that she had come at the correct time. I agreed but said I was unable to work with her that day. She left perplexed. I felt terrible, knowing that she had suddenly and unexpectedly approached my limit of containment.

Waiting to see what the following session would bring was agonising for me, especially as I expected her to potentially enact a further assault by attempting suicide. I did nothing but stay with the aloneness of pain and the paradox that, in my opinion, the best help was to dare to leave a gap and to trust in the patient's capacity to survive my destruction of her, rather than arranging a hospital admission. I was assailed by my own demons in my countertransference enactment that I was not a competent analyst, and imagined I would be struck off the medical register and thrown out of my analytic society, yet I decided to not contact the patient over the weekend.

The patient arrived on time for the Monday session. She looked considerably better in a more alive way and no longer dangled bloody bandages. She began by saying that she was very grateful for what I had said and done in the previous session, as she understood it as recognition that I cared about her. Implicitly she also meant that I was not simply allowing sessions to continue in some sort of unconscious collusion with the idea that she could just continue seriously to cut herself, as if her body did not matter. I, unlike her perverse parents, could not bear the show. She never cut her body again and the transference alliance was considerably strengthened.

Of course, interpretations about her state had been made in all manner of ways, always falling on stony ground. Historically this was a repetition, as it seemed that her parents had had no concern about any pain inflicted physically on her. Her response to my act was being able to begin to heal the pair of us. It was the first such recognition. Such a piece of analytic work, akin to the alarm for the analyst of falling into a deep black hole, was the clinical terrain of a potential for creative recovery. The point of being able to enter such an emotionally evocative blackness that was a recreation of her history was that now we could work together more on her historical traumatic narrative, whereas in the past and for most of her life, she was profoundly alone, repressing her knowledge. Such a clinical atmosphere cannot be taught but requires a good-enough capacity to bear being in that moment and accepting one's fate—a position true for both analyst and analysand.

In the presence of such destructive unconscious relationships, if the analyst remains in a clinical position of being only the observer, looking at and commenting on, then the patient realises (often quite quickly) that the analyst is not *alongside* their emotional analytic journey. Rather the analyst is perceived as speaking a commentary—you are doing this or that and even linking it to the transference "to do something to me". For those patients who have had a surfeit of destructiveness in life that has left them barely alive emotionally, the process of healing necessitates the revelation of the impact of that destructiveness, both on themselves as a form of expression, and on the analyst, with each of the pair taking on the different sadistic and masochistic positions as the object is made use of. It is only later in the analysis that these can be interpreted, once the patient is in a state of object relating rather than alone.

The analyst must be extremely thorough in examining his own desire for revenge against such mental and physical assaults. Of course, such patients expect to be attacked back, as this is the life offered by primary objects. The patient may be constantly in a state of expecting that the treatment will just be stopped and may take the opposite form of the patient trying to stop therapy in order to pre-empt her phantasy of the analyst's punishment of her coming true. Sometimes the patient's expectation of the analyst's desire for revenge (in identification with the patient) is an accurate reflection of the analyst not being able to stay further in the analytic quagmire. The patient's wish and expectation of being too much for anybody to cope with can then come true. The analyst may think that he or she has done enough in an impossible case, but this needs to be perhaps understood as a revenge motif. Instead, the analyst can continue to do analysis with a realisation that another picture exists beneath the blackness. In-patient psychiatric care needs to be considered. However, if the home situation is amenable enough, analysis of the psychotic state (to include such violent phantasies, with the analyst taking all necessary precautions in order to stay with the storm) can result in an analytic movement to a benign state in which interpretative work and the lifting of repression leads to deep depression for the agony of such an early life. That work on coming to terms with the depressive state is for a later stage of the analysis.

In this chapter, I have not dwelt on the many and various oedipal interpretations subsequent to the patient having left the one-person state (Rickman, 1951, p. 218). The meanings of knives, cuts and blood alongside the undifferentiation of the phallus and the womb are left for later in the analysis. Mother, father, sibling, incest, cruelty and sadomasochism follow this early state of the analysand emerging into daring to trust the dyadic relation.

So, back to the beginning. In "The aetiology of hysteria", after describing how traumatic memories of sexual experiences of childhood resurfaced during the treatment, Freud wrote:

> It is exactly like putting together a child's picture puzzle: after many attempts, we become absolutely certain in the end which piece belongs in the empty gap; for only that one piece fills out the

picture and at the same time allows its irregular edges to be fitted into the edges of the other pieces in such a manner as to leave no free space and to entail no overlapping. (Freud, 1896c, p. 204)

I had, by sudden action when I "murdered" the analytic session and without thought, found the missing unconscious piece of the puzzle that stopped the perverse game. In her mind was her parents' (mis)use of her and her brother at the paedophilic parties they arranged, with their children at the centre of any sort of perverse coupling imaginable and in the reality beyond phantasy. We could now begin to understand that the diagnosis that several psychiatrists had formally made years before—that she had a paranoid schizophrenia—was itself a cover for the severe paedophilic perversity that was laid on her and her younger brother. Psychotic medication only helped suppress the role of hateful parenting, as if the parents had just been victims themselves by way of having "mad kids" who grew up to have a psychotic and apparently untreatable psychiatric illness.

Balint's "harmonious interpenetrating mix up" (1968, p. 66) was a description of benign states. He also theorised about malignant states found in severe states of regression. However, in *The Basic Fault* (1968), he provided no vignettes for a malignant regression and I am trying to fill that lacuna with this case.

His wife Enid felt distanced from some of his findings about the "basic fault", especially in the area of technique about how the analyst deals with or stays alive in regressive states, and was expecting to further her husband's work in their next book, unwritten due to his early death. Rickman, who had experienced analysis with Freud, then Ferenczi, and later with Klein in London, was her training analyst, although her analysis with him ended after two years with his sudden death in 1951.

> Subsequently she went into analysis with Donald Winnicott for three years until she qualified as a full member in 1954. Thereafter, she resumed seeing Winnicott once-weekly for a year from 1962 while she was preparing for her training analyst panel (which she passed in 1963) and then again once-weekly from the time of her husband's last illness from October 1969. Winnicott died in 1971. (Wolf & Antonis, 2023, p. 158)

She was interested in the theories of both her analysts, around the "use of an object" as well as creative life. She published her papers in *Before I was I* (1993) including the seminal works "On being empty of oneself" (1963), "Unconscious communication" (1990) and "One analyst's technique" (1991).

My patient was in a one-person state a great deal of the time but also acutely observed me and my availability to be in the room with her. The one-person state that she was often in was not mirrored by the analyst, who was potentially available at any time during the sessions, by observing, whilst having his own reverie and an unspoken expectation of work happening at the level of unconscious communication. She knew, for instance, that I was always there for every one of her sessions as well as potentially in the gaps of treatment if she needed it, something of which she never availed herself, nor did she have crises in the gaps. Rather she managed her self being in analysis.

I will, before ending here, look at Mrs B's own ending. She had survived, managed and eventually coped with many summer breaks, but this one was different. She returned as usual and told me that she had noticed a growth in her breast within a few days of the break. She wanted to inform me about this before seeing her general practitioner, which she did the following day. I was very upset by this start of term, knowing that such pathology requires an urgency in diagnosis and that she had deliberately delayed having a consultation. She now quickly discovered that she had a very malignant breast carcinoma, taking the news with an astonishing calmness. This was the opposite of my inner distress. I came to realise that she had deliberately used the summer break to think about her life and death, working out her solution. In view of the aggressiveness of her cancer, only severe treatments were offered and were quietly, firmly, refused. She was in a quiet and peaceful existential state, as she organised her affairs.

I came, reluctantly, to realise that, although she knew that analysis had profoundly changed her from being alone in the world, unreachable in the pain of her horrific childhood with paedophilic parents, and despite knowing that in our work she had found she could trust another, the aggression she had suffered was too much for her to accept as psychic pain. It seemed that the internal aggression had returned as a severe somatisation attack on her breast that was unstoppable, and she quickly died. Her death left me pondering for many years, and it is only now that I can bring closure by describing the end of her analysis. She was able to have a quiet and even impressive going towards death that was a mark of deep respect for the analytic work we had both participated in.

So is this a return of the death drive? For Freud, the death drive was characterised by compulsive repetition and destructiveness, and although it may be attached to pleasure and excitement, it is not governed by the logic of wish fulfillment. Paula Heimann, writing after the schism with Melanie Klein, when she was a member of the Independent group, wrote:

> What, then, is the death instinct? There are many situations when our patients tell us and show us that they want to be dead. I believe it is more correct to say that they want to be dead than to say they want to die; indeed, analysis reveals that the wish in question concerns a state that is painless, while the fact of dying is usually strongly invested with phantasies of pain. Behind the wish to be dead what one really finds is the wish to be free of pain, whether physical, or psychical, such as shame, guilt, intolerable fears, anxiety, depression, confusion, despair, and so on, or we find phantasy wishes to be revenged upon or to kill an object with which the patient has unconsciously identified. A fairly typical revenge phantasy, that is pre-conscious, consists of imagining one's parents in a state of terrible guilt, suffering from remorse, accusing each other over their child's grave: here an Oedipal wish is concealed behind the wish to be dead. (Heimann, 1989, p. 253)

Here Heimann is turning away from Freud's description of a return to an inanimate state. Being inanimate for her is an expression of negativism, indifference, contempt for pain and lack of self-interest. These are states of mind of an opposite formation to that of creative life, the fragmented, dissociative mind—as found in psychosis, severe manic-depressive states and perversion formed in the actual traumas of infancy and childhood. Heimann eventually states, "Personally, what

I no longer find convincing is the relation between the hypothetical death instinct and the primary destructive drive" (ibid., p. 255). The importance of this later work lies in its descriptions of her giving up the seductive pull of inertia and primary destructiveness. Kleinians regard the latter as a central concept and view an analysis without such introspective theoretical discussion as superficial. I would argue that such a position diminishes the historical findings of the various intrusions into the body and mind of babies, children and adolescents, discovered through transference and countertransference (and also distancing from Balint's primary love). Heimann's clinical description, like Winnicott's child covering the colourful painting with black, reveals the possibility of finding in an analysis what used to exist before the true self was protected and covered over by the false self.

And now I suggest it would be worthwhile to read or re-read Ferenczi's seminal extraordinary paper "Confusion of tongues between adults and the child—The language of tenderness and of passion" (1932) and to compare his descriptions alongside that about Mrs B. So much of the paedophilic cruelty that she had sustained in her childhood and adolescence had been faced in analysis, with the repetitive viciousness of her self-attacks mitigated. Yet as Judith Butler has written:

> The death drive works in fugitive ways, and is fundamentally opportunistic: it can be identified only through the phenomena on which it seizes and surfs. It may operate in the midst of moments of radical desire, pleasure, an intense sense of life. (Butler, 2019)

Perhaps the seed had been sown earlier when she articulated her knowledge that I cared about her, such that during the break she might have decided to release me from my task of caring for her. I don't know much about how *she* mourned, but *I* did. And I have realised that the quiet, brave confrontation she had with death was a measure of her found maturity from the analysis.

I would like to mention that my patient had trained as a teacher and in time was a gifted headmistress who established a very well-regarded school. She could recognise similarly damaged children and kindly helped them to some recovery, respite and protection, which her school allowed. She was very well known to be committed to helping "impossible to help" children.

I will leave the last sentences to her, with a poem of hers containing a deep metaphorical description of her living with her destroyed self, the act of poetic formation itself being a strand of her recovery and of her death.

> I do not live in the past
> The past lies in the present here
> With me.
> Not past are the hands that
> Tear and claw,
> Not past are the torments and the
> Unshed tears.
> The past envelops and smothers the present
> And reaches out to pull the wings off the
> Future.
> I cannot say
> "Bury the past", because
> The dead rise from their corruption
> And the stench of decay
> Continually deflowers me
> As I suck the final trumpet of
> Despair

CHAPTER 9

Early Covid writings

At the beginnings of Covid, in April 2020, I wrote some short pieces about how I was thinking and feeling about the state of incarceration and sensory deprivation of family, friends and colleagues. Life had suddenly changed for all of us, in ways that we were only just beginning to explore, imagine and understand. It was also incomprehensible.

These writings were akin to the old ways of sending out messages in a bottle to try and connect. I sent them to many colleagues and friends from around the world in an email. Here is what I wrote:

> I hope you and your families are safe and hunkered down in these times of global contagion.
>
> I have written a couple of pieces in the last few days and hope that they might interest you. Please feel free to pass them on to colleagues and citizens.
>
> This email is also by way of my being isolated in London lockdown and desiring to be in touch with friends around the globe.
>
> Moreover, I am hoping to encourage colleagues to write short pieces about how they see our pandemical environment, from

the cities and countries that you live in. I would be pleased to have any writing sent also to me so that they might be collected. They would make an interesting and even valuable analytic set of views and a record of Dark Times.

Warmly
Jonathan

These are the pieces that I sent.

A-tishoo, A-tishoo, We all fall down

25 March 2020

Ring-a-ring-a-rosies
A pocket full of posies
A-tishoo, a-tishoo
We all fall down

The king has sent his daughter
To fetch a pail of water
A-tishoo, a-tishoo
We all fall down

The robin on the steeple
Is singing to the people
A-tishoo, a-tishoo
We all fall down

The wedding bells are ringing
The boys and girls are singing
A-tishoo, a-tishoo
We all fall down

All of society does not fall apart at once. We are mainly used to being on the comfortable side of the equation rather than the other side. It can be very wretched being on the other side, living near the edge of a falling life, or worse, being over the precipice with no employment, very little money, cramped home conditions or living on the street. Those in some comfort can look over to the other side and locate the problem over there. We can split our thinking into a them and us mentality that can absorb any personal guilt and more comfortably blame the other. Trump now continually blames the "Chinese" virus, giving it his particular "innocent" spin and covering his guilt for ignoring knowledge given to him months ago, leaving Great America very vulnerable. Yet we all have variations of this theme, blaming others while we bask in our own sustained, steady, comfortable position in society. For so long the separating off of the other from the self has existed in racist, anti-Semitic, misogynistic tropes trying to locate any undesirable function of one's own onto another group. In analytic parlance this is unconscious splitting and projection as defence mechanisms against the outside getting into us. Some of our undesirable qualities or phantasies are located onto the other, in order to leave us free and cleanly innocent.

Now it is we, all of us, floating in a global boat that is holed, as our world is falling apart—the country that we live in and our own complex lives within it. We all have the level playing field now, with equal possibility of catching Covid-19. So much of the world is in lockdown, with most of us contained in our own spaces in apartments and houses. For others, their fate is to be forced to be tightly packed together, like the refugees and those in Gaza with a significant risk of contagion. While we can mitigate our chances, we still live in the state of not knowing our fate, which is to quickly die. Worse is to die alone, without loved ones, our body carted off to be dealt with, without family, who are left alone to grieve and begin mourning without the human expression of coming together for the dead. This is a terrible reality, which is very hard to know and face, however intelligent and sophisticated we think we are. We sneeze and the whole world really is falling down. It does not even matter if our pockets are filled with posies.

In the children's poem the king loses his daughter. Those high up in the steeple of life will fall, as will the lovers too, despite the ringing of wedding bells. No, we are more in the territory of Hemingway's *For Whom the Bell Tolls*.

Hemingway's title is from John Donne's *Meditation* XVII (1624) and is particularly pertinent for our time, not least because Donne wrote it as he came very close to death himself in December 1623 in an outbreak of spotted fever, which killed thousands.

> No man is an island, entire of itself; every man is a piece of the continent, a part of the main. If a clod be washed away by the sea, Europe *is* the less, as well as if a promontory were, as well as if a manor of thy friend's or of thine own were: any man's death diminishes me, because I am involved in mankind, and therefore never send to know for whom the bells tolls; it tolls for thee.

Leading authorities on nursery rhymes, Peter and Iona Opie, thought the *A-tishoo* poem derives from the Great Plague of 1665 in England, a rosy rash being a symptom of the plague and posies of herbs carried for protection. So it seems a strange tale to find in a poem sung to young children. Winnicott saw it as the good-enough mother unconsciously paying out the baby for having such an immense impact on her life, accepted without retaliation. With Covid-19 we have no way of getting revenge on the virus itself. This is very different to our usual range and panoply of tools to obtain revenge against the other. This makes us human beings even more vulnerable psychologically as we pull up the drawbridge to our homes, awaiting the arrival of the modern-day plague. Our forebears dealt with horrific and widespread contagions and had the humanity of creative urge, as now, to bring meaning and solace to all of us undivided and together in the face of so much death.

So, what do humans do about the impact of life catastrophic? We can regress in our thinking, which has many forms. By regress, I mean to return to earlier and significant times in our life—babyhood, childhood and adolescence—when our character is developing in relation to family life and later the world beyond. If the good-enough mother of our early life is one who predominately held, fed and looked after, the baby imbibes an environment, a mental structure, that is generally safe. It is not perfect and any gaps and calamities in ongoing care can create a storm leading to quick reconciliation as the world is restored to its usual state of ordinary all-rightness and safety.

And if the baby's state is one of fragmentation, sensing that a feed is not instantly forthcoming and the wait is too much, what then? Then the baby has to manage alone, and depending on the roughness of early life, survive, at the price of developing a false self. Those citizens who have had to deal alone with early collapse of their world when small may now fear its return as more dangerous than those of us more lucky to have imbibed an internal mental holding that allows us a certain resilience. For others, the repressed aloneness from early in life suddenly returns as a severe taunting, as if they imagined they could really manage alone. The imposed isolation may well contain them for now, but in the aftermath there may be an eruption of overt psychic pain that will need to be understood and held.

For most of us, this long-enforced period of isolation may lead to a wave of adaptation and creativity that will aid our captivity. We will find that we can, surprisingly, manage the unimaginable and even enrich our capacities to survive.

And we will also have to all deal with the deaths and the desolation of mourning, most of which will have to be put off till later.

A recent news item on TV showed a forlorn football supporter sitting alone in his car outside his beloved club, Liverpool, suddenly closed. Nobody else was around. All was deserted. He had come by himself to play "You'll Never Walk Alone", the club anthem. Strange behaviour and totally understandable as one means of coping today.

Today somebody in my building suddenly died— a meditation on death (Sklar, 2020a)

30 March 2020

On a recent Thursday evening, a few days ago, in cities, towns and villages all over the UK, people gathered by open front doors, windows and balconies in their locked-down homes to applaud by extensive clapping the doctors, nurses and ancillary workers of the NHS. Some even were heard to blow trumpets!

It was a spontaneous event, emerging from emails, Twitter, Facebook and street gatherings on WhatsApp groups—our modern non-touch communicative tools. And it was done to honour our present-day heroes, manning the clinics and hospitals, all on an emergency footing to protect us, trying, if at all possible, to keep our citizens with Covid-19 alive.

Yet the emotionality behind this pleasurably impressive outpouring of rapture had a shadow. It was becoming clear from several accounts from nurses and doctors, often unattributed, that being on the frontline, they expected some colleagues to die, having caught the virus due to their close proximity to disease. That, as part of the medical ethic, they were prepared for, but to do so without the necessary protective armour was almost too much to bear. The British Medical Association today wrote: "The continued failure to provide an adequate supply of personal protective equipment to health workers is putting doctors and patients alike at risk of serious illness and even death" (BMA member update 30/3/20).

This brings to mind the Spartans at the battle of Thermopylae in September 480 BC. Some 5,000–6,000 Spartans, Thespians and Helots rushed to the very narrow pass at Thermopylae, which was the only road, in order to contain the invading Persian army of 150,000 troops. Vastly outnumbered, they held their ground for seven days. Leonidas, the Spartan King, aware that his small force had been outflanked by a betrayal, dismissed the bulk of the Greek army, leaving just 300 Spartans and 700 Thespians as the front line to fight to the death. This gave time for the Greeks to gather their forces to defeat Xcrxcs later at the sea battle of Salamis, when the Persians withdrew, losing most of their forces in the retreat.

Ever since, mythology has taught us the profound value of selfless sacrifice at certain times of national crisis. At least the Spartan citizen warriors went into battle fully armed. Our frontline medics and nurses were not properly protected, as the cry was heard from the smallest to the biggest countries in the world for more masks, gowns and gloves. Also needed were thousands more intensive-care beds and respiratory ventilators. The world watched China in amazement as it built hospitals from scratch, looking on with a critical eye, but without much intelligence, that a virus does not have to show its passport at the border to enter all our states. What complacent narcissism our leaders mainly showed. We basked in the pleasant thought that "it" was over there and not here. This easy-enough unconscious defence apparently protects us by the phantasy that the bad is somewhere else than with us.

The splitting in the mind between us and them, a potent force for denial, can be found in many, perhaps all, of the deep conflicts in societies, by which I mean the racism, misogyny and anti-Semitism that sucks up our hatred and locates it elsewhere in certain groups of citizens, or abroad. If the virus had been discovered first in America or Europe, would the same laxity have applied? I think that the contagion would have been more psychologically understood as potentially affecting all of us, rather than something alien and imagined in part as an unconscious phantasy of a "Yellow Peril" of political and economic concern about the modern strength of our neighbour China. Trump, of course, in his usual way, wanted to take down and humiliate any opponent, as he spoke of Covid-19 by a different name—the Chinese Virus. His explicit message was that it belonged to one nation who was giving it to the rest of us, leaving himself squeaky clean.

The "Yellow Peril" is a colour metaphor that East Asians are an existential threat to the Western world. It is a racist trope that uses an ominous existential fear of a faceless horde of … well, really this is a description of the new virus that we cannot even see, and which knows no boundaries of nation states. Even the internally borderless European Union was in fear of infection from its neighbour states. This may be right in trying to isolate communities, but it can breed rivalry and nastiness between allies when we all need to help each other, even applaud each other's great struggles with the same viral enemy.

But where is the death in the title of this piece? Well, first I want to think through the subject of narcissism and with it the projection of bad elsewhere, anywhere but in me. We are usually lulled into thinking too little about death. Looking at our image as reflected by the water allows us to avoid seeing a larger picture beyond one's reflection. Now the full horror of huge numbers of dead cannot be avoided.

In the shadow of the wonderful applause for our courageous health service workers lies the thought that some, perhaps many, will, like the 300 Spartans, have to die in their mission to help most of us survive. Without the medical front line accepting the very ill for triage, there would be total chaos in the country. Yet we know a real price will be paid, with rising numbers of Covid-19 deaths of medical, nursing and ancillary staff.

Were we not applauding their courage to be standing in that place where they too might die? As of 30 March 2020, twenty-five per cent of

British doctors were off work, sick or in isolation themselves or with a family member ill due to coronavirus.

> At Columbia University Irving Medical Centre in Manhattan half the intensive care staff were already sickened by corona-virus. In China more than 3000 doctors were infected, nearly half in Wuhan. In Italy, the number of infected health workers was now twice the Chinese total, and the National Federation of Orders of Surgeons and Dentists compiled a list of 50 who have died. Nearly 14% of Spain's confirmed coronavirus cases were medical. (Schwirtz, 2020)

Today, somebody I knew in an apartment in the house that I inhabit did not wake up from his last night's sleep.

Suddenly a door opened to the actuality and reality of death. This was not the near-incessant run of news from afar, to which I am listening less and less. My doorbell had rung, and it was the London ambulance service. They asked if I had called them, and I said that I had not. I was perplexed that it was not the post or an Amazon delivery of books. My phone soon rang, and my neighbour told me the news. I knew that the man who died had a serious heart disease. The ambulance crew, arriving in four minutes, later told me that he and the person living with him had both been coughing in recent days and they suspected a Covid-19 death. My first thought was "and it's in my building!"

The other man was a very vulnerable character, able to make a cup of tea, but not much else, and had had his autistic life looked after for many years by his now-deceased friend. The ambulance crew and police, who were obliged to attend a sudden death, if only to rule out the rare possibility of murder, had not grasped the still-alive man's fragility. His very distraught sister rang, as her brother declined to pick up her calls. Knowing his diagnosis of Covid, she knew she was not able to bring him to her nearby home. The daily delivery of meals was now difficult in the city due to excess demand.

But more to the point, where might social services look after otherwise-well Covid-19 patients unable to manage their own lives by themselves? So much for opening a Pandora's box of impossibilities. I was struck by the actual tragedy, not, as usual, far away, but in my own house. My own front door was in use by virus carriers. Did I have to urgently move out, to become a displaced person? Chaos needed a moment of quiet reflection as well as the good advice of a colleague, in case I had missed out on anything that was dangerous to my own life.

Curiously, I had been pondering on how sixteenth-century Venice had dealt with contagion from carriers of disease from faraway lands, in the sailors, merchants and traders coming daily to the great city. The plague of 1576–1577 killed 50,000—almost a third of the population. In 1680, the bubonic plague killed 80,000, with 595 Venetians killed on 9 October of that year. Later, in 1776, the Venetians set up a quarantine island, Poveglia, to house those suffering from the plague. The place became a checkpoint for all goods and people coming to and going from Venice and acted as a temporary confinement station. It is thought that over 100,000 persons were buried in plague pits on the island. It is interesting to note that later, in 1922, it morphed into a mental hospital, which finally closed in 1968.

Now, every accident and emergency hospital unit is a plague island. But what facilities are there in social services to look after the Covid-infected but otherwise well, who cannot look after themselves? I discussed this possible provision with the policeman on temporary duty in our house and we wondered why the plague island in Venice did not have a well-known modern-day counterpart in London. Not knowing, our house and the ill person's relative were left waiting, while the dead man lay silent in his bed in the flat.

I had been on a journey beyond the endless news descriptions on Covid-19, eventually realising that my being touched by this story is multiplied by the many personal human stories—in their thousands—in countries all around the world. These sad human stories suddenly happen, like the angel of death visiting the Egyptians with the tenth plague, the death of the firstborn, for failing to let the Israelites leave. Death passed over (hence Passover) the Israelites, who had painted a sign in lamb's blood on the door lintels of each Jewish household.

However many people tragically die in the UK of Covid-19—today the possible number from the government is perhaps 20,000—it is important to note that the total number of registered deaths in 2018 was 541,000. I have deliberately merged the daily news about death of citizens and doctors with what happens to the people in a block of flats when someone suddenly dies, near the eve of Passover with its potent myths about who will live and who will die.

Responses to my essays

In response to my thoughts on Covid, I received many emails from friends and colleagues who were delighted and touched with the communication "out of the blue", or more realistically the grey, including this one from China.

> Dear Prof Sklar,
> That's GREAT!
>
> We are following the news about Europe, the number is still increasing, and it is a difficult time in coping with the virus outbreak. Take care and we sincerely hope you and your family keep well and safe.
>
> In China the situation seems to become better, and China has come out slowly from total lock-down. We much appreciate your great support in the dark time, about 5,000 people read your beautiful paper[1] in our official We-Chat account and were inspired by what you said about You Will Never Walk Alone. Many people were moved by it and some of your students left words to say that this article reminds them of the touching silence in the end of the training last spring.
>
> In total, over 10,000 people read this article after sharing in the public platform. The unit and all the Chinese are very appreciative of your contribution for supporting us in the dark time!
>
> We will never walk alone, and are waiting for the end of the storm.
>
> Wish you all the best and warm regards.
>
> Yours,
> Prof Wang

* * *

In addition, the following short pieces were returned to me, gratefully received, and providing much pleasure.

Clearing a space

Philip Hewitt
Psychoanalytic psychotherapist, British Psychotherapy Foundation

Before Covid-19 became the burgeoning daily headline, there were pervasive concerns about the state of the world. For long we have had alarms about climate change and evidence of worldwide life-threatening pollution. The trends are worrying and at a vulnerable moment, I received Jonathan Sklar's first paper, "Atish-oo, Atish-oo" (2020b), catching me by surprise. I was taken back to childhood. My parents could always account for how they managed adversity, though I realise now that much of it was with welcome persuasive hindsight. The slow response of governments, seemingly reluctant to be reflective, without radical lockdowns as now, suggest they do not really know what to do faced with the obvious need to cut back and change our ways of life. As in "Atish-oo, Atish-oo", life is made to go on because there is no other way of thinking about the situation. This is the most daunting of all things. Is this really how things are? Is wisdom in such short supply?

The experience of working with a colleague who is studying "physician-assisted suicide" (PAS) has been challenging the fundamentals of how we live and may choose to negotiate our end. It also reveals the deepening insecurity about the no-longer held "sanctity of life" and it is as if PAS anticipated this pandemic. My own thoughts have gone very much towards questioning whatever it is that holds me or does not hold me. This is to say, what keeps me going? I always claim that I do not want to be a trouble to anyone but have I also been saying to myself until now that I am frightened of being too much trouble to be held. Winnicott postulated the existence of the "object-mother" and the "environment-mother". I take the liberty here of running with the "environment", which has become such a frequently used and emotive term. Winnicott describes this complexity of experience in the development of the child. As the thinking developed, he extended understanding beyond Freud in terms of the primary-process thinking of the mother who "imaginatively elaborates" her understanding of the child as part of an environment (Joyce, 2019).

"It takes our breath away" draws on Winnicott's important idea of the "transitional object" (Sklar, 2020c). This is central to the holding maternal relationship, and also the search for new understandings of how to live with *mother earth and mother nature*. Yet some of the material that has been broadcast from relatives of those who have chosen to end their lives under legal medical supervision is mostly rational, objective, lacking the lingering grief and awareness of consequences which accompany death, and rather just tidied away. Is there pride being taken in facing what is believed to be reality in order to control *transitional discovery and experience?*

Reported in the media at the height of the pandemic crisis were examples of "older, vulnerable people" being phoned by their doctor and having discussions about whether they wish to be hospitalised or stay at home if infected by "the virus". The idea was also there that the NHS had to be saved. We all agree! One measure suggested was to opt out of NHS care if you were of a certain age. It is difficult to know the actual circumstances, but it feels rather too close to Harold Shipman, who murdered his patients. This sounds dramatic but it is shocking, as is the epidemiological term of "harvesting". At the same time, we have to hold on to the fact that many people in the NHS and those looking after people in care homes and other places like prisons are in the frontline of infection and most vulnerable. Something important is happening about a sociocultural change in our relations with each other and our doctors and nurses who carry so much responsibility. Above all, currently we appear not to be looking after them, let alone people working in other situations.

So where do I go with "Atish-oo, Atish-oo"? Whenever we played this, the fall-down was the fun; I always got up again with a degree of ease so that we could repeat it, which would not actually be possible now. I mean, "not easily", but still possible! The pragmatics of choosing death are one thing, but there seems to be the threat, under great pressure, of a big step being taken as social policy emerges, about which Jonathan Sklar warns, "For so long the separating off of the other from the self has existed in racist, anti-Semitic, misogynistic tropes trying to locate any undesirable function of one's own onto another group".

So much has changed in our society, and I express this from being "held" in a particular British-conditioned–Christian/Jewish background from which, over the years and through analysis, I have had to excavate my post-colonial foundations. In Jonathan's Sklar's most recent paper "It takes your breath away" (11 April 2020) he describes the spectre of a Zombie world, objects which are easily identified but not invisible and serve the purpose of embodying our terrors. This however does provide precedent; "the object of Zombie" is something that can occupy our minds. In various reports from different sources the word "unprecedented" is so often urgently used. Such a stable word, disguising the unimaginable "objectless state of mind"—but nevertheless *"unprecedented"*. The precedents we do have, such as Spanish Flu (1918) and more recently AIDS, SARS and Ebola, seem less in relation to the present pandemic. For the most part, those bad objects were "them", not "us". It is time now to accept that this is "us". There is no counter-phobic escape from this pandemic by being a doctor or a prime minister or a psychotherapist or even as a patient—we are all responsible for what we carry.

The current pandemic raises the curtain of denial about the nature of our existence on Earth and our relationship with the planet. My search has been for ways of trying to think about this: precedented ways of thinking and maybe finding new ways, though that is far less likely. In the opening of *Radical Hope: Ethics in the Face of Cultural Devastation*, Jonathan Lear (2006) wrote:

> Shortly before he died, Plenty Coups, the last great chief of the Crow nation, reached out across the "clash of civilizations" and told his story to a white man. Frank B. Linderman had come to Montana ... as a teenager and was intimately associated with the Crows. [Linderman wrote:]
>
>> Plenty Coups refused to speak of his life after the passing of the buffalo, so that his story seems to have broken off, leaving many years unaccounted for. "I have not told you half of what happened when I was young," he said when urged to go on. "I can think back and tell you much more of war and horse-stealing. But when the buffalo went away the hearts of my people fell to the ground, and they could not lift them up again.... After this nothing happened. There was little singing anywhere. Besides," he added sorrowfully, "you know that part of my life as well as I do. You saw what happened to us when the buffalo went away" (Linderman, 1962).

With this possibility in mind, one can see Plenty Coups' gesture in yet another light. He is witnessing the death of the Crow subject, to be sure—but he does so in order to clear the ground for a rebirth. For if the death is not acknowledged there will most likely be all sorts of empty ways of going on *as a Crow*. Only if one acknowledges there is no longer a way of going on *like that* might there arise new genuine ways of going on *like that*. This impasse would explain Plenty Coups' eagerness to tell his story to a white man. For in a time of cultural collapse, living memory of that living way of life will last only a few years. The most important artefact the white man could offer the Indian—much better than guns—was writing and printing. (Lear, 2006, p. 1, p. 2, p. 51)

I drew from this some hope, which includes moving on from where we are and not simply repeating *"like that"* or just *"back to normal"*. Yes, hope of survival, but in a way more than that, the hope that I could "clear a space" for myself and join with others who struggle to untangle the muddles of history. This muddle is history, but is also now, is tomorrow. Plenty Coups has to face the end of a way of life as the railroad carved up the land and the buffalo and whole way of life were destroyed. In the face of ending through the other of Linderman, his scribe, like Plenty Coups we are left with a chance for ourselves. As "we all fall down", I am writing now for the record, hoping to clear a space in order to get up again.

19 May 2020

Mask of the Red Death

Endre Koritar
Training and supervising analyst, Western Canada
Psychoanalytic Society and Institute; Assistant Professor,
University of British Columbia; Associate Editor, American
Journal of Psychoanalysis; *board member, International Sándor*
Ferenczi Network; in private practice, Vancouver, Canada

Jonathan Sklar's recent missive about the Covid pandemic has inspired me to consider how we and those around us respond to such a massive rift in our social fabric. For a species that is naturally a social animal, social distancing and isolation is an unnatural hardship to endure for months on end with no relief in sight. In my imaginary meandering, I chanced upon a remembrance of a time when I was enthralled with Edgar Allan Poe's morbid fascination with the macabre. There, in a corner of my mind I recalled reading, "The Masque of the Red Death".

This is a story of how others in times past dealt with the plague.

The story goes like this. A plague called the red death wreaking havoc on his kingdom, Prince Prospero had been cooped up in quarantine for what seemed like a long time. This was a particularly lethal disease, which manifested as a rosy rash, spread on the body quickly and killed the person within a day. Prospero, feeling bored and longing to return to his former lifestyle, moved to his castle in the country with a hundred of his subjects to keep him entertained. There, they continued their merry lifestyle as if there was no plague. At a masked ball he noticed a strange person wearing the mask of the red death. Enraged that the intruder would ruin his contrived oblivion of the tragedy unfolding outside the walls, he approached the red-masked wraith and ripped off his mask, intending to run him through with his sword. But underneath the mask was the same face as on the mask. Prospero immediately got the rash and dropped dead. His merry company, now terrified, each in turn developed the dreaded rash and died. "Ring around the rosies … they all dropped down."

Now, we might consider this as a cautionary tale of the fate of those who would seek to shut out the reality of there being a killer in our midst and wish to live life as if that reality did not exist. This coping mechanism might sound familiar to an analytic audience. An iteration of Freud's paper "Negation" (1925h), argues that negation can be used to negate the presentation of an external reality that is held in abeyance. This might be useful, say in the situation where soldiers are ordered to rush into battle facing a hail of killing bullets, or a tightrope walker without a net below. In a pandemic, the realisation of an external presentation of danger is held in abeyance for the purpose of continuing to be able to function as if there was no threat to one's survival. This negation of reality can be readily seen in primitive psychotic states of mind, as in schizophrenia; however, the temporary loss of reality testing can be time-limited as in a neurotic condition, or it may persist for hours or days as in personality disorders.

With this dynamic in mind, we might now consider that Prospero was suffering from a narcissistic personality disorder and under the influence of delusional thinking of omnipotent invulnerability, rendering his judgement impaired to the real danger that the Red Death presented in a crowded Bacchanalian celebration.

In the current pandemic situation, there are those who delude themselves into the belief that they, and by extension their country, is invulnerable to the external reality of pestilence. Their hour of glory will come and go, as predicted Shakespeare of Macbeth:

> Life's but a walking shadow, a poor player,
> That struts and frets his hour upon the stage
> And then is heard no more: it is a tale
> Told by an idiot, full of sound and fury,
> Signifying nothing

The tragedy, however, is that deluded Prospero led his cohort into the jaws of the Red Death, and ambitious Macbeth left a trail of bodies behind while bellowing his sound and fury.

We are now listening to the sound and fury of powerful figures like Trump and his minions. We can only hope that they will be identified as idiots bellowing their sound and fury and it will signify nothing.

Mortality salience, the fragility of the human condition, and Covid-19

Danielle Knafo
Clinical psychologist, psychoanalyst, professor and author,
NYU Postdoctoral Program in Psychotherapy and Psychoanalysis,
New York, USA

With the entire globe grappling with a viral monster that is taking and threatening lives while inciting anxiety and even panic, there could not be a better time to contemplate death.

Surely what we are living though is a new situation, yet I believe it is surfacing repressed feelings that we defend against because they are simply too much to bear. These feelings have to do with the terror of death and the insult of human fragility. During "normal" times, when we entertain thoughts of human fragility, we conveniently place them in the other: people starving in a far-off country, distant war-torn areas, persons with serious illnesses, refugees, the homeless, and so on.

Today, with the Covid-19 virus encroaching upon all aspects of life, everyone is feeling the presence of mortal threat, which tells a simple truth: *I am fragile*; life is ephemeral: things can change in an instant, even for great numbers of people; control over life and the future is more illusion than reality. As more people are mandated or selecting to stay home, they are turned inward to their deepest thoughts and emotions. They are facing realities that are usually avoided by focusing on the external world with its work and social activities. Solitude breeds reflection and insight, the latter usually gained through angst. This is why we do our best to avoid it.

Today we face a core truth about the human predicament, starkly revealed by the complete disruption of the social and economic order. Ernest Becker wrote in his 1973 masterpiece, *The Denial of Death*, "What does it mean to be a self-conscious animal? The idea is ludicrous, if it is not monstrous. It means to know that one is food for worms." He goes on to say that the essence of normality is the refusal of animal reality. We need our defences. We need to be ensconced in a normative social order. We need to be free of death anxiety in order to function and not go mad.

As a clinician who works with people diagnosed with psychosis, I have witnessed the daily terror that accompanies awareness of the precariousness of human life and human relations and the uncertainty and confusion that emerges from feeling overwhelmed by the human enterprise. Think of persons with psychosis as those who comprehend on a profoundly visceral level that their very bodies are a menace to themselves, that everything in life is fragile and can come to an end at any moment. In other words, they *really* know what we only come to know at times like this. However, the psychotic solution to such insight is understandably extreme. They are God. They have special powers.

They fear being contaminated or contaminating others. They see the end of the world. It is interesting how in the age of Covid-19, many of us may be entertaining similar thoughts and feelings.

What can we learn from this psychotic state of emergency without going mad?

We learn that we are all interconnected and that we rely on each other to survive and to have a good life.

We learn that we need very little to live, and to value and not waste what we have.

We learn to be alone and, in this case, to gather our strength and courage.

We learn to nurture our relationships at a distance.

We learn that we need to work together to conquer the threats to human life. Irreversible changes caused by climate change will cause much greater damage to human and animal life than Covid-19. We must collectively make the necessary changes to prevent grave damage to our world.

Most importantly, we learn that we flee our awareness of annihilation, but that that very awareness is what allows us to live life more fully.

As Theodore Roethke keenly observed, "In a dark time, the eye begins to see".

Thoughts for the times on distance and death

Victoria Hamilton
Retired psychoanalyst, International Psychoanalytical Association;
retired child, adolescent and family therapist, Tavistock Clinic;
PhD psychologist, UCL; painter and designer, Glasgow School of Art;
illustrator—for further information and current activities,
please visit http://www.victoriahamiltonarts.org

Thank you, Jonathan, for initiating this dialogue and for your two most interesting and thought-provoking pieces. I was fascinated by the connection you made between the Atish-oo nursery rhyme (which I never understood as a child falling out of a circle to the floor) the plague and our current Covid-19 pandemic.

In the second piece, I appreciated what Jonathan wrote about "selfless sacrifice". Doctors, healthcare workers, police and fire fighters, bus and subway drivers, post-office personnel, grocery store and delivery workers demonstrate this day after day, as they see their fellow workers fall sick and die. It is very difficult to make this selfless sacrifice when you are filled with fear of the unknown and of dying.

Although I affiliated myself with the Independent group in British psychoanalysis, my primary education in psychotherapy was at the Tavistock Clinic in the seventies, caught between, and hopefully benefiting from, the teaching of John Bowlby during the time that he was developing his attachment model and the Kleinians, mostly ardent followers of Esther Bick. And it is two aspects of these two diverse teachings that I find myself returning to when trying to understand the various responses to the current pandemic.

To take Melanie Klein first—whose theories, like those of Freud, were developed in a wartime and anti-Semitic environment and therefore may be most pertinent to the current times as outlined by Jonathan. Melanie Klein described the earliest and most primitive state of the human infant as one of "persecutory anxiety" which she characterised as the "paranoid–schizoid position". The infant suffers from paranoid anxiety and easily resorts to splitting into good and bad, idealisation and denigration. Under good circumstances, the young child reaches what Klein described as the "depressive position" or "age of concern" (Winnicott).

Applying these ideas to the current pandemic situation, the enforced isolation and social distancing can easily make us paranoid and avoidant of the other. We resort to "splitting", idealising perhaps one person or group whilst denigrating the other—a Trumpian world of goodies and baddies.

Klein's theory of infant development has long been challenged and refuted as a model of *normal* infant development. Her theory was not developed from direct infant–parent observation but was a projection backwards from her work with disturbed adults. She understood that adults can suffer from paranoid anxieties that wall them off from care and kindness.

In his attachment model of human development and behaviour, Bowlby demonstrated the propensity to orientate towards the familiar over the strange. Now, except for those living in the familial environment, we are forced day after day, minute by minute, to orientate towards the strange. We suffer interminable "stranger anxiety". We are afraid to go out in case we breathe the breath of friend or foe. This goes against our basic instincts. Bowlby also described another parameter that guides us from cradle to grave—anxiety and exploratory behaviour. When anxiety is high, we have no desire to explore the environment. We shut down. Or we take flight. Today, even if we did feel like going on an expedition, we cannot. So we are walled in by stranger and persecutory anxiety. Sadly, those who live alone have "no shoulder to cry on" (Bowlby) and may find themselves stuck in anxious, avoidant attachments.

The current fearful environment preys on primitive anxieties, on splitting into good and bad, on paranoia about the other, and cuts across the powerful desire to live amongst the familiar and familial. We long for the warmth of companionship.

What can we do?

How to stay sane if we are neither a lifelong solitary artist for whom isolation is the familiar state nor part of an absorbed, affectionate family unit? Perhaps one can hold onto and nurture whatever shreds of familiarity are available. For instance, I have found that a walk through the woods (in upstate New York) gives me a feeling of familiarity as long as I trudge up the same "weary" path every day (Tennyson, *In Memoriam*). I see a bright little crocus pushing its way through the dead leaves and branches, I hear a new bird call, a cock crow in the distance. Once on a warmer day I heard the first cuckoo. Maybe the best one can do is to hold on to something very ordinary and simple that previously one had taken for granted or did not see. Whatever it is, it can become familiar and can guide us in today's strange world—a small, ordinary thing that slipped our attention in the old world before Covid-19. A tiny bud becomes a "beacon of safety" (Bowlby). And when it fades, we find another source of greenness, reminding us that life springs and the birds still sing.

On yesterday's walk, I saw no beacons. I felt heavy and lonely. It was a cold, grey, day so maybe the little beacons on previous days curled back up, waiting for the warmth of the season to open again. No birds sang, only the dry "pock pock" of the woodpeckers pecking in duets and trios on the broken trees.

Figure 26. A newborn miniature pine tree, springing out of the protective bark of an old tree root. Copyright © Victoria Hamilton. Reproduced with permission

The next day, still no flower beacons but I saw a newborn miniature pine tree, already manifesting its full-grown adult form, springing out of the protective bark of an old tree root, surrounded perhaps by the arms of its grandmother. Thankfully, I found it the next day, shining green in the sun in the wizened bark cradle. From now on, I hope to see it every day, growing stronger and greener, even on days when no flowers bloom.

Coronavirus and production of subjectivity: me and humanity in the face of the unexpected*

Marcelo N. Viñar
Psychoanalyst; trauma expert; coordinator of research groups
on adolescence and marginalised young people; former Professor,
Faculty of Medicine, Universidad de la República, Montevideo
(1968–1997); and President of the Latin American Psychoanalytic
Federation (FEPAL)

In the days when there was time for leisurely and anodyne talk, in one of the last conversations I had with my elderly father, a phrase appeared whose age gave it testamentary value. He solemnly said something like this:

> I was a foresighted man: I always worried about anticipating and preparing for tomorrow. But that morning never fit my prediction. There came another with its surprises, good or bad … so I no longer encourage or advise you to be foresighted.

Surely his status as an emigrant from distant lands and cultures sealed a childish mark of insecurity or fragility where it germinated into a reaction formation of being cautious.

With this legacy, I can think of reaching the think-tank about the future of psychoanalysis, having lived a life whose logic and commitment was effective in placing myself on the enjoyable side of the human condition, avoiding the chasms of precariousness and exclusion, unemployment and marginality.

Arriving safely to the final stretch of our lives, the Covid-19 virus burst into our lives, cancelling habits, longings and projects, which we had designed and were working on in the current year; in addition, except for Mariano Horenstein, the rest of us are inscribed in the highest risk area, which underlines the adherent to the only measure that has been recognised as effective and active to reduce contagion:

---

* First published in *Psychoanalysis.today, 11: Psychoanalysis in the Time of Pandemics*, July 2020. https://www.psychoanalysis.today/en-GB/PT-Articles/Vinar-108460/%E2%80%8BCoronavirus-and-Production-of-Subjectivity-Me-and.aspx. Reprinted with permission of the editors.

quarantine and social confinement. Hence Jonathan Sklar's testament as he wrote that to diminish the virus's spread we must mitigate in isolation, testifying to the experience we are all experiencing, spontaneously and in the heat of the moment.

Badiou calls the *event* a derailment that derails the expected and forces us to invent and design other itineraries of life. Learning, Heidegger says, is not to inform someone of something he didn't know before, but to make of someone a being who didn't exist before. Infatuation, falling in love, the birth of a child, are universal models of this experience. Prison during the dictatorship and subsequent exile were for me experiences of that kind. I suppose the emergence of a serious illness can be added to the list.

Social isolation is an imperious necessity and a painful experience; it pushes us to the condition of the lepers of the Middle Ages. The price of preserving health maims us in the most human way of the human condition, our condition of relational beings. Perhaps for young people, the natives of the digital revolution, the code-changing will be less violent. In what is personal to me, the virtual encounter is radically different from the face-to-face encounter. But if there is no bread, cake will do, and today thanks to the informational venues we can be less alone than years past.

The first reaction to the epidemic is egocentric, self-referent, as if it had been conceived by a diabolical being to interrupt our lives, our longings and our projects, which we had undertaken to feel alive.

Between negotiations and denials, we know that aging and dying are part of life. But this experience—like love—is conjugated in the singular. The pandemic comes to beat down that singularity and plunges us into the plural, the massive into being an anonymous number and to rob me of my singularity, at the very least, it comes to dilute it.

Almost immediately, the shame of egocentrism and self-centeredness erupts, shame of feeling unique (and privileged) in the abolition of the collective dimension of a historic trauma … After a short silence, we call upon humanity as a restorative remedy of repugnant egocentrism. I have a home, food, books, money to get through the tragedy, where there are millions of people that lack what I have. Consolation is necessary, but shortly after we begin to navigate it, becomes overwhelming when humanity becomes present in its massive and opprobriate inequality, which the pandemic stresses.

I understand that confinement is not the same in the favela as in a comfortable house; I think of the posters of Bolivia's slums in dictatorship, writing posters and shouting, "Better to be killed by the virus and not hunger". How can I combine the gaze towards the intimate and the world without falling into the cheesiness of humanism? Since human diversity is infinite, each one is entitled to his own version.

As Bifo Berardi says in the compilation entitled *Wuhan Soup*, the extreme pandemic experience will leave indelible marks on the planetary village and presumably it will not be the same before and after the extreme experience, the little "Jair B flu" experience, will leave its deep footprints. I leave to political scientists and sociologists the analysis of the ongoing phenomena that forces the rethinking of the damage of an extractive and always expanding economy and its replacement with the difficult balance between ecology and a sustainable economy.

I read that the epidemiologists think that the genesis of the latest pandemics can be attributed to a combination of human factors, a demographic and an ever-expanding economy that destroys forests in their ecological diversity in order to encourage agricultural production and the exponential growth of large cities that squeeze millions of inhabitants in limited space. I leave this specialised knowledge to the epidemiologists, virologists, political scientists and economists. Let's go back to the specific field of construction of subjectivity. In his *Discipline and Punish: The Birth of the Prison*, Michel Foucault gives us some clues or walkways: the school, the factory, the hospital, the asylum, are common spaces or scenarios that sentence the uniform, to think about breaking that barrier of uniformity and assuming the limits and pains of confinement, and to do with these creative elaborations.

The real-time and experiential experience of confinement is slower. Between delight and boredom, we realise to what extent we were addicted to epileptic rhythms that devoured us and now we recover moments of silence and loneliness. Although reading, music and cinema accompany us—hooray for modern life—nonetheless, the painkiller does not calm the total of what we have lost, forbidden to come close, to embrace, to kiss, especially and above all, our loved ones. We evoke Walter Benjamin's reflection here: sharing experiences and day-to-day life experiences and narrating them is as necessary for the soul as drinking and eating is for the body.

Perhaps the time has come in this psychoanalysis of the twenty-first century not to be cloistered in the world of internal objects that founds psychic reality but instead open our minds and ourselves to the multi-determination of cultural and sociopolitical realities, while maintaining customs open between the two registers.

Translation: Monica Lachman from the original Spanish

Shelter in place

Drew Tillotson
Psychoanalyst, San Francisco; past President,
Psychoanalytic Institute of Northern California (PINC)

Dearest Jonathan,
Thanks so much for including me on this. I found your writing very powerful and moving.

It is hard to balance the outrage at the power structure who "should" have known better how to protect us, with the fear and heartbreak over the enormity of this kind of global experience. The inequities. The luxuries of those who can watch from safe havens, the sheer trauma of those who are helping on the front lines of disease, with limited resources. I have come to refer to this as "the great leveler".

I am including here below a portion of a letter I posted to colleagues the first week we were "sheltered in place" here in San Francisco, and indeed California as well. It is almost like a diary entry. I just wanted to respond to you sooner than later, with something, in the spirit of appreciation and solidarity.

Warmly, and to all of you, safety and health,
Drew

Wednesday, March 17, 2020*

It is difficult here in San Francisco. We are officially in "shelter in place" mode, encouraged to remain at home. We expect our situation to be similar to what Italy has gone through. We're told the onslaught is a matter of time, not if, but when.

I am at home conducting phone and camera sessions only. This frame requires a lot from both sides of the electronic chair/couch/computer/home/kitchen/dining-room/playroom. Betty Joseph meant something quite different in her idea of "the total situation", but this is indeed a very 2020 total situation. Transference is only one part; there are many objects, dangerous, loving, dead, overstimulated, terrified.

In Bion's version of "catastrophic change", the process of relinquishing old object ties, the terror and survival of that, of coming alive, is internal. Yet, I keep thinking about it … it seems very apt at this moment. Now, all is new, hour by hour, literally. The old must be relinquished in order to take in the reality of calamity, but the terror of surviving it is not only psychic at this point. It is bodily, a literal danger. A catastrophe of being forced to bend. Of contending with a body that won't be ignored. Of being forced to contend with each other as vectors of disease.

Today was Day Two here from "Sheltering in Place". Yesterday, Day One, I struggled with sessions, restless, annoyed, sleepy, coffee tasted stale. Today something shifted. At moments in both phone and camera sessions, it was like meeting a whole new patient, a different version. I worked to open my mind, to dilate the frame. I kept turning to analytic intention as a mooring line. I started having reveries of holding sessions on the street, in a cafe, in a meadow, on the moon.

As the day went on, the work became freeing. Something powerful was occurring in the disruption of asymmetry—the fact that we were facing the same catastrophe evoked very playful, loving, surprisingly erotic moments. All amidst a tsunami of terror and disease moving towards us. It was a paradoxical soup of pain and pleasure, of love, great disappointment, impatience, crawling out of and into our skin.

---

*This letter first appeared in print in *ROOM: A Sketchbook for Analytic Action*. Issue *ROOM: 6.20.* Analytic-room.com. It is reprinted with permission of the editor.

The frame has to shatter and reconsolidate right now, from my little home office, in a corner of San Francisco. If it can't bend, I can't help or think. If I can't help or think, I will be forced to disappear in Netflix or Googling factoids of terror.

So, here's to the resilience of our minds. We can do analytic work from a lily pad, a flatbed truck, a dancehall, or billiard room. At least I am counting on that.

Warm solidarity from a heavily endangered, beautiful city by the Bay,

Drew Tillotson—San Francisco

* * *

A month after I sent those first pieces on Covid, I wrote this third essay, still from a perspective of lockdown.

It takes our breath away—the first day of lockdown[2]

London, 10 April 2020

We take breathing for granted, as being ordinary, normal and natural. We usually do not give it a second thought. This is where Covid-19 attacks humans, in a vulnerable place we take for granted. Take our breath away and we suffer instantly. Not being able to "catch our breath" causes immediate mental suffering, leading to feelings of being distraught, severe anxiety, fear of dying. Now we are beginning to know that any early sign of impediment to our usual respiratory rhythm may lead to a sense of terrible slow strangulation.

One of my daughters wrote to me about her experiences at the very start of lockdown:

> On the first day of lockdown, I felt a rush of emotions as I was planning to leave the house. The virus wasn't just on the television—it was outside my front door. How do you protect yourself against something you can't see? I thought I must be able to see something and the only way I could understand the virus was to imagine a world full of zombies outside my

front door and that we had to find our way to get past them! My thoughts then shifted to the heroes in zombie movies and how they survived. I was reliving the film *28 Days Later* for real! In the film one lives out a terrible and devastating epidemic, moment to moment.

I picked up my backpack and started to pack it for the day ahead, packed so much stuff … food, drink, sanitiser, layers of clothes, I packed it all! As I drove my children, I kept looking at people thinking they looked different in some way. I was actually looking for zombies in the street! It sounds crazy but that is how I lived my first day. Three weeks later I still pack too much in my backpack when I leave the house but I've stopped looking for zombies on the street; the global impact of Covid-19 is so much scarier to me!

Ghosts

We are in the territory of ghosts and ghouls, an imaginary system of daydreams that turns the invisibility of the virus into a visual representation full of imaginary terror. Hollywood has poured out a diet of such images for many years to titillate our pleasure as it comes close to great fear, in the knowledge that it's just in the imagination. Yet an alternate reading might be that the film industry in the guise of entertainment and profit has been offering us images and stories about the terrible potential calamities of global warming, as if at the core of such entertainment there is a subtle message of concern.

The virus can take away our lives, but much more than that is scary for many other reasons too. The pandemic is taking away jobs, destroying commerce, savings, factories and shops, and potentially destroying much of the way we live our lives.

So many of the world's population, being under thirty years of age, have an intimate acquaintance with the spirits of our times. The Dementors of Harry Potter infest the darkest places, glorying in decay and despair as they drain peace, hope and happiness out of the air around them. Dementors, if one gets too close, suck out every happy memory inside one's mind, reducing one to being soulless like them. It is a modern take on vampiric phantasies that are directed at sucking blood out rather than breath, but the effect is to dominate and wipe out our internalised stability of good-enough memories as the very stuff of our insides is removed, leaving us empty. Such phantasy is about wiping out the mind, especially our ability to think, discriminate and to eventually become free of its shackles. In the midst of what seems a long campaign to fight for the next breath, it is very hard to think about anything else in that continuing moment.

Ghosts, phantoms, wraiths are often the spirit of the dead, haunting us, the living. The word ghost denoting spirit is linked to the Latin *spiritus*, which also means breath. Ghosts can be demonic as Dementors or holy as in *Spiritus Sancti*, which includes the idea of taking in breath as in inspiration and hence linked to creative life. They also may contain vague shards of more painful memories from the past, now ghosted as a form of staying away from very unpleasant thoughts from perhaps earlier on in our life.

Could we try to define madness? asks Enid Balint.

> Is it a state when you are on your own, but in order to maintain the boundaries in your life you have to be creative? To be on your own without being creative is not being alive. Being on your own and being creative might be mad but it is being alive. (Balint, 1993, pp. 233–234)

Here is an example of a Winnicottian paradox that can help us make sense of how citizens in the privacy of their own particular lockdown can be creatively alive or on the edge of being emotionally deadened by their attempts at being alive. For my daughter it required a shift from seeing and expecting to see zombies on the streets beyond home, a visual hallucination of alive madness on the path to realising the reality of the scary object that Covid-19 really is. Her momentary madness was a journey to realising the horror of reality.

In lockdown cities we can no longer visit museums and art galleries, cinemas, theatre, concert halls and opera houses. Those places in which we congregate to come close to the arts as manifestations of human thoughtful achievements that touch us contain manifest supplies of another invisible product—the pleasure of play within a cultural object. There is an avalanche of online communications to help us survive solitary imprisonment, which now allow us to look at Michelangelo in the Sistine Chapel or take a virtual tour of the British Museum or an exhibition of paintings, or film archives. Great orchestras are freely opening their archives and pianists are playing live online. A huge mass of wonderful moments to suck up and to fill up our emptiness. We can be touched, but not physically. It is nearly enough, but human beings need physical presence as much as breathing.

In time, when the virus has been overcome, the importance of cultural objects as mechanisms to keep us sane and thoughtful to the resonances beneath the surface need to be remembered. Financial support for such actions and in particular our artists is an essential part of our complex life. Van Gogh, mad–alive and invariably struggling, sold but a single canvas in his lifetime (*Red Vineyards near Arles*, to Anna Bloch, sister of his friend Eugene Bloch).

We can ride the flow of these cultural envelopes into our homes in our captivity and we have time on our hands to take advantage of such rich themes. It is a force that can fill up our emptiness with extraordinary creative influences, sounds and ideas. Families locked in together can begin to be and play together in new ways as our timetables have, of necessity, altered. Such possibilities of playthings can be a bulwark against our despair and can even, in the moment of our recreation with them, take our breath away in the form of inspiration for now and the future.

CHAPTER 10

Bloomsbury and the early evolution of British psychoanalysis*

I am going to examine some of the overlapping early groups to develop British psychoanalytic thinking. Whilst it begins with stories about academic men in Cambridge and Bloomsbury, two women, Alix Strachey and Karin Stephen, became important independently minded female analysts alongside their husbands James Strachey and Adrian Stephen. Bloomsbury values informed their independence and the importance of having freedom of mind. There were others, too, like John Rickman, Sylvia Payne and Ella Freeman Sharpe,[1] who were not Bloomsbury, but equally committed to Independent values. Blooms-bury members contrived their own legends by continuously writing about themselves in their intricate relationships with each other, and the part that several of them played in disseminating Freud and shaping the psychoanalytic profession is undeniably significant. Likewise, the Cambridge group was one of many groups to stand against a prevailing

* A version of this chapter was originally published in E. Wolf & B. Antonis (Eds.), *Independent Women in British Psychoanalysis: Creativity and Authenticity at Work* (pp. 35–45). Abingdon, UK: Routledge. Copyright © 2024 by Routledge. Reproduced by permission of Taylor & Francis Group.

Victorian orthodoxy but is of particular interest for, unusually, taking in Freud and his early ideas about the unconscious and dream life, and for being part of the development of psychoanalysis in England.

Beginnings

The London Psychoanalytical Society was founded in 1913 by Ernest Jones. It changed its name to the British Psychoanalytical Society in 1919, when Jones expelled what he described as "the Jung 'rump'" (Paskauskas, 1993, p. 328). In Cambridge, G. E. Moore, Arthur Tansley,[2] Bertrand Russell, John Maynard Keynes, Leonard Woolf, and Lytton and James Strachey were all friends and belonged to the long-established and invitation-only Cambridge Apostles society, which met regularly to discuss truth, sex and ethics, amongst other topics. Freud's contributions on the importance of an unconscious life and understanding the roots of sexuality in the mind were regarded by many as polluting, yet this group was very taken with his ideas on psychoanalysis from about 1910, when those ideas began to be published.

Alongside the London Psychoanalytical Society, the Medico-Psychological Clinic, better known as the Brunswick Square Clinic, opened its doors between 1913 and 1922 and developed the first training programme in Britain, as well as offering psychoanalysis to a range of patients, including shell-shocked soldiers in particular. As Suzanne Raitt writes:

> Nowadays the Clinic is almost forgotten: Ernest Jones, in his zeal to establish his own primacy as father of the British movement, fails to mention it in his published reminiscences, even though some of the leading lights of the British Psycho-Analytical society under his presidency including James Glover, Sylvia Payne, Ella Freeman Sharpe, Mary Chadwick, Nina Searl, Susan Isaacs, Iseult Grant-Duff and Marjorie Brierley, received their first analysis or training there. (Raitt, 2004)[3]

Post-war Cambridge and Bloomsbury

It was after the war that Cambridge/Bloomsbury became a major locus of interest in psychoanalysis. The Cambridge group that met from 1925 included James Strachey, John Rickman, Arthur Tansley,

Harold Jeffreys, Lionel Penrose and Frank Ramsey, who were dedicated to putting psychoanalysis on a scientific footing. Many of them were in or close to the Bloomsbury group, which was by that time the major culture carrier of psychoanalysis, both in private discussions within the group and by widely disseminating psychoanalytic ideas into their writings on topics such as economics (Keynes' *The Economic Consequences of the Peace* (1919) and his 1936 *The General Theory of Employment, Interest and Money Economics*[4]), history (Strachey's *Elizabeth and Essex* and his various biographies containing psychoanalytic insights including *Eminent Victorians*), philosophy and living an ethical life (Moore, Russell[5] and his student Wittgenstein), and sexuality.

A bohemian group, many of them lived close to each other in houses around Gordon Square and always had various friends and scholars staying. The group was loyal to itself, often in love with other group members, both hetero- as well as homoerotically and was at the centre of artistic and political life in England. It was an inside–outside group that was very well connected to society while rejecting Victorian morality and frankly confronting sexuality in its webs of relationships, which often contained complex shifts, with friends becoming lovers without concern for gender. Keynes himself described himself as an "immoralist". G. E. Moore was deeply concerned with individual experiences as well as an aesthetic life.

The Hogarth Press had been set up in 1917 by Leonard Woolf and his wife Virginia Woolf, also members of Bloomsbury, and was importantly at the forefront of bringing Freud and psychoanalysis to the English-speaking world, with its many translations by the Stracheys. In 1952, it would begin the project to publish the *Standard Edition* of Freud in English, and under the editorship of James Strachey, in collaboration with Anna Freud, assisted by Alix Strachey and Alan Tyson, the complete works were published between 1953 and 1974. It was different from the *Gesammelte Werke* as it contained critical footnotes by the editors.

James and Alix Strachey

James Strachey and Alix Sargent-Florence, a member of the Bloomsbury Group, had met in 1919. On 31 May 1920, James wrote to Freud asking to begin analysis, and received his acceptance on 4 June, the day that he and Alix married. In October 1920, they both went to Vienna for James to start analysis, which continued until June 1922 for him.[6] Alix had not intended to be analysed herself but had an attack of palpitations at the *Staatsoper* [State Opera House], became alarmed and requested James to inform the Professor, who soon took her on full time (Meisel & Kendrick, 1986, p. 30). They were both invited to translate Freud's works into English, along with John Rickman. Alix's first assignment was "A child is being beaten".

Alix's analysis with Freud was interrupted by her having to be hospitalised with pleurisy in 1921. There, she was attended to by Felix Deutsch, Freud's personal physician. Despite that, James wrote to his brother Lytton on 22 June 1922 that they were both "passed as fit to practice by the Prof" (ibid., p. 30). By 1924, following Freud's advice, she had moved to Berlin to have analysis with Karl Abraham, until he became very ill in the autumn of 1925. Meanwhile Alix attended lectures there by Frank Alexander, Sandor Rado and Otto Fenichel (ibid., p. 36). She also met Hans Lamplight, Helene and Felix Deutsch, Lou Andreas-Salomé, Wilhelm Reich, and Ernst and Anna Freud (ibid., p. 36). It was in Berlin too that Alix's closest friend became Melanie Klein, who, following on from her first analysis in Budapest with Ferenczi, was now also in analysis with Abraham.[7] The analytic vision that Bloomsbury brought to British psychoanalysis broadened when Alix invited Melanie Klein to lecture in London in 1925 to the British Society, where she was warmly received. In 1926, following Karl Abraham's early death, meaning a disrupted analysis of only nine months, Klein moved permanently to London. Alix later translated Klein's *Psychoanalysis of Children*, published in 1932.

By 1929, James Strachey was a training analyst. He was, with Ella Freeman Sharpe, the most successful training analyst of the entire inter-war period, with three candidates successfully qualifying (Sharpe had five, Klein had one, Rivière two, Glover two, Jones one) (Forrester & Cameron, 2017).

Adrian and Karin Stephen

Meanwhile, in 1914, Adrian Stephen, the younger brother of Virginia Woolf and Vanessa Bell, had married Karin Costelloe, a philosopher at Newnham College, Cambridge. He was a conscientious objector during World War I and wrote a paper on pacifism. Conscription upset many in the Bloomsbury Group. Stephen's stance was in association with Bertrand Russell's high-profile views,[8] and he was familiar with Quakerism from his wife's family. That tradition expected quietness until someone was moved to speak; perhaps it was an early direction of quiet dignity with the other—and the later postulate of the psychoanalysis of free association could also find here a ready atmosphere for analysis to develop (John Rickman was also a Quaker and a pacifist). Adrian Stephen did not object to those wanting to go to war but preferred not to be part of it himself. Towards the end of the war, both Adrian and Karin trained medically prior to training as psychoanalysts, at the request of Ernest Jones, who was trying to persuade the British Medical Association to regard psychoanalysis as scientific.[9] They were elected to associate membership in 1927, which was the year Sándor Ferenczi lectured to the Society and was made an honorary member.

In the 1930s, the four Bloomsbury analysts, Adrian and Karin Stephen, and James and Alix Strachey, all had analytic private practices whilst also translating Freud and others into English and writing themselves. D. W. Winnicott began analysis with James Strachey in 1924. In the same year, James wrote what became a classic paper on technique, "The nature of the therapeutic action of psychoanalysis". For Adrian Stephen, the aim of psychoanalysis was to enable more freedom in the patient's mind. While freedom was a fundamental concept in analysis for Freud, Adrian Stephen further highlighted its centrality, resonating his Bloomsbury culture alongside psychoanalytic values, and it was to become a key component of Independent British analysis as the culture of the British Psychoanalytical Society from the early 1930s. Thus the goal of greater mental freedom, a liberal political position, transposed into a core idea of psychoanalysis in London.

In the Second World War, Adrian Stephen was so angered by Nazism and anti-Semitism that he abandoned his pacifist stance, and in 1939 volunteered to become an army psychoanalyst. He felt it important for reasons of transparency as well as fighting for a cause he saw as just. It was in his paper "On defining psychoanalysis" (1936) that Stephen argued for allowing more freedom of the analysand's own mind. He was active in promoting reforms of the BPAS, especially the idea of transparency of its rules as well as the long control that had been wielded by Jones as its president.[10] During the Controversial Discussions, he became the Society's secretary (1945–1947).

The Controversial Discussions 1942–1944

James Strachey characterised the battle between Melanie Klein and Anna Freud in the Controversies in his own wryly sensible way.

> My own view is that Mrs. K has made some highly important contributions … but that it's absurd to make out (a) that they cover the whole subject or (b) that their validity is axiomatic. On the other hand, I think it is equally ludicrous for Miss F. to maintain that (Psychoanalysis) is a Game Reserve belonging to the F. Family. (Appignanesi & Forrester, 1992, pp. 298–299)

The four Bloomsbury analysts were on neither side of the Controversial Discussions, and joined with Sylvia Payne, Ella Sharpe, Marjorie Brierley, William Gillespie, John Bowlby and Michael Balint in trying to find common ground for all the Society.

This did not mean that the BPAS meetings could only be about the theoretical differences between the two women. Karin Stephen wrote rather than spoke[11] at an extraordinary Business Meeting to discuss the state of affairs in the Society about the entrenchment of power leading to resentment and intimidation and non-cooperation: "We are now witnessing the second phase, open revolt and ill-will, which requires courage, independence and free exchange of ideas. Both are fatal to creative work" (Forrester & Cameron, 2017, p. 571). Here, she was arguing about the sense of resentment due to economic dependence on having referrals if they were deemed to be critical or "even by vigorous indecent thinking" (ibid., p. 572). She went on to examine the problem of training analyses:

> It is unsatisfactory in the extreme that so many members should be in the patient–analyst relation with one another over periods of years and years. Straightforward adult equality relations, such as should hold between fellow scientists, are hardly possible in these circumstances … (ibid., p. 572)

Karin Stephen also wrote that members of the Society should vote "in favour of altering our methods of election in such a way as to make it impossible in the future for any individual or group to capture power over the Society for more than a limited period" (ibid., p. 572). Ernest Jones, as president from 1913 of the first London Society and then the BPAS from 1919—a period, by then, of 30 years—was chairing the debate, meaning that Karin had considerable courage to openly speak truth to power. She ended by stating:

> It is not good for human beings to wield unchecked power: they become dictatorial and arrogant and there is too much temptation for them to favour supporters and penalise opponents or rivals. And it is humiliating for those who allow themselves to be ruled in this way: either they become subservient, or they become aggressive, or they become depressed and apathetic. (ibid., p. 573)

These statements from Karin Stephen demonstrate her capacity to pinpoint particular issues within groups, issues that were and are potentially available to be thought about in all analytic Societies and in particular the BPAS, from that point until today.

One could argue that, despite these critiques, Strachey, with his liberal views, stood somewhere in the middle, and that the BPAS did invite important foreign analysts to give their theories and debate metapsychology. Following this argument, much of the prevailing culture derived from the Bloomsbury openness to think and the freedom to express views, especially on the unconscious and sexuality, which were made available as core values within the analytic Society.

During the Controversies, Strachey, in relation to the powers of the Training Committee, thought that psychoanalysis

> keeps close to the facts in its field of study, seeks to solve the immediate problems of observation, gropes its way forward by the help of experience, is always incomplete, and always ready to correct or modify its theories.[12]

Strachey was arguing that technique was not so closely aligned with theory and that the Society's problems were insoluble because of theoretical differences, bound up in training due to unresolved webs of transference–countertransference around the groups. He fought for compromise in the Society in order to protect psychoanalysis from external political forces. Training candidates was not about teaching affiliation with one theory against another theory but

> For the Candidate, in proportion as he has been freed from his unconscious prejudices, will be able to accept those of the analyst's views which can be confirmed, to supplement those which prove incomplete, and to correct or reject those which seem false. (Adrien Stephen, quoted in Forrester & Cameron, ibid., p. 588)

Here we can value Strachey and Stephen's view that psychoanalysis is aimed at mental freedom, the same structure of their liberal political ideas, and the template both before and after the Controversies of the position of the Independent group, which took neither of the two sides.

Bloomsbury and the concept of freedom

John Forrester describes the Bloomsbury group as providing a ready-made atmosphere of a non-judgemental aesthetic that was also very curious about the unconsciousness of relationships, one's individual history and its impact on sexual life and in particular within an envelope of truth-seeking. It was this small group of friends, the Bloomsbury group, which particularly took psychoanalysis into itself, using it across different disciplines to examine unconscious process in an atmosphere of freedom to think—freedom to free-associate and to bring freedom to engage in life beyond the harsh realities and dictates of two World Wars. It has been remarked that the Bloomsbury group lived in squares and loved in triangles (ibid., p. 553). They were also able to examine ideas about control and freedom of citizens and individuals through the prism of psychoanalysis. This was unusual in many strands of family life and intellectual pursuits coming out of Victorian England—the control of children, discipline and corporal punishment, the homosexuality of the British boarding school experience, the lives of women and even suffrage in the UK.[13] Unusually, the Bloomsbury set was alive to the thinking together of the men *and* women within the group.

Tradition in the British Psychoanalytical Society accepted women to train in psychoanalysis probably more than elsewhere in Europe. It is hard to understand how that came about alongside the prevailing British attitudes about women and the bitter fight for suffrage. It certainly did not happen by the sort of ongoing incremental progress that is a common trope to defend against giving away male privileges. Married women and women over the age of thirty obtained the vote in 1918, and equal adult suffrage, the so-called "flapper franchise", came in 1928. But what was the history of these complexities? The franchise to vote prior to 1918 was property-based. Between 1884 and 1918 about a third of adult males as well as the entirety of females were excluded. However, suitably qualified women, which meant women who were ratepayers (predominantly women living independently, such as spinsters or widows, plus married women who owned property independent of husbands) could vote in municipal elections from 1869 and in county council elections from 1888, vote and stand as candidates in school board elections from 1870, and stand as candidates in county council elections from 1907.

It was also very difficult for women to go to university and have a professional life. It was not until 1876 that the UK Medical Act repealed the previous Medical Act in the United Kingdom and allowed the medical authorities to license all qualified applicants irrespective of gender. In 1877 an agreement was reached with the Royal Free Hospital that allowed students at the London School of Medicine for Women to complete their clinical studies there. The Royal Free Hospital was thus the first teaching hospital in London to admit women for training. The arrival of a teaching hospital for (initially) only women helped to enable the establishment of women doctors and in time for them to become specialists, yet the prejudice must have long continued.

It seems that there were fewer barriers to women pursuing a career in psychoanalysis. Maybe this was because of the analytic discussions around the Oedipus complex, which accepted primitive states of mind for both men and women; yet for a long time the prejudice persisted that the phallic was more "important", and that women were the lesser and might have penis envy. The respect to be found in Bloomsbury for intelligent women was also part of the picture. The early female analysts in the British Society, later joined by the powerful views of, first, Melanie

Klein, and then Anna Freud, secured a firm position for women who wanted to train in psychoanalysis in London.

The point to be made is the value of freedom for men and women, freedom for citizens, freedom to think and write about the unconscious mind, not only for psychoanalysts but for others, then bringing together analytic texts in Europe and beyond, translating the papers and publishing them in English, as well as the great project of the *Standard Edition* for the English-speaking world. These were all acts of freedom beyond one country or language. Keynes wrote decades later:

> We repudiated entirely morals, conventional wisdom. We were, that is to say, in the strictest sense of the word, immoralists. The consequences of being found out had, of course, to be considered for what they were worth. But we recognised no moral obligation on us, no inner sanction, to conform or obey. Before heaven we claimed to be our own judge in our own case … It resulted in a general, widespread, though partly covert, suspicion affecting ourselves, our motives and our behaviour. This suspicion still persists to a certain extent, and it always will. It has deeply coloured the course of our lives in relate to the outside world. It is a justifiable suspicion. Yet so far as I am concerned, it is too late to change. I remain, and always will remain, an immoralist. (Keynes, 1938, pp. 447–448)

Now put that description alongside that of psychoanalysis to speak one's mind to the analyst by putting aside one's distinction between good and bad values and behaviour and to put aside the listeners' (both analysand's and analyst's) prejudices. Morality was put aside and replaced by the hegemony of the personal and the aesthetic of what is human experience. The requirement of absolute honesty and a boundary-less confrontation with human passion and sexuality. Analytic listening without prejudice was the atmosphere of psychoanalysis in its early formation in the BPAS. This was before the eruption of the Controversial Discussions, which demanded the setting up of theoretical walls for the Kleinian and Anna Freudian trainings within the Society, and that atmosphere continued towards the Independent group, which was seemingly transposed to being in the *middle* of the warring pair.

Adrian Stephen's trenchant position that psychoanalysis was to allow more freedom in the patient's mind kept the concept of freedom as the key value of the Independent group in the British Psychoanalytical Society.

The name of the group

How might we understand some naming the group as "Middle"? Change came about with the need to find a new political balance in the wake of the Controversial Discusssions, which was first described by Glover as the so-called Middle group (King & Steiner, 1991, p. 681), or as the non-aligned or Independent British analysts. The new model, the Gentleman's Agreement[14] was of a Kleinian and Anna Freudian wing of analytic training—either side, as it were, of the original independent matrix of the society, which was indeed perceived as being in the "middle". Those not inside the two new training formations had the freedom to sift competing theories that worked for them and their patients without the burden of allegiance. The central political issue was who had control over training: training analysis, supervision and curriculum—and is still the central political issue today.

It is still a strange conundrum that the British Psychoanalytical Society had a determination to learn about all kinds of developing theories within Europe, then later in the United States and after that, South America. It welcomed colleagues to teach and to stay and develop theory and practice. The core of such an atmosphere was certainly taken from Bloomsbury and followed a somewhat incandescent idea of having the freedom to develop oneself; not just one's internal object relational system but the open atmosphere of the early Society. John Rickman was curious enough to go to Vienna for analysis with Freud, then later to Budapest to have analysis with Ferenczi, and further took the opportunity to have analysis with Melanie Klein when she practised in London. Such attitudes were about being independently minded. The group invited into its midst Melanie Klein and later Anna Freud, who warred within the Society. But to push the original analysts of the Society into a position of being in the middle, between Klein and Anna Freud, was a political act.

Many years later, when some colleagues who had trained in the Independent group had a desire, for personal reasons, to have a second and

Kleinian analysis, it was not uncommon for that theory to be imbibed too. This could lead to a theoretical dissonance unless one changed one's group. In the late 1990s this led to a schism in the Independent Training group, as those colleagues who were theoretically now functioning with a Kleinian theoretical approach were still members. Yet it was not at all clear if their candidates who wanted an Independent analysis knew this. When challenged, one training analyst spoke to ask where else could one have a home, as admission to the Klein group was barred, membership being only through one's primary training analysis. Here we meet another political act that caused much difficulty to Independent training.

And what of more modern times? Michael Parsons wrote in 2014:

> [The concept of] the Independent tradition does not coincide with the Independent Group. There is a large overlap, in that the majority of analysts who have exemplified and developed the tradition have been part of the Group. However, there are members of the Independent Group that do not stand within the Independent tradition. Conversely, the Independent tradition is not limited to the Group, or even the British Society. (Parsons, 2014, p. 187)

The old core of the British Society was and is the Independent group continuing the atmosphere of enquiry and respect for differing theoretical views as well as respect for its own history and its core value of freedom of mind.

* * *

A book on the Independent tradition, *Independent Women in British Psychoanalysis: Creativity and Authenticity at Work* has recently been published,[15] to which I contributed a version of this chapter, and I will add some thoughts on some of those early colleagues, who although not Bloomsbury, were, as I wrote at the beginning, equally committed to Independent values.

Ella Sharpe advised beginning where Freud started, not where he left off (Robinson, in Wolf & Antonis, 2023). This is particularly good advice on how to learn Independent theory and technique; it was similarly made clear by Enid Balint that Ferenczi could only see a bit further by standing on Freud's shoulders (personal reminiscence). Sharpe left her mark on writing about listening closely to words also as metaphor.

Marjorie Brierley wrote an Armistice Letter that led to the setting up of the Controversial Discussions that demarcated the political terrain of the British Psychoanalytical Society (Abram, in Wolf & Antonis, 2023). She, like her friend Ella Sharpe, made use of different techniques and theories for each patient, related to their particular pathology. Brierley tried to foster an openness of dialogue in the Society that has remained a hallmark of the Independent tradition.

Paula Heimann began her "change in philosophy" in 1955 from being Melanie Klein's "crown princess" to being asked to resign the Melanie Klein Trust whilst simultaneously saying that she wished to be free of its control (Alster, in Wolf & Antonis, 2023). This was a pivotal political and cataclysmic event in the BPAS. Heimann had had analysis with Theodor Reik in 1929 until she had to leave Berlin in 1933. Klein[16] had already arrived in London in 1925 when Ernest Jones invited her to give a series of papers on her work, and settled permanently there in 1926. Heimann went to London in 1933 and by 1934 was Klein's secretary—the two had already met in Berlin. A little later, Klein invited her to be her analysand—a very unusual occurrence indeed. In 1983, Heimann told William Gillespie that she had been seduced into treatment (Grosskurth, 1985, p. 385). There is evidence that Heimann did not feel free to develop her own theoretical ideas whilst in analysis (ibid., p. 384).

Heimann's view on the death instinct became a central tenet of Independent theory, as she argued for the importance and analysis of hate and neglect in early object relationships, not just instincts, as responsible for early emotional problems, adding her rigour and penetrating insight to the analysis of early trauma. I can add an addendum to her late paper "On the necessity for the analyst to be natural with his patient", as the supervisee was myself. The young patient had arrived sodden wet while bicycling through an icy storm prior to starting his analytic session. Heimann quickly commented in relation to my seemingly not caring for his physical state and asked what I would say if I did not have the whole weight of the analytic Society on my shoulders. I instantly knew the answer and replied that I would have asked him to go to the bathroom, find a towel and dry himself off. I knew the natural answer was about a human care that he neither had much of growing up or could give to himself now. Heimann kindly pointed out my initial failure to put aside the finding an interpretation, as if that was all to consider and taught me the great lesson of being natural with the patient as well as not enacting a rough countertransference. It is in line with Freud starting a session note of the Ratman "He was hungry and was fed" (1909d, p. 303). Heimann knew the profound importance of the analyst being her- or himself in conjunction with being analytic rather than mimicking a theory or the training analyst.

Pearl King started her clinical advice to Ken Robinson to "not act differently but that I be different" (Robinson, in Wolf & Antonis, 2023). This directs attention for the necessity for the analyst to be free to locate him/herself "alongside the patient, both inside and outside the patient's world". She, like Enid Balint,[17] had been analysed by Rickman. Robinson makes clear that Pearl King was the heir of both Brierley and Sylvia Payne's leadership of the group in and beyond the Controversial Discussions, and also heir to Heimann and Sharpe theoretically. Together with Riccardo Steiner, she wrote the famous and formidable volume on the Controversial Discussions (King & Steiner, 1991), ensuring that her love for and concern about history became a central component and archive for that enormous and hugely important upheaval in the BPAS.

The artist Marion Milner, according to Maia Kirchkheli (Kirchkeli, in Wolf & Antonis, 2023) functioned as a "pliable medium" for her patients. Milner's concepts of illusion, symbols and the creative process itself were very important to developing independent theory and in particular the importance of the "gap" (as in "mind the gap"). And the idea of the surrender to painting, to playing, to free-associating, to nothingness as a state of mind in an analysis were further elements of her range of theoretical ideas. Milner was deeply thoughtful about the "rhythm of psychic growth" and her reflections were far more located on the internal state of an internal culture rather than contending with the politics of a tripartite analytic society, as Milner's quest for authenticity in finding a creative lived life was far from wrapping analysis in theory.

Nina Coltart attended to the patient with a capacity to "continuously observe, watch, listen and feel in silence." She, like her supervisor Bion, had a special aptitude for silence. Negative capability is brought power-fully to light from the dark in her famous paper "Slouching towards Bethlehem … Or thinking the unthinkable in psychoanalysis," as fear, dread and an awful feeling of ignorance are familiar companions on the analytic journey. She described the issue of daring to go along to the unconscious edge and being there alongside the analysand and wait-ing, rather than interrupting in order to make the analyst feel more comfortable by issuing an interpretation (and often enacting a previous unconscious early history). She too prized authenticity and was con-sulted by a large number of people wanting her advice on who to be referred to for analytic treatment. Paula Somaini has grasped the total picture of Coltart's life including her death with a similar Coltartian attitude (Somaini in Wolf & Antoni, 2023).

Enid Balint, another of this extraordinary group of female analysts was quietly observing, taking in, silently thoughtful and "being in the experience" of analytic work (Wolf & Antonis, 2023).

Enid was thought to be an appropriate other when the analytic society tried to construct clinical seminars with training analysts from different groups and was paired with Hanna Segal. For several months there was a quiet tussle of ideas between the two in their dif-ferent clinical evaluation of the clinical material. Near the end of each seminar Segal would sum up by saying "and this is how we understand the material." Enid Balint would find time before the end to say that there was also much that was as yet unknown. It was a profound differ-ence of analytic attitude: one of knowing where the analyst and patient were at the session's end, showing how analysis was working; the other, of the quiet solitude of hanging on to that which was unknown, and being in the experience of it as analytic work. The issue of knowing and not-knowing was enacted between the supervisors. Being of a quiet, albeit resolute character, Enid declined to continue another term of clinical seminars, and that particular experiment in ecumenical teach-ing quickly, quietly, ended.

It is probably clear that she was my analyst, and I will tell a further story that was part of the analysis. Near its end, Enid once remarked that she expected that I would be curious about what lay beneath the couch. This was perplexing, as I had never had such a thought. I was invited to explore, and saw an old leather suitcase, which when opened revealed the original letters that Freud had written to Ferenczi. Ferenczi had given them to Michael Balint, hoping he would publish them, together with those written by Ferenczi and held by Anna Freud. Long after the end of my analysis, their correspondence was published in three volumes (Brabant, Falzeder & Giampieri-Deutsch, 1993). This was her way of passing on legacy for me to take up or not, a very important history on the developing understanding of early childhood trauma and authenticity in analysis, and many other matters that Freud and Ferenczi had discussed, argued, agreed, and on Ferenczi's "Confusion of tongues" paper (1955) disagreed with each other in ways that I believe have shaped the contemporary dialogue in psychoanalysis ever since.

Enid Balint was deeply influenced by Winnicott, and being married to Michael, intimately knew the work of Ferenczi and the mutual respect between him and Freud. After Michael's death she carried forward the project of managing the publication of the Freud–Ferenczi letters as well as Ferenczi's *Diary*—both of these important subjects for the renewal of interest in Ferenczi, long buried by his analysand Jones. The trajectory from Rickman being analysed by Freud, Ferenczi and Klein and imbibed by Enid in her first analysis, together with her second with Winnicott, and the impact of Michael Balint's knowledge and culture of Hungarian analysis through Ferenczi, is a formidable backdrop to the Independent tradition. And Enid, standing on their shoulders, found her own analytic mind and her contributions to femininity, mutuality and early unconscious object relationships.

Finally, I want to note that by far the major work in this volume is by the current female contributors of the Independent tradition, the Third Wave of Independent Female Analysts.

I am grateful to John Forrester's work with Laura Cameron: *Freud in Cambridge*; also for Ken Robinson's skill as a historian of British psychoanalysis. I am also grateful for cogent comments from Phillip Waller, Fellow and Tutor in Modern History, Merton College, Oxford.

CHAPTER 11

Apocalyptic times and the missing debate*

> *The evil of modernity begins with the disappearance of the community of listeners.*
>
> Walter Benjamin (1970)

If one speaks with anybody it is likely that they too will be worried about the present state of the world. Many things are the matter and are frightening all of us. The problems are enormous, from global warming, Covid and its vicissitudes, and also the lurch to the right towards fascism and totalitarianism. How can people speak and listen to each other in times of a culture of deeply embedded lying and attacks on truth— and whose truths? I will try and examine how and what psychoanalysis might contribute to our polarised world of "us and them".

Introduction

The tradition of apocalyptic prophecy was developed in the Middle Ages, first by Jews and later Christians to "console, fortify and assert

---

* This paper was presented at the European Psychoanalytic Federation's 2023 annual conference "Illusions", and is published in EPF *Bulletin* 77, 2023.

themselves when confronted by threat" (Cohn, 1972). Messianism and debates about the Antichrist were further developed during the Crusades. Later the division into a good–bad dichotomy was enacted by the thousands of penitents masochistically scourging themselves across Europe in response to the plague as well as their mirror image of the Torquemadian sadistic persecutions of certain citizens. All the major European powers used such cruel display, as it was socially, politically and economically expedient to those in power. Unconscious manifestations of human cruelties find expressions in societies, and presently cruelties have engulfed the world again, particularly in the current politically (Dis)United States and the recurrence of protest by Black Lives Matter, reiterating the historical unconscious traumata of unmourned racism.

The claim to be Christian can be a surface cover of what is a ruthless and cruel "us and them" system containing a desire to establish a politically totalitarian control. Believers engage in a narrow set of apparent religious terms. *Join us, we want your soul, we want you to be born again; if you are unwilling to be like us, we have nothing to say to you, you are on the side of the Devil.* Armageddon is the place where the final battle between good and evil will be fought. Christians will be saved through Christ's resurrection, and they journey straight to the Garden of Eden; others go to Hell.

There is no sense of concern for the other. There is instead a viciousness, and all badness is projected into the other(s). Historical examples abound, with many connecting to the 1930s, when Nazism was intent on turning Jews and other groups into the *Untermenschen*. For this to be successful, the Nazis needed to get most of the people—the *Volk*—to be against Jews. Some Christian fundamentalists regard this punishment by God for the Jews' killing of Christ. The Holocaust also ushered in the gathering of the Jews to the Promised Land, which is seen to be the creation of Israel in 1948, but also the harbinger of the prophecies of Armageddon.

In those years, psychoanalytic ideas, analytic Societies and analysts were attacked; many killed or displaced, leaving the analytic world reeling from the 1930s and beyond the end of the Third Reich in 1945. Perhaps not enough work was done by the analytic community to come together and deeply examine the traumatic landscape of what was left of our analytic environment. Perhaps the idea of the return of the massive individual, group, societal, country and world traumata are too unthinkable even for psychoanalysis, such that overall, despite many islands of creative thought about the happening of the Holocaust, we as a profession fear the return of the repressed.

How can the community of psychoanalysts engage when we too are frightened? Psychoanalysis has knowledge of hate and perversity that can be applied to help pre-empt violence through examining states of truth and false narrative that includes understandings of the unconscious in individuals, families, groups and societies, which can, at times, nurture deep and vicious hatred of the other. I will examine people's fears today, which predispose towards fundamentalist patterns of thinking, using conflicts in America as the exemplar.

For many Christians the imagined is more important and even more real than the lived life now. How can we tell what is real or what is knowledge or even know anything for certain? What can society do with a severe clash of values, words and meanings? Individual freedom within a set of liberal rules is opposed by a more secretive system within particular religious sets of beliefs of an apocalyptic nature. One group accepts experts in the community on all manner of investigations, whilst the other eschews "expertise" and replaces these with particular biblical texts, particularly the *Book of Revelations*; by just quoting a biblical sentence, views are justified as "His expertise" as written in ancient texts. Substantial views about the truth of life are spoken not only by church leaders but many millions of their followers with a righteous dogma that theirs is a particular and absolutely accurate and correct understanding of truth with no place for doubt. Yet today the clash of cultures between the liberal desire for a society with rules and governed by free elections is being savagely contested by a differing series of theological "truths" that is causing violence and severe schism within the politics and leadership in the United States and other countries.

Important questions as to how society and politics engage citizens are not being discussed due to mutual contempt without debate—us and them. Discussion fails. Fake news is restated millions of times within the internet and on TV, as if mass of reiteration makes meaning clear. It does not. It is a form of bullying tactics and a dissent towards experts and expertise, rather than God-given words. These words are worshipped by the apocalyptic followers as the true measure of what is necessary in order to achieve certain "religious" goals. The believers regard everyone else on Earth as apostates and wicked. The far-right conspiracy group QAnon alleges a secret cabal of Satan worshippers: cannibalistic paedophiles running a global child sex trafficking ring that plotted against the former President Trump. Strangely, such a bizarre phantasy is believed by millions of Americans, as a delusional conspiracy takes over the mind of people as Covid can do to our bodies. The cult predicts "The Storm" and "The Great Awakening": concepts of religious millenarianism and apocalypticism. Trump, the flawed Christian, forgiven his sins, is seen as a messianic messenger from God. The 2020 US elections had to be understood as stolen and fake as a prelude to ushering in the coming of the Messiah. Such "religious" wrapping paper is the cover that white supremacists are using to develop totalitarian governance.

One can understand such violent, eruptive, millennial phantasies as being a massive defence against individuals' huge anxieties about living in today's increasingly complex world and feeling lost, poor, vulnerable, alone and near to being wiped out; and hoping for a powerful force that will nurture, control, regulate and punish. Messianic phantasies provide a security, once one has accepted the entry ticket of being born again, now into the care of "new parents". The prediction of the future apocalypse can be well understood as a projection into the future of a catastrophe in babyhood/childhood/adolescence *that has already happened*. This is a common fate for children brought up in poverty, as the gap between rich and poor drastically widens.

The idea of the Church and its leaders functioning to look after the children in the flock is age-old. The idea of rebirth allows an individual to lose their particular suffering and instead be part of an idealised large group. Any violence suffered in the original family is instantly projected into the rest of the non-believers. It is they who will go to hell. Some sense can be made of QAnon being so determined with the subject of paedophilia and labelling Democrats and socialists as the vicious attackers towards children as coming from their own projections (i.e., their own intergenerational trauma).

Many people taken with the possibilities of being born again can unconsciously perceive that their personal sense of humiliation, and the burden of an impoverished early childhood and adolescence, provide them with a vulnerability to being promised the garden of Eden.[1] This is well known as cumulative trauma and identification with the aggressor, which fuels transgenerational traumas. Such adults feel safe in their born-again container inside the right-wing politic whilst allowing the pain of the past to automatically project onto a violent scenario, while the rest of the population is now consigned to hell. Bollas has described such a mental structure as "Violent innocence" (Bollas, 1992, p. 165). The reborn disciple is as innocent as a newly born baby, turning a blind eye to support projections of violence wherever the political leaders direct it.

Not a single Republican in either House voted for President Biden's huge pandemic relief stimulus package in March 2021, even though it established a guaranteed income for families with children and has the makings of a policy revolution to care for the nation's impoverished. Well, of course—because if the millions of impoverished families are really beginning to be cared for financially by the State, it may lead to a withering of support for the Republican Party.

Bion and catastrophic change

On 4 May 1966, Wilfred Bion presented to a Scientific Meeting of the British Psychoanalytical Society his paper "Catastrophic change" (1966). He was bringing attention to a pattern he had been observing in psychoanalysis and outside it in the form of container–contained, as something contains something, each impacted into the other. As Chris Mawson explains in his introduction to Bion's *Collected Works* (2014), this "relates to two forms of the relationship between the pattern of existing knowledge and the impact of new perceptions or ideas" (Bion, 2014, vol 6, p. 24). Here, Bion cites the necessity to notice Keats' Negative Capability, "when a man is capable of being in uncertainties, mysteries, doubts, without any irritable reaching after fact or reason" (Keats, letter to George and Thomas Keats, 21 December 1817). Bion points to the analyst's toleration of feelings in letting go momentarily of facts and reasons in existing theories.

In an Independent psychoanalytic context, it would privilege the analyst's free-associative state of mind, receptive to new experience but not necessarily spoken. In such a state, new meanings can dare become accessible to becoming represented. Bollas' "unthought known" is an example that refers to preverbal, un-schematised early experience, including trauma that may determine one's behaviour unconsciously, barred to conscious thought. Such activities in an analysis and elsewhere are highlighted by a sense of disorientation which may include something as absent, despite it having disruptive potentials. This is the territory of Bion's concept of container–contained.

Bion goes on to describe the appearance of mystics or men of genius in many different fields: Christ, Genghis Khan, Einstein. "Some attract notice as outstanding personalities, but some must be supposed to attract no attention because conditions for their existence is not propitious. A similar fate attends on ideas" (ibid., p. 31). Mystics are not so uncommon over the centuries, and are known in all religions and contain ideas that may be called messianic. Bion thought that one function of society was to make such ideas available to members of groups, either by laws in society or dogma in religion or laws or rules in mathematics and science. People have a problem that moves towards the catastrophic if these different applications of potentially genius perceptions become muddled up in the three different categories (laws in society, rules and laws in science, and religious dogma). This is especially so if dogma leaps from religious mysticism into the other categories.

This is the territory of attacks on science and expertise and knowledge. In apocalyptic millennialism, an extreme mystic view in a sect is pushed into other categories and structures of human existence. Global warming may be seen, felt and only believed as an expected and anticipated sign that the end of the world is nigh. The scientific view is that we need to urgently change our uses of coal, oil and meat-eating, which pours carbon dioxide into the atmosphere of our container as the delicate biomass of the Earth is in danger of severe and imminent irreversible climate change. The rules governing society are now seen to be in conflict and the incremental moves towards a scientific new beginning within the liberal imagination brushes against the seeking of a millennial cruelty to tip the globe into the particular mystic violence—which some 100 million Americans believe in. And an electoral war broke out between the millions of citizens, such that with seven million more votes, Biden won the presidency by 306 to 232 Electoral Votes. Instantly, and as predicted by Trump for months, this authenticated election become a conspiratorial "steal" believed by half the electorate, now contaminated inside a messianic phantasy. The insurrection against Congress became the sharp violent edge of a catastrophic uprising.

"The reaction of the Establishment is to prevent the disruption" (Bion, ibid., p. 33). This time it failed. Bion goes on to write: "The problems of the Christian Establishment developed even in the times of Jesus. The first were: 'delineation of the borders of the group, selection and training and stabilisation of the hierarchy'" (ibid., p. 35). Who are the sects' followers—are they religious converts, or do they sail under a Christian ideological cover, but with their own extreme right-wing white totalitarianism (Proud Boys, etc.) masquerading as supporting and being the shock troops to bring about a catastrophic age of a new Republican messianism? Does the Christian Right really believe that such extremist bully boys have God in their heart? Or do they make use of extremists just as they see Trump as having a leadership role, for now, in accessing more power for the millennial church. Trump has fully supported misogynistic and racist views of society.[2]

Depending on whether the mystic is nihilistic to the community or being disruptive or creative and appearing to eschew violence, Bion saw the work of the Establishment as preventing disruption. Yet who would be qualified to speak and to lead? This becomes a near intractable issue if "the mystic work is available to ordinary members who do not have the mystic's qualifications for atonement to the deity" (ibid., p. 34). However, the problem of such containment is particularly difficult if there are 100 million followers with a very large number speaking on behalf of the deity, mainly with a false expertise, just because they have "God in their heart." Devout followers may even want to join civil unrest for their own particular reasons and grievances. Of the Klu Klux Klan, neo-Nazi groups, Proud Boys, White Aryan Resistance, Atomwaffen Division, etc., many of whom have fought in the US military, it seems reasonable to think that they do not speak from God but are part of millennial Christianity, now awake and disruptive in society.

For Bion, thoughts can be independent of the thinker, such as ideas floating in the zeitgeist. Thoughts can become propaganda when followers sloganise them. The recent explosion of "fakeness" proliferates falsity until it becomes a known and ignored lie. "The barrier of the lie increases the need for the truth and vice versa" (ibid., p. 39). So messianic ideas can cover political, insurrectional, racist ideas and destroy the rules of democracy. It should be possible to intuit the messianic ideas of the container from the myriad of forms contained, which together become dynamically toxic and extremely dangerous.

Yet, although we are confronted with these dangers at present, such historical moments of impending and impactful catastrophic change are part of human history: the advent of the first millennium, the Crusades, the Black Death, Pizzaro conquering Peru,[3] 400 years of slavery, Hitler and the Holocaust, the Atomic Bomb, the influenza pandemic of 1918–1919, the second millennium and, of course, global warming—such long events might be seen as some of many harbingers of catastrophic change.

What can psychoanalysis do when faced with times of catastrophic change in the world? Freud wrote in 1924:

> I perceived ever more clearly that the events of human history, the interactions between human nature, cultural development and the precipitates of primaeval experiences (the most prominent of which is religion) are no more than a reflection of the dynamic conflicts ... which psychoanalysis studies in the individual—are the very same processes repeated upon a wider stage. (Freud, 1925d [1924], p. 72)

This differentiates psychoanalytic thinking of social and political phenomena from the clinical process in a psychoanalysis. Writing presumptuously, as if a leader can be "analysed", the press brings us to false diagnostic assumption. It is necessary to underline that expertise can be real, and that truth has to stand up against being faked. If the expert can be debunked just by a false statement being re-tweeted thousands of times, then that needs to be resisted and addressed despite its difficulties. Often this requires bravery. In the light of two opposing and contemptuous groups knowing that each is unheard and unrecognised by the other, the analytic position is to be in the position of listening as the third. It is only in that space that the profound anxieties of expecting to be wiped out can be addressed. The paradox is that the oppositional groups, not hearing the other, each suffer mirror-like anxieties. Instead of being revolted by the other's stance, recognition and understanding is required of the underlying history and impoverishment of their situation.

Dialogues

As part of a MacArthur grant that Charles Strozier and Robert Jay Lifton received in 1988 to study how ordinary Americans imagined nuclear threat, they sought to learn how Christian fundamentalists' apocalyptic orientation connected with nuclear threat. Strozier attended five different NYC sites to do in-depth interviews: a mainstream Baptist church, a Pentecostal church, a large African American church in Harlem, an Upper East Side Bible study group, and Riker's Island. Each religious setting welcomed him because he was a prospective convert. He was immediately taken into the fold and taught about the Bible as it supported apocalyptic thinking. After nine months, his failure to convert despite his impressive store of religious knowledge was recognised and no more interviews were given. He proved to not "have Jesus in his heart". A standout aspect of the research was that it changed *him* but none of the interviewees. He became more attuned to the "complexity of human experience" (Strozier, 1994, private correspondence, 2021).

When it comes to the feeling of love, we human beings can often get such love states quite wrong. Yet if we take it as a true feeling, it does have a powerful meaning within the particular religious group, and it is a statement that one believes, thus becoming a group member. That meaning further expands to: "I am loved by God" by being born again and so can you. Moreover, if you decline, you are headed for hell and damnation. If one ignores an offer that seemingly comes from a felt divine presence then the members of the group who feel it will have nothing more to do with you. Perhaps there is a certain arrogance in their apparent knowledge, as they instantly leave the lost soul alone to continue to wander. The gaze on one is withdrawn, as one has no value in boosting the number of souls they are desiring to save. Identify with us or nothing.

This cannot be about dialogue. It is not like discussion with friends or colleagues, which expects disagreements, and then the links and friendships continue. In this apocalyptic dialogue, unless one joins, one is wiped out as an enactment of the fallen status in the eye of the believer. The sudden withdrawal brings to the surface the falsity of the friendliness, revealing a selfishness, as getting too close to the non-believer might now taint their special status and expected privileges in the life hereafter. To my mind, this is a small enactment of a totalitarian position, which either embraces the newly born-again recruit as a fellow member, or one becomes nothing. Human kindness is not then available because of a triumph of cruelty over the other. Such a scenario applies to all Republican believers, except Liz Cheney, who was recently voted out of Congress, wiping out freedom of expression, of thought and the freedom to debate with a venom that is still hard to believe. Such negative control systems are not, of course confined to the right.[4]

The present clash seems inevitable without common space to enquire into these profoundly different ways of expressing ways to live, as well as imaginings of death. If one is a millennialist then all men and women do not have certain inalienable rights. Not being a believer means that it is fine and even appropriate to remove voting rights in order to facilitate the apocalyptic Trumpian prophet—such that the Capitol was the site (sight) of a vicious insurrection. The millennium vision demands that believers expect and pray for a huge war, as such conflict will deliver a messianic new beginning. Such an omnipotent religious phantasy might be seen in contrast with Michael Balint's view of a creative new beginning.

In apocalyptic thinking, there seems to be a thread of grievance that draws the individual to the idea of being reborn. The thinking appears to be forward-moving in that the rebirth and the blessing of the new belief will make certain that one will live a life without grievance in heaven. One of the problems with grievance is that the issues are so difficult and awful that the grievance structure demands a sense of entitlement. So huge numbers of folk expecting at last to be cared for, look to the leader to make some sort of American dream come alive for them. Yet when it does not happen, they are invited to blame Democrats, or the anti-Christ, rather than the Church and Trump, who had been leading them on. Eventually the required changes may become so huge that it may only be assuaged by the power of God. The need for a dialogue with the other, who may listen carefully and helpfully, is of no consequence because the other is already known to be of no help. Joining a group of grievance-driven fellows and together signing up with a dictator, as we see in Trumpism, or Bolsonaro-ism, means the individual supporter melts into the group. The other is not needed to discuss and dialogue any individual issues. Yet there is a clue within the desire to be reborn.

As Winnicott described, the idea of future trauma is because past trauma has not been held, understood and mourned. The issue is one of cumulative trauma, and I will include also generational racism and anti-Semitism, which keeps huge groups of people "unable to breathe" while falsely entitling white supremacists, fascists and Nazis. As the past cannot be changed, the direction is unconsciously spun into future times. However, this sleight of time does not confront the real traumatised early life—being unwanted, perhaps coming to life from a failed abortion, not being loved, left alone, starved, beaten, incestuously molested. And all the time an expectation that someone would notice, see, hear and do something about the child's plight can be carried as a severe chip on their shoulder. That provides the probability for the development of other coping strategies, such as identification with the aggressor, becoming cruel oneself and finding victims to project one's own earlier victimhood onto. And the pull to being reborn allows belief that God has now taken special interest, while leaving aside the painful question of why the child had not been heard during childhood and adolescence. It only works if a new victim is found who will go to hell instead.

Town Hall meetings

I want to describe the value of so-called Town Hall meetings for citizens to discuss what is on their mind and of concern to them. After the publication of my 2019 book *Dark Times: Psychoanalytic Perspectives on Politics, History and Psychoanalysis*, I was invited by psychology and psychotherapy groups as well as bookshops around the UK and beyond to come and discuss my writings. Of course, this was a way of eliciting book sales. The meetings had common elements. The attendees, in groups of twenty to forty, were concerned about not understanding what was going on in present politics, about Brexit, global warming and deteriorations in society. The expected expert was going to explain it all so that the audience would "know".

Instead, after a brief description of the content of *Dark Times*, alongside my concerns that had led to its writing, I turned the meeting into discussion. I wanted to hear their concerns and I would listen, as long as it was understood that I was not going to answer questions. In addition, I hoped that everyone would dare to join in and speak together. I was determined to change the unconscious teacher–pupil hierarchy in order to think horizontally together. A group experience formed of discussing and thinking together. This activity allowed a sense of aliveness to emerge as individuals found their silent thoughts and dared to share them. Nobody was damaged, it seems, from being part of a thinking group, and whilst the very difficult conflicts in life were, unsurprisingly, not solved, an energy was sustained in the group to carry on thinking rather than waiting passively for an expert to explain it. If attendees could talk together, then such group discussion could grow, and citizens might begin to dare to think and speak and come to feel more alive in the moment instead of being full of despair in the absence of a capacity to think.

In 2018, I had been very impressed with Michael Moore daring to hold Town Hall meetings in some rust-belt towns in the United States. He was able to dialogue with committed angry Trumpian supporters who detested Hillary Clinton. Managing to create a space for discussion rather than polemical point scoring and destructive and nasty comments allowed for a growth in self-thinking away from the propaganda usually fed to eager subjects. Later, I was struck that Hannah Arendt, too, thought very highly of this form of political engagement. Elisabeth Young-Bruehl wrote in her splendid biography of Arendt, of

> her *amor mundi*, that underlaid her enthusiasm for "the council system", the political form she considered an antidote to totalitarianism. She judged the council system the best form for genuine political life, allowing action and reasoning speech. (Young-Bruehl, 1982, p. xxiv)

As well as studying such meetings, Arendt examined ward and voluntary associations, popular societies in the 1871 Paris Commune, the Russian extra-party workers' councils or *soviets* appearing in 1905 and 1917, and the councils that emerged in the Hungarian revolution of 1956. As Arendt wrote, "spontaneous organs of the people, not only outside of all revolutionary parties but entirely unexpected by them and by their leaders" (Young-Bruehl, 1982, p. xxv). Her biographer in a preface wrote:

> Arendt began to think that the gravest danger in American political life was a kind of thoughtlessness or not-thinking,

specifically a lack of historical memory about America's revolutionary origins and constitutional tradition, which protected its council formations. (Young-Bruehl, 1982, p. xxv)

Arendt was concerned about America's fear of further revolutions and wrote:

> Fear of Revolution has been the hidden leitmotif of post-war American foreign policy in its disparate attempts at stabilising the status quo, with the results that American power and prestige were used and misused to support obsolete and corrupt political regimes that long since had become objects of hatred and contempt among their own citizens. (Arendt, quoted in Young-Bruehl, 1982, p. xxv)

The deep fear of another revolution wiping out their own seemed to contain an unconscious phantasy of, say, a return of the French revolutionary practice of guillotining those in power that was then projected to American power, pre-empting unconscious fear by chopping off foreign heads instead.

Speaking up

In 1931, the League of Nations set up exchanges of letters between representative intellectuals "on subjects calculated to serve common interests of the League of Nations and intellectual life"; this led Einstein to invite a conversation with Freud (published as "Why war?", 1933b). Whilst Freud was trenchant that mankind was aggressive, he failed to address possibilities of dialogues between the dissonant parties prior to war. The thought of questioning particular belief systems is perceived as an attack on inalienable basic assumptions. Being unable to question destructive racist premises in the Constitution and for those left out of the phantasmic miracle of the afterlife is a reason indeed for sentient debate. Such phantasy is cruel to the millions of US citizens who are not fundamentalist believers, let alone the rest of the world. We are left alone in such an enquiry, as the true believers decide we are not like them and refuse to engage, unless they imagine that converts can be made out of such scriptural conversations.

Who then is to have such debates? We have witnessed the near impossibility of this being achieved in a political frame in the United States, as the Trumpian far right has captured any middle ground for discussion. The lie of a false election is believed by the majority of Republican members of both Houses of Congress. This leaves all types of religious leaders rather silent, such that the control of the Second Coming is left in the hands of a very narrow range of theology. What would happen if religious leaders came together to express a solidity and solidarity on the present, very dangerous, millenary views of most of mankind that include many in their own flocks? Religious leaders together in a commission could show that the many theological views differ from a too-simplistic politic, resting on God residing or not residing in the heart, which is being used as propaganda to deliver the United States and other countries into the hands of dictators. Yet, as in the 1931 initiative, the intellectual debate does not impinge on an aggressive rush to destructiveness and war.

Psychoanalysts have skills to evaluate the complex thinking between truth, lies, phantasy and reality as perceived in religious expression, freedom of thought, and the demands of a cruel sadomasochist totalitarian governance that is entwined underneath the surface with rhetorics of cruelty that diminish groups to being *Untermenschen* as their basic human rights are wiped out. After all, our analytic profession has deeply trawled the unconscious spaces of sadomasochism in human relationships and can use its experience beyond the couch as an evaluative tool to understand unconscious meanings and metaphor in society. We can examine who speaks on behalf of whom in the unconscious object-relational system. In Bion's terms: to delineate the leader's views from the parroting disciples, as dysfunctional splits in the unconscious mental apparatus.

Some societies, such as the Mayans and the Incas, searched for redemption through sacrifice, as an inclination to try and control death through death as sacrifice. It was found in the annual Cretan ritual of feeding young men and women to the Minotaur. The significance of sacrifice as a means of protecting a society from death by "doing" death establishes a powerful and cruel apotropaic, as evil towards the population appears to have been averted. Such societies embrace cruelties as the victims are regulated to being inconsequential as lesser humans—the sacrifice is "not us", but of "them". By understanding much more about the unconscious meanings of cruelties and murderous violence, attacks on others might be pre-empted by understanding the sadomasochistic unconscious roots of apocalyptic thinking. Acknowledgement of the sources of misery that result in violence are in the history of both them and us. As understandings unfold of specific historical positions that require the warring sides to demand further blood sacrifices (over the centuries) the positions are stuck and fixed, with each projecting hate and blame onto the other. Destruction is central for fundamentalist-apocalyptic thinking. Hope is embalmed in annihilatory thinking. There is no room for ambiguity, as the difference between belief and no belief is obliterated. There is no space to think and feel either about oneself or the other. Instead, a violent formality, a *Totentanz,* or dance of death, is seductively available.

The Christian imperative of "Love your enemies" can, of course, be exceptionally difficult yet enemies deserve to each have a hearing. And things can be recognised rather than just reacted to. John Alderdice, working as leader of the small Alliance Party of Northern Ireland 1987 to 2004, and Speaker of the Assembly, was able to have a vision of understanding and giving recognition in Northern Ireland between the Catholics feeling abused, ill-treated and misunderstood for centuries and the ruling Protestants feeling that if they give up anything it is a *nil sum* game. When both sides have the chance and possibility to hear the misery of the other, there is a potential for compromise if both sides obtain something that they did not have before—respect and the potential for peace.

Out of these dialogues between the warring parties, enticing them both to meet and hear out the other, Alderdice positioned himself as the analytic third. Each side received fleeting glimpses of a sense of mutuality and respect that a peace process might then deepen. It also meant that the reliance on an unconscious sadomasochistic mechanism that continuously binds the two sides together, constantly desiring blood sacrifice from the other through murders, could develop a new control system that both sides adhere to, with a letting go of the double-jeopardy of aggression. And so, the Good Friday Agreement was born. Instead of becoming captured by death-givers, devouring the soul that goes with knowing one has murdered for "the cause", those celebrated historical blood sacrifices began to be mourned. Such mourning projects allow the young to dare to imagine that a creative life awaits them instead of the celebration, annually, of death.

So much of the political conflict in the world presently is of the "us and them" variety. Psychoanalysis may be very beneficial in understanding how to listen contrapuntally such that the potential rewards of befriending vicious enemies can be part of a new solution to interminable conflict by accepting reality and reckoning it in the dyad.

To be engaged in such delicate work requires finding new forms of space to contain a different type of dialogue emerging. Winnicott's concept of transitional space is valuable in the context of conflict resolution, where creative, imaginative play can reframe matters, rather than reiterating the age-old versions of destructive histories. Ironically the stuck-ness is due to an incapacity to play together with different ideas. Holding such a frame also means constructing the space as safe for *all* participants who fear the deadly reiteration of violence and brutality wiping out any space for thought.

Ferenczi wrote a paper on "The problem of acceptance of unpleasant ideas" in 1925, utilising and going beyond Freud's important paper on negation of the same year. The act of a negation of reality is a transition-phase between ignoring and accepting reality. Ferenczi writes that "first an attempt is made to deny it as fact; then a fresh effort has to be made to negate this negation, so that the positive, the recognition of evil, may really be assumed to be the result from two negatives" (1925b, p. 368). It is the necessity to deny reality and then in addition to negate the negation that is the core of the difficulty in accepting reality. One might say that this is the nub of the denial of reality when Trump and others double down on the phenomena and project the problem onto the other. The acceptance of reality then must emerge from a double denial— "always a two-fold mental act" (ibid., p. 368).

> The stage of negation has an analogy, as Freud has shown, in the behaviour of a patient during treatment and especially in a neurosis, which is similarly the result of a half-successful or unsuccessful repression and is actually always a negative—the negative of a perversion. The process by which recognition or affirmation of something unpleasant is finally reached goes on before our eyes as the result of our therapeutic efforts when

> we cure a neurosis, and, if we pay attention to the details of the curative process, we shall be able to form some idea of the process of acceptance as well. (ibid., p. 368)

The patient discovering, for instance, very painful parts of their histories allows the possibility of accepting reality in the present and future as a double negation can become a positive, as mathematics shows (two "minuses" equal a plus).

It is necessary for human beings to do the hard work of thinking as the prelude to having a freer life. The times are complex, for sure, but this is nothing new in world history. More pertinent is that time for thought is running out, due to humankind's insistence on pillaging Planet Earth of resources while the vast majority of citizens is left, mainly silently, perplexed and feeling powerless. Not thinking allows us to avoid the confrontations with judgement. We all need to acquire the energy and knowledge to make judgements on what we want for the future, without the simplistic polarities of hiding from radical thoughts or joining totalitarian groups who will think for and on our behalf. Or we can suffer a banality of non-thinking in accepting life's fates. Psychoanalysis is not a special discipline, other than it contains the possibility of an evaluation of unconscious, hidden history: one's own, the family, and how one has taken or declined decision-making in life. Psychoanalysis's vitality is in the dyadic nature of discourse, privately held, such that by speaking one's mind and hearing such internal thoughts spoken out loud, a shift can occur in our capacity to think.

Applying this to develop skills in becoming the third to the conflictual sides seems an essential growth for and of psychoanalysis. Judging then and now is an alive position, and in particular allows the possibility, through the freedom to think, of creating new possibilities for the future. This does require judging one's life, the family, and finding new answers to combat the unconsciously "safe" position of living in an expectation of a return of the repressed. Or beyond that, just an emptiness in the core of humanity. Having knowledge of the past, knowing that history enables analysands to recover the possibility of a different future, and, by extension, for citizens in groups to have knowledge through their own capacities for freedom to think, imbues politics with new meanings and goals for the pursuit of truth and happiness for all.

All such discussions, together with radical programmes of social, economic and environmental renewal, especially to give greater resources to caring for babies and children through political actions, would provide safety and security in these threatening times, through the caring of all people, adults and children in this very damaged and damaging world.

Of course, I am over-optimistic.

An addendum on the great little man

The problem of Trump's charisma is relatively easy to solve. It is the fanatical faith this man had in himself and rested on the well-known experimental fact that Trump must have realised early in his life, namely that modern society in its desperate inability to form judgements will take every individual for what he considers himself and professes himself to be—and will judge him on that basis. Extraordinary self-confidence and displays of self-confidence therefore inspire confidence in others' pretensions to genius and waken the conviction in others that they are indeed dealing with a genius. This is merely the perversion of an old and justified rule of all good society according to which everyone has to be capable of showing what he is and of presenting himself in a proper light. The perversion occurs when the social role becomes, as it were, arbitrary, when it is completely separated from the actual human substance; indeed, when a role consistently played is unquestioningly accepted as the substance itself. In such an atmosphere any kind of fraud becomes possible because there appears to be no one at all left for whom the difference between fraud and authenticity matters in the least. People therefore fall prey to judgements apodictically expressed because this tone frees them from the chaos of an infinite number of totally arbitrary judgements. The crucial point is that not only is the apodictic quality of the tone more convincing than the content of the judgement, but also the content of the judgement, the object judged, becomes irrelevant. To assess correctly charisma in Trump's case, we have to remind ourselves that in present day society it is not really all that difficult to create an aura about oneself that will fool everyone—or just about everyone—who comes under its influence. In this respect Trump behaved no differently than have many less talented charlatans. It goes without saying that under these conditions the rule of a good upbringing which says one must not blow one's own horn has to be ruthlessly put aside. The more the vulgar practice of unbridled self-praise spreads in a society that for the most part still adheres to the rules of good upbringing, the more powerful its effect will be, and the more easily that society can be convinced that only a truly "great man" who cannot be judged by normal standards could summon the courage to break rules as sacrosanct as those of good breeding.

In the prevailing chaos which that inability to form judgements created, however, Trump's superiority went considerably beyond the fascination, the mere "charisma" that any charlatan can emanate. The awareness of the social possibilities offered by the modern inability to judge, and the ability to exploit them were supported by the vastly more telling insight that in the modern world's chaos of opinion the normal mortal is yanked about from one opinion to another without the slightest understanding of what distinguishes the one from the other. Trump knew from his own most personal experience what the maelstrom into which modern man is drawn was like, in which he changes his political or other "philosophy" from day to day on the basis of whatever options are offered him as he whorls helplessly about. He is himself that newspaper reader of whom he says that "in a city in which twelve newspapers each report the same event differently he will finally come to the conclusion that all is nonsense". If you really hang on to any of the current opinions and develop it with "ice-cold" consistency, then everything would somehow fall back into place again. Trump's real superiority consisted in the fact that under any and all circumstances he had an opinion and that his opinion always fit perfectly into his overall "philosophy". In this social context (and only in this context) superiority is indeed increased by fanaticism because obvious and demonstrable errors no longer undermine it. What immediately reasserts itself after any demonstrated error is the fact that one not only has an opinion but also embraces that opinion and is capable of judgement. And in politics, where one constantly has to act and therefore constantly has to make judgements, it is indeed altogether correct in a practical sense and more advantageous to reach any judgement and to pursue any course of action than not to judge and not to act at all.

Taken together, these traditions made appear quite plausible a curious equating of purely technical capability with purely human activity, the latter of which has always had to do with questions of right and wrong. Once the moral basis of the knowledge of right and wrong, unarticulated as it was, began to crumble, the next step was to measure social and political actions by technical and work-oriented standards that were inherently alien to these larger spheres of human activity.

If logic is defined as the capability to press on to conclusions with a total disregard for all reality and all experience, then Trump's greatest gift was one of pure logic—as in "thinking exists only in the giving or in the execution of an order". He is with that one statement drawing the last, valid conclusion that follows not so much from all philosophies of power as from the opinion that rules in the chaos of opinion, namely that everything is "none sense". His listeners, fascinated as they were by the seamless coherence of this world view no doubt had only in the rarest of cases enough practical imagination to grasp the true meaning of this unswerving logic. Only in the rarest of cases would they have understood that Trump was providing what was in his view an altogether adequate justification for organised murder.

At the table with Hitler

And now dear reader—a confession. I have just challenged you by taking out of context, while being perfectly in context at the same time, a piece of writing that was a book review that Hannah Arendt wrote in German in 1951–1952 as "Bei Hitler zu Tisch" ("At the table with Hitler"). All of the addendum above was written by Hannah Arendt on Hitler, substituted by me as Trump. I suggest Arendt's review of seventy years ago of the narcissistic incoherence of Hitler's self-adoration offered to the people as a form of thinking and then the national politic, is found in identical forms in Trump's selfish and inconsistent behaviours whilst disregarding good sense, good manners and logic other than an underlying racist hatred that his millions of supporters swallow as he offers them carte blanche to murder the constitution to allow his racist agenda.

The cloth that fits Hitler then shockingly fits Trump. Please read the essay from the beginning again, now knowing that in truth it was written describing Hitler. Trump was voted out of office too early—so far—to continue his racist, murderous politics. And, of course, we know that he, mirrored and admired by some seventy million of his supporters and voters, still regards the election as a fraud against him, rather than the reality of him attacking the constitution, trying to do away with it as irrelevant. I think that it follows that Arendt's description of the vacuousness within Hitler, which led to his dangerous cruelties, is why we still need to be very afraid and concerned about Trump's continuing quest for power. The threat is, as yet, not over.

CHAPTER 12

Thoughts about dancing bears— psychoanalytic thinking to understand present-day problems of inner and outer reality

My book, *Dark Times: Psychoanalytic Perspectives on Politics, History and Mourning* was published in 2019, and it was written with an urgency that now seems presumptuous. It seems a faraway time: pre-Covid and prior to a new and very dangerous war in Europe. Putin wants Europe and the world to accept his phantasy that Russia alone beat Hitler, and that, in his view, the West took over Nazism from the Nazis. So it is timely to think with the perspective of these times we live in. This requires locating cruelty masquerading as fun in life. The foundations of sadomasochism and its forms of enactments that I have long been investigating in psychoanalysis are to be found in society.

Analysands, when they begin to consciously realise the painful and often fragmented phantasies and illusions that are the life that they have been living, invariably find the quest for a new beginning to be an arduous task. The giving up, even prising apart, of defensive structures in past and present relationships is a deeply painful part of the analytic journey of discovery to new forms of object relations. In a similar fashion, looking ahead to the difficulties citizens may find when a freer life becomes a possibility is a very difficult and serious task.

This is particularly true in the aftermath of the severe effects of the cruelties of war on a besieged population and in particular the impact of war privation on children.

The issue I want to draw attention to is one that is well known in psychoanalytic treatment—that, despite much progress and knowledge about the ailment, letting go of negative states of mind or desperately holding on to impossible object relationships can be profoundly difficult. Or reckoning on what to do with the revealed truths. It is as if holding on to a near-sinking vessel can intensify a closeness, like a perverse umbilical connection to the negative. Similar issues can be found in the citizens of and children brought up in totalitarian societies. In such social-political states of mind in these societies parents know not to talk about politics in front of the children, for example at mealtimes, as it can be very dangerous if the children reiterate their parents' conversations about the regime beyond the home. So, despite the overthrow of the old and terrifying regime, many individuals continue to stay fearful, left unable to move to a new creativity in their lives, even staying silent about some matters in their analysis as being too painful, or even irrelevant, as "the world has moved on".

Since the 1990s, Bulgaria has established a sanctuary for bears rescued from captivity from circuses and performing in towns and hamlets, the end of communism giving rise to hopes that bears might enjoy freedom too. Young bears had for centuries been taken from their mothers in the wild and domesticated by keepers by attaching chains to rings driven through their noses, beating them and knocking their teeth out as a means of training them to dance. They performed tricks, imitated celebrities and, claws trimmed, gave back massages as entertainment. Worse, was forcing the bears to follow human customs, living with their keepers on a diet of bread and alcohol and working all year round without winter hibernation. They forgot how to hibernate, to hunt, to attract a mate or to move freely, as their limbs were chained and then pulled to make them seem to dance. This is described by Witold Szabłowski in *Dancing Bears: True Stories of People Nostalgic for Life Under Tyranny* (2014).

Some keepers, not noticing that they had done anything wrong, badly missed their confiscated bears, which they thought they loved.

How were the bears retrained, understanding that freedom must come gradually? First their nose rings were removed, then, in a special fenced-off section of the park, they gradually became accustomed to the smell of other bears, without yet eating together. Later, they roamed within the large fenced-off area in the hope that there would be a return of natural instincts—hunting, mating and hibernating. However,

> it was only a semblance of freedom as the bears could not survive. Either they would die of cold, incapable of finding a place to hibernate or the first male, whose territory they entered, would kill them. Or they would look for food in trashcans and someone would shoot them. Some were so infected with the prisoner mentality that for years they start to dance when they see a human being. They would stand up on their hind legs and start rocking from side to side, As if they were begging, as in the past, for bread, candy, a sip of beer, a caress or to be free of pain. (Szabłowski, 2014)

The description of the chained bears, cruelly forced against their nature to identify with their aggressors, and putting on a show of obedience in return for scraps, is a powerful metaphor for what humans may need to understand of their traumatic histories. Humans brought up in specific, severe, traumatic environments, citizens living in totalitarian states, living all of their lives under the Nazism of the Third Reich, Stalinist Russia, racist South Africa, totalitarian regimes in Argentina, Venezuela or Myanmar, the Isis genocide on the Yadzidi and, of course, the Holocaust, do not find the possibilities of freedom easy to bear. In order to stop being dominated by the past, they, like the bears released from the external chains, can only slowly let go of the old paranoid control structures by being understood. This can be in groups and through new politics that understand the lack of trust in these people, induced by the domineering aggressive regime.

Similarly, as the analysand comes to realise that the prison door of their inner life is no longer barred shut but is ajar, it does not mean that the cell can be easily left. This can be perplexing for the therapist. Yet why should one "get better", in case the perpetrators will be delighted and might suggest that there had never been any capture? Or the more obvious position of continuing to stay in the masochistic identification formed through multitudinous cruel practices and the continuation of deep fear. The aggressors are still in mind to identify with and thereby available to identify as a form of holding on to the impoverished past. As well as developing new democratic structures, it takes a long time for citizens in damaged societies to begin to trust again, like the bears.

History matters for the individual in psychoanalysis as well as for the citizens of a state. The recent continuing wave of momentum in the Black Lives Matter movement reconnects with the complex histories of racism well known to historians. Racist crimes have for several centuries been hidden from the narratives of many countries. The recent pulling down of statues in the UK has drawn attention to the lack of narrative of the racism and wealth of those slave traders. The UK was hugely enriched in the seventeenth and eighteenth centuries by sugar profits from the slave trade. It is often stated that to find the crime one needs to follow the money. Several thousand slave owners became hugely wealthy off the backs and lives of their black African and Caribbean slaves, cruelly captured from their ordinary life.

This has been meticulously researched by Catherine Hall in her book *Legacies of British Slave-Ownership 1763–1833*. In Europe, Spain, Portugal and Holland also became fabulously wealthy, and riches were poured into building great houses and estates. In the UK we can enjoy visiting these, many now owned by the National Trust. The wealth led to the establishment in 1694 of the Bank of England to act as the English government's banker and later probably providing the seed corn for the Industrial Revolution. Many politicians had slave fortunes and their descendants still profit.

All this history is now unconcealed and on view, similarly to the Stasi records in East Germany after the Berlin Wall came down. It reveals that social systems developed and continue to be influenced by the master–slave relationship, which still consigns the other towards poverty and second-class citizenship in all aspects of society. Covid has been a great revealer of the link between poverty and death. What was known, was hidden in front of us and disavowed. For instance, the sole reason that the UK begun a National Debt was to fund the vast payment to the British slaveowners. The capital sum was only paid off very recently, with interest having been paid annually since its inception.

The task in analysis—to make conscious the unconscious—can also be examined in the social and political and financial deceits as the re-finding of what has been social-political disavowal, now becoming conscious as a necessary part of a new beginning in our lives and for all citizens. I am describing the re-finding of history in the individual in analysis and its associated task of re-finding such vicious histories that have been corrupting societies, mainly unknowingly, for centuries. Think about the apparently sudden knowledge that we the people have of climate change, which industry, business and governments have disavowed for a very long time. The greed of the political class and the industrialists raping the earth for their profit can now being seen as an attack that impoverishes the planet and most of its inhabitants. It is a form of sadomasochistic bind, as if it is an ordinary people not only do not matter but they passively accept their fate. Both situations are about an untenable white entitlement.

In contrast to the tendencies of control, deceit and linguistic rigidity within a master–slave mentality, psychoanalysis offers a path towards truth and reconciliation, and away from paranoid discourses towards alterity. The development of the ability to tolerate the other without allowing domination, and at the same time recognising complexity, is the modern heritage of psychoanalysis, and we can offer leadership to citizens and some politicians. We can call this, after Marie Langer, the "return of the social–political repressed" (Langer, 1989). I am describing the importance of transgenerational trauma and the necessity for a truth-telling to be a vital and often brave unravelling of strands in the transference–countertransference.

To my mind, the paranoid–schizoid theory laid down in the mind through three to six months old is theoretical, leaving out, as it does, all the multitudes of fine moments of loving/hating that etch with perplexity into the dream life, the ego and superego and developing character from pre-birth through childhood and adolescence. It is such matters that are discovered in analytic work as a truth-telling in the history of the analysand's object relational system, which is about transgenerational stasis or development, and it is a similar quest to look at the relationships in society between cruelty, dictatorships and how citizens, from their private unconscious histories, flock to join the bullies or become the oppressed. The vast and cruel damage by Russian soldiers against the invaded Ukrainians damages the minds of the victims who live to tell the tale. It also damages the minds of those soldiers who explode to rape, pillage, kill and defecate over their enemy.

Such states of the traumatic contain paradoxes: "At the start is an essential aloneness. At the same time this aloneness can only take place under maximum conditions of dependence" (Winnicott, 1998a, p. 132). The quest for a new beginning in those who have suffered severely is, like with the dancing bears, an arduous and necessary process. As a young former analysand recently wrote to me

> I think it is becoming more difficult to ignore the ghosts and inheritances, though they spring up in new and insidious ways co-opting the language of freedom. Though in vigilance I think there can be some joy, or really there must be, because survival is not enough—the art of the possible, as you say.

Acknowledgements

Lockdown was a place where I began to develop and put together a series of essays which I later realised connected with the importance of culture. Observations on Covid times elicited return messages of survival and I am grateful to my friends and colleagues who have provided their thoughts and ideas from their lockdown experiences.

As with much of my writings, the parallel worlds of history, politics and philosophy entwine in several of these essays, as well as one chapter about what we can conceptualise about standing up and speaking out to the large numbers of silently anxious people in the hope that the silent majority can find forms of discussion to discover all our voices in our devastating and devastated world. I would like to thank those who came to discussions around my previous book *Dark Times: Psychoanalytic Perspectives on Politics, History and Psychoanalysis*, perhaps expecting just to hear my thoughts on present politics and the state of our society, but being willing, once invited, to voice their own perspectives.

I am very grateful to my editor Catherine Hall for being on this journey with me. And for Kate Pearce, my publisher at Karnac.

Thanks to Yiota Panagiota for her deep knowledge and resonances of Greek language and myths. Bernard Jacobson for interesting me with a writing project on the art of William Tillyer, and to Robert Grossmark at the Bernard Jacobson gallery who was so helpful in collating images of Tillyer's work. Thanks to Phillip Waller for information on socio-political issues around suffrage.

My thanks also go to Luke Griffin who collated the artwork and delivered another fine cover.

And to my analysands for patiently teaching me so much.

I also give my thanks to those who invited me to present these papers at conferences and offered me the occasion to write and develop my ideas. The giving and re-giving of lectures over recent years, and especially with the ensuing discussions, was very helpful in developing and expanding my understandings of the entwining of culture, history, politics and psychoanalysis. Details on where I presented these papers follow.

"Velázquez and the transmission of psychoanalysis" was first presented at a memorial conference at University College London, 2019.

I am grateful to Jorge Canestri when he was president of the European Psychoanalytical Federation (EPF) for encouraging me to present two analysis and politics papers at the EPF congress "Beyond the origin of life: Memory and trauma in society", 2018.

And to Heribert Blass for continuing that direction when I gave "Apocalyptic times and the missing debate" at the European Psychoanalytic Federation's 2022 annual conference, "Illusions".

I was invited to give papers over recent years to the seminars of both Lene Auestad and David Morgan—each of their programmes is interested in examining psychoanalysis and politics.

Papers presented at Lene Auestad's Psychoanalysis and Politics seminars:

7 October 2020 – The Nazification of psychoanalysis: Velázquez and the transmission of power
1 December 2021 – Francis Bacon and the radicality of free association
4 June 2022 – Berlin Conference: Apocalyptic life and the missing debate
14 September 2023 – Stranger, visitor, metaphor

David Morgan's Political Mind Seminars held at the Institute of Psychoanalysis:

29 May 2018 – Hatred and racism: Evocations of the Confederacy in today's America
19 May 2020 – Velázquez, power and the Nazification of psychoanalysis
18 May 2021 – Authoritarianism and dancing bears: Implications for a New Beginning
11 July 2023 – Apocalyptic times and the missing debate: The evil of modernity begins with the disappearance of the community of listeners. Walter Benjamin (1995 [1970])

The chapter "Psychosis and the true self" was presented at Winnicott: A Present to the Future, London on 25 September 2021.

The chapter "Stranger, visitor, metaphor" was first presented at the 9th Delphi International Symposium in August 2022.

British Lectures at the Peruvian Psychoanalytic Society, Lima, 21–24 June 2023: I presented the papers "Metaphor in psychoanalysis" and "Violence, destruction and survival—independent theory and clinical practice".

"Violence, destruction and survival—independent theory and clinical practice" was also given to the British Psychoanalytical Association 5 March 2022 and to the British Psychoanalytical Society on 28 March 2023.

I would also like to thank the following publications for publishing earlier versions of some of the material in this book.

"It takes our breath away—the first day of lockdown" is also published in *Mind in the Line of Fire: Psychoanalytic Voices to the Challenges of Our Times*. IPA, 2023.

Marcelo N. Viñar's response to my early Covid writings, "Coronavirus and production of subjectivity: Me and humanity in the face of the un-expected", was published in the e-journal *Psychoanalysis.today*, Issue 11: 'Psychoanalysis in the Time of Pandemics', July 2020, and Drew Tillotson's response, "Shelter in Place", was published in *ROOM: A Sketchbook for Analytic Action*: 6.20. Analytic-room.com

A version of the chapter, "Bloomsbury and the early evolution of British psychoanalysis" is included in *Independent Women in British Psychoanalysis: Creativity and Authenticity at Work*, edited by Elizabeth Wolf and Barbie Antonis. London: Routledge, 2023.

The chapter "Apocalyptic times and the missing debate" is published in EPF *Bulletin* 77, 2023.

Postscript

How a cultural age ends and the repressed returns[1]

Dictatorships always ask, actually demand, of their cultural icons and their staff to make statements in favour of the regime at war. It is a form of letting the people "know" that core values of the State are supportive of the leader and to give the regime a form of legitimacy. Hours after Russia's invasion of Ukraine began, the Meyerhold Centre, an experimental venue in the centre of Moscow, became the first theatre to protest. "We can't not say it," read a statement posted online. "We can't not say: No war".

Within days about 2,000 Russian cultural workers had signed an open letter to the government opposing the war. Some went to the streets, including young playwright and festival director Yury Shekhvatov, who was detained by riot police, beaten, and spent fifteen days in jail. A handful of theatres added peace doves to their logos. Russia's top Shakespeare scholars issued a joint statement. Legendary director Lev Dodin pleaded in the Kremlin on the pages of industry magazine *Teatr*: "I beg you, stop!"

Within two weeks of the war, many staff of theatres and music venues were given disciplinary conversations. This is significant as most theatres are formally government institutions and state censorship is still a hangover from Soviet times. Within hours of the protest, Elena Kovalskaya, the Meyerhold Centre's artistic director, resigned. Four days later, the ministry fired her colleague, the director Dmitri Volkostrelov. The new director ordered the theatre's media team to delete all anti-war statements. The media team then all quit. Within a week, the theatre was subsumed under another institution and the famous name was again lost. The Soviet theatre named after director Vsevolod Meyerhold had been shut down in 1938 during Josef Stalin's Great Terror.

In 1934, Dmitri Shostakovich's opera *Lady Macbeth of Mtsensk* was performed initially as a success but detested by Stalin, and was condemned by the Soviet government. Shostakovich lived for years fearing the knock on the door. And, despite his constant anxiety, wrote String Quartet No. 8 after visiting Dresden in 1960, dedicating it "to victims of fascism and war". In a conversation with members of the Emerson String Quartet he said,

> Through listening to the silences and the desolation, the violence and the tragedy, and using that to imagine his world … like a letter from a forbidden place that we know nothing of. These pieces stand as an aural representation of an incredible spectrum of human tragedy and suffering, with occasional glimpses of hopefulness. At the opening of the fourth movement … there's a sustained tone in the first violin, and then all of a sudden three dissonant chords are played … it sounds like a knock on the door in the middle of the night that so many Russian people dreaded …[2]

Dozens of the leading Russian artists of their generation have today been denounced by colleagues and purged from their jobs. Censorship has returned to smother Russia's free-thinking theatres, devastating the cultural scene.

Once the artistic intelligentsia had freed themselves from the upper classes by the mid-nineteenth century, the community of artists, writers, architects and actors had become the arbiter of taste and the centre of society's attention.[3] Now the director of the famed Tretyakov art gallery had been fired by the culture ministry and replaced by Elena Pronicheva, the daughter of an FSB general, who had a career at the state gas company Gasprom. Stalin brought repression to the artistic endeavour, binding its explorations to state control. This is now happening again in Russia. Artists are on blacklists, purges of the cultural leadership continue by drilling down to rake in the smaller fish. So many have fled Russia and many of the rest have again packed a suitcase ready for departure.

As self-censorship switches on within an atmosphere of paranoia, it has become the time of the talentless, again.

Of course, this is what dictatorships and war can do to states. It is not too far away in time to remember the intentional destruction of cultural heritage by Daesh, the four UNESCO World Heritage sites in Iraq (Ashur, Hatra, Samaria and Irbul Citadel), especially the capital cities of Nimrud and Nineveh.[4] By May 2016, forty-one buildings of Islamic heritage had been severely damaged or erased in Mosul. If we go back in time to 2003–2004, the US military base established in Iraq by the coalition invasion forces sat on top of the Babylon site, significantly damaging the archaeology there.[5]

Or further back to World War II, during the siege of Leningrad between December 1941 and January 1944, the German army killed 800,000 of the city's inhabitants, destroying much of the city. It was not just the incessant firepower but also the starvation during two very cold winters that killed so many in the besieged city. Shostakovich wrote the Leningrad Symphony No. 7 in C Major and it was played there on August 9 1942, to honour the citizens of the city. Several members of the orchestra had succumbed to famine, so many that the Russian military command released any soldier able to play. The concert was transmitted by loudspeaker around the perimeter of the city to both hearten the Russian citizens and to tell the Germans surrender was not at hand. Empty chairs in the orchestra represented its fallen members.[6] Here we have the use of culture for the purposes of morale.

Wiping out history is a consistent activity alongside killing populations and completely destroying the towns and cities, as we see in Russia's present offensive in Eastern Ukraine. What is left is heaps of rubble. The projection of rage from the wiping out of so much of Russia by the Nazis is now being applied by Putin as the inheritor of Stalin's power to similarly "to rubble" the people, cities and culture of the Ukraine. This, after all, contains the same territory as the many concentration camps of the Nazis.

The Victory Museum in Moscow is dedicated to the Soviet Union's defeat of Nazi Germany and is a showcase for children and adolescents to visit in order to learn their history. One new exhibit explains "NATOzism: the purpose of creating NATO was to achieve world domination". Another, "Everyday Nazism", includes artefacts from Ukraine's Azov battalion,[7] which has far-right connections, as evidence for the false assertion that Ukraine is committing "genocide" against Russians. Putin cast the invasion as near-holy for Russia's very identity, declaring that it was fighting to prevent liberal gender norms and acceptance of homosexuality from being forced upon it by an aggressive West (Troianovski & Hopkins, 2023). One might imagine that a passive, supine Russia is being homosexually raped by NATO and the West. As so often in the aggressive language of totalitarianism, the attack is projected onto the other and showing a grievance-ridden Putinesque paranoia.

As Timothy Snyder claims,

> Practically everyone who dies in the Holocaust either called Poland or the Soviet Union home before the war or was sent to German-occupied Poland or German-occupied lands of the USSR. Ukraine was home to the largest Jewish populations in Europe. In 1941, the Nazi Einsatzgruppen began to kill by mass shooting an estimated one and a half million Jews. Poland and Ukraine was the territory that the Nazis established the concentration camps that killed most of the Jews from Europe.

So it probably is not surprising that elements of aggressive anti-Semitism and homophobia return from the repressed unconsciousness of Ukraine and also that other huge country that had the rest of the killing camps, that of German-occupied Russia. According to Timothy Snyder, "the Holocaust is integrally and organically connected to the attempt to conquer Ukraine. Had Hitler not had the colonial idea to fight a war in Eastern Europe to control Ukraine, had there not been that idea, there could not have been a Holocaust" (2017). Snyder goes on to comment that US frontier colonialism built an empire by slave labour and when Hitler spoke about the United States, it was generally, before the war at least, with admiration. And it was a question for Hitler: who will the slaves be in the German Eastern empire? And the answer that he gave, both in *Mein Kampf,* and in practice in the invasion of 1941, is the Ukrainians. (ibid.)

For Snyder, Ukraine was the centre of Hitler's ideological colonialism. The same area is now being fought over but this time the attack comes from the east, from Russia, but it is the same lands where the fighting and battlefields were before. Ukrainian commanders have been closely examining the minutiae of the defended towns and hamlets as well as the avenues of attacks from Nazi times as the territory has not altered. Here we can see at work the well-known analytic unconscious formation of the *return of the repressed.* In this light, one can see through the smog of war that it is now Russia that demands the return of Ukraine to be enslaved by colonial Russia who desires to recapture the Bread Basket, not for Europe but now for Russia.

And, as this book has made clear, there are many links, political and historical, to the rise in fascism again throughout the world from the Nazi times of the 1930s in Germany. Today there is a new danger, that of rebranding Holocaust remembrance and imagery to delegitimise communism. As Jelena Subotić makes clear in her excellent book (2020), the equation of communism and fascism, and then the appropriation of the Holocaust, "has occurred throughout Eastern Europe, with much historical revisionism resulting from the attempts of Eastern European countries to deny or cloud their participation in fascist crimes, including the Holocaust by delegitimising anti fascism, and in so doing legitimising resurgent neofascism" (ibid., p. 6). And this takeover proceeds in plain sight.

In 2014, Victor Orbán declared a Year of Holocaust Commemoration, in which the Holocaust was incorporated into the larger contemporary political narrative about twentieth century totalitarianism and used to condemn the worse variant, that of communism. The Law and Justice government in Poland prevented the opening of a new museum on WWII in Gdańsk as it did not express "the Polish point of view". After it finally opened in March 2017, the director was replaced by a political appointee in order to project more "Polish" history. "These moves were all part of the new Polish politics of memory, the purpose of which is to highlight Polish heroism and sacrifice throughout history and not dwell on negative episodes such as, well, the Holocaust" (ibid., p. 7). It jars the new memory if Poles are implicated in the killing of Jews.[8] Similarly, the Katyn massacre in 1940 of 22,000 Polish soldiers shot by the Soviet army in death pits has seen its name invoked in 2009 by the Polish president Lech Kaczynski, who "claimed that the Red Army's 'treacherous attack' in 1939 brought 'the night of occupation, the essence of which was the Holocaust, Auschwitz, Katyn'" (Fredheim, 2014). As Subotić wryly comments, "the message is not only that Auschwitz and Katyn are one of a kind, bur also that communism *caused* Auschwitz. There is hardly a better way to delegitimise communism than to blame it for the Holocaust" (Subotić, 2020, p. 8).

So the Holocaust is being used to filter out and obfuscate any serious addressing of one's own responsibility for mass atrocities in more recent times. But it also clouds memories that do not fit the current political moment, such as those extensive Nazi crimes against communists and partisans. Such politically formed screen memory allows the re-formation of Nazism and enables fascistic return to many countries. Europe in 2024 is being potentially destabilised by the rise of fascist parties seeking to share or take over governance in France, Germany, Italy, Spain, Denmark, Sweden, Poland, Hungary, Serbia and Norway. The UK is in an impoverished condition following fourteen years of right-wing Conservative government. The Republican Party is now a very right-wing party in the United States and still expects Trump to be re-elected President. And though in South America Bolsanaro is now no longer President in Brazil, Venezuela is in a parlous and undemocratic state and fascist Peronism remains the dominant political ideology in Argentina. Such political manoeuvrings do not give much of a priority to climate change.

The most insidious political manoeuvrings in post-communist states is memory appropriation of the Holocaust where the Holocaust is remembered as a cypher for remembering something else, such as communism. In Serbia, there is a memory inversion where

> the Holocaust, its crimes and its images are directly appropriated in order to make space for the discussion of crimes of communism. The Holocaust is not denied—it is not even obviously

> trivialised—but it is only remembered heuristically, as a vehicle for remembering the crimes of communism. (ibid., p. 25)

There is an inversion of the suffering of the Jews and instead other ethnic victims are cited. This strategy enables Holocaust remembrance and memorial to now be displaced and replaced by concern with nationalistic needs. For example, in 2014, the Historical Museum of Serbia had a much published exhibition, titled "In the Name of the People—Political Suppression in Serbia 1944–1953," displaying new historical documents as evidence of communist crimes of assassinations, detentions in camps and repression. Yet the exhibition showed detexualised photos of "victims of communism". One photo in particular, far from showing the crimes of the communists, displayed

> a well-known photo of prisoners from the Buchenwald concentration camp, including Elie Wiesel, taken by US soldier Harry Miller at the camp's liberation in April 1945. In the Belgrade exhibition, this canonic image was displayed in the section devoted to a communist-era camp for political prisoners on the Adriatic island of Goliotok. (ibid., p. 5)

This postscript is an invitation to continue to carefully examine various strands of evidence that ruthless politicians and governments utilise to manipulate us away from thinking beneath the surface of the image and the political argument—to keep the people quietly sleeping while the fascistic states steal our freedom again. In times of artificial intelligence, this becomes even more critical for the world.

Freud, in describing the German concept of *Weltanschauung* (1933a), thought that as well as a scientific *Weltanschauung*, there was also a mystic *Weltanschauung*. In this case, Freud said, "a psychological explanation does not help. This one is the real enemy of the future. Our science is powerless against it. It is based on the belief in the irrational. People have a need to preserve a piece of mystic *Weltanschauung*".[9] The world today appears to be drawn to mystic politics and with Trump as an exemplar, the more he is found guilty in multiple court arraignments, the more his millions of supporters ignore reality and continue to believe in his powers. Reality does not dent the mystic container.

At a later meeting on March 20 1930, the topic was *Civilization and Its Discontents* (1930a). Freud put considerable emphasis on spending his whole life endeavouring to uncover truths. "I had no other intention and everything else was a matter of indifference to me. My single motive was the love of truth." Then he continued:

> Actually, the truth is that we do not have so much culture that we could really feel uncomfortable in it. My book is the outcome of the insight that our theory of instincts was insufficient. It has been said that I am trying to force the death instinct upon analysts. However, I am only like an old farmer who plants fruit trees, or like someone who has to leave the house and leaves a toy behind so the children will have something to play with while he is absent. I wrote the book with purely analytic intentions, based on my former existence as an analytic writer, in brooding contemplation, concerned to promote the concept of the feeling of guilt to its very end. The feeling of guilt is created by the renunciation of aggression. Now it's up to you to play with the idea. But I consider this the most important progress in analysis. (1930a, pp. 186–187)

We must continue exploring the human necessities for the aggression of our species that is now destroying our civilisation. The task is to turn sadistic mischief in politics into sublimation that benefits mankind. And that strange word "mankind" does indicate a separation from the feminine and the necessity to include womankind in fixing solutions to man's aggression.

And we have support in our endeavours to look and see with a critical eye and ear. I have cited the bravery of Shostakovitch in relation to Stalin and I will add Picasso seeing through the fascist ideology with his huge painting *Guernica*. The destruction of the town was planned by Reichsmarschall Göring as a present for Hitler's birthday on April 20 1937.[10] The attack was to test the Luftwaffe's ability to annihilate a city. Franco and his Nazi allies denied that any bombing had taken place, claimed that the Basques had destroyed their own city and accused the Nationalists of attempting to win support for the anti-fascist cause. Sounds familiar, as Putin uses the same playbook in destroying towns and cities in Ukraine. Now Picasso had his theme for his World Fair commission. Dora Marr, who had witnessed and documented the making of *Guernica*, said that Picasso had told her: "I know I am going to have terrible problems with this painting, but I am determined to do it—we have to arm for the war to come" (Richardson, 2022, pp. 139–140). Josep Renau, his friend watching the painting progressing, proposed, "What would he think, I asked him, if after the war, we prepared a special gallery at the Prado in which *Las Meninas*, his *Guernica* and (Goya's) *Third of May* were exhibited together?"

Such is the soft power of culture …

Notes

Prologue

1. National Gallery, London.
2. https://en.wikipedia.org/wiki/Myra_Hess
3. T. S. Eliot, "Sweeney Agonistes", in *The Complete Poems and Plays*. This volume was given to me as a goodbye present in January 1978 by the patients of the Halliwick Day Hospital where I had worked as the ward psychiatric registrar for two years. I learned much from them.

Chapter 1: Stranger, visitor, metaphor

1. *Xenos* is also a word that can contain the paradox of being alone in a foreign place as well as being taken inside, looked after and potentially developing relationships.
2. Walter Benjamin in a letter to Scholem, 17 April 1931.

Chapter 2: Velázquez and the transmission of psychoanalysis

1. https://www.pablopicasso.org/las–meninas.jsp
2. I am grateful to Trudy McGuiness, Anne–Marie Sandler's stepdaughter, for providing me with a copy of this private autobiography.
3. Encyclopedia.com
4. *documenta: Politics and Art in Berlin*. Prestel. Deutschland Historiches Museum 2021. https://www.dhm.de/en/exhibitions/archive/2021/documenta–politics–and–art/

Chapter 3: Francis Bacon and the radicality of free association

1. This idea comes from John Rickman ("Number and the Human Sciences", 1951), who was analysed at different times by Freud, Ferenczi and Klein. See *No Ordinary Psychoanalyst: The Extraordinary Contributions of John Rickman*, Ed. Pearl King. London: Karnac, 2003.
2. "How could he endure to perceive the echo of innumerable shouts of pleasure and woe in the 'wide space of the world night', enclosed in the wretched glass capsule of the human individual, without inexorably fleeing toward his primordial home, as he hears this shepherd's dance of metaphysics?" Friedrich Wilhelm Nietzsche, *The Birth of Tragedy* (1886).
3. Harry Houdini observed one of Carrière's seances and asserted that they were fraudulent. He was never convinced by her and likened her performance to the magician's Hindu needles trick. See Wikipedia and H. Houdini (2011).
4. John Rothenstein writes, as quoted by Winnicott:

   … to look at a painting by Bacon is to look into a mirror, and to see there our own afflictions and our fears of solitude, failure, humiliation, old age, death and of nameless threatened catastrophe. His avowed preference for having his paintings glazed is also related to his sense of dependence on chance… His dark blue pictures in particular, I heard him observe, gain by enabling the spectator to see his own face in the glass. (Alley & Rothenstein, 1964).

5. In *Oedipus and the Sphinx*, for example, it is the bandaged and bloody right foot that is encircled.
6. Translation: "Excuse me, Monsieur Consul–General, there is nothing to be done. Mr Bacon likes it".

7. National Gallery show: *Titian*. 16 March 2020–17 January 2021.

8. On the Gagosian website: https://gagosian.com/exhibitions/2017/cy–twombly/ but originally said by Cézanne (Letter to Roger Marx, 23 January 23 1905, as quoted in John Reward, 1995, p. 313).

9. The quotation from Read's text is from T. S. Eliot's 'Ballad of J. Alfred Prufrock', of "ragged claws scuttling".

10. A corollary sculpture of Michelangelo, *Dying Slave*, was in Bacon's mind in an early painting of 1950 simply called *Painting*, of a twisted muscular nude and its shadow of death (Wullschager, 2019). Together Michelangelo's pieces represent freedom and life versus dying and death.

Chapter 4: William Tillyer: against nature

1. "How does one make a landscape painting that recognises two fundamental facts, the impact humans have had on the landscape and the main currents of twentieth and twenty first century art—the readymade, anti–art, abstraction and, more recently, the digital realm—without devolving into parody, pastiche or irony?" John Yau in his 2021 catalogue essay in *William Tillyer— A Retrospective*.

2. See John Yau (2021), p. 7:

   According to *The Guardian* (May 31, 2017), Hockney's 2017 retrospective at Tate Britain 'was the most visited exhibition for any living artist ever held at any of Tate's four galleries'. Tillyer's work, on the other hand, has never been included in a group show at Tate Britain, let alone a solo exhibition. According to the artist, the museum owns around eight or ten of his prints, mostly etchings, which were acquired during the late 1970s by Sir Norman Reid who was director at that time. None of his paintings are in the Tate's collection.

3. *William Tillyer: The Golden Striker* (James, 2022). Film, available on Vimeo.

4. Georges Braque (1882–1963) joined the French army on 2 August 1914, a day after general mobilisation was declared. His artistic partner and aesthetic collaborator, Pablo Picasso, a Spaniard from a neutral country, famously said, "On 2 August 1914, I took Braque and Derain to the station at Avignon. I never saw them again". Picasso's statement was not literal, of course; both Braque and André Derain (1880–1954) survived the Great War, but both men would be profoundly altered as human beings and as artists. However, Braque would not last a year in this war. After his regiment was transferred to the area around Vimy Ridge, on 11 May 1915 Braque was caught up in an

explosion of a shell and went down in no man's land, where he lay unconscious until stretcher bearers found him. In the interval, he had been "left for
dead", and his family was informed of his death. His lover, Marcelle Lapré,
refused to accept what turned out to be a false report. Braque survived but
was temporarily blind, a terrifying fate for a painter, and his skull had to be
trepanned to relieve the pressure on his brain.

5. Frieze Masters is an annual London exhibition in Regents Park that presents
museum-quality artworks from the ancient era right through to the end of
the 20th century. This leading fair thus offers a unique look at the relationship
between historical art and contemporary work.

6. "In Velázquez's *Las Meninas* and my own *Mesh Paintings*—this dark narrow space between the wall and the back of the canvas or panel serves to
dramatise, by shadow, the action on the canvas, and additionally sends the
viewer back 'beyond', out to the start again of what is a visual obstacle race.
This 'haven', as I call it, behind the more public statements of the canvas can
only be reached by literally breaching that surface" (Tillyer, 2002, p. 38.)
I can add to his description by offering to change the obstacle course to
the metaphor of Freud's *fort–da* in which the cotton reel object is gone/lost
and then/found, the age-old game of hide and seek now found within *Las
Meninas*.

7. He had been an altar boy and had been taught church ritual.

8. *William Tillyer: The Golden Striker.*

9. ibid., end of film.

Chapter 5: Psychosomatic reflections in the analysis of a heroin addict

1. Medication administered by means other than through the alimentary tract,
as by intramuscular or intravenous injection. The word, of course, contains
the word *parent*.

2. Tausk goes on to describe a patient of Freud's, Emma Eckstein:

> Miss Emma E felt herself influenced by her lover in a singular man-
> ner; she maintained that her eyes were no longer properly placed in her
> head but were entirely twisted out of position, and this she attributed
> to the fact that her lover was an evil, deceitful person who twisted eyes.
> At church one day she suddenly felt a thrust, as if she were being moved
> from her place, which had its cause in the fact that her lover disguised

himself, and that he had already ruined her and made her as evil as himself. (Tausk, 1919, p. 35)

Tausk regarded this material as representing the stage in the development of the delusion of reference preceding the projection that later is the bridge between an internal change and attributing it to the powers of an external person as a delusion of reference.

Chapter 7: Psychosis and the true self

1. Quoted in Parker (2019, p. 238).
2. Freud hints that the game was beneficial to Ernst as, even though he was not free from feelings of jealousy upon the arrival of a new sibling, he was able to cope with the death of his mother a short time later. Nonetheless such meanings of death may be deferred to adulthood as guilt–driven anxiety.
3. As I have written in my book *Landscapes of the Dark—Trauma, History, Psychoanalysis* (Sklar, 2011), Freud's paper "Neurosis and Psychosis" (1924b) is seminal for the way it allows us to understand not just the notion of a gap in the ego, but the struggle by the unconscious to make good the gap and to attempt repair: "In regard to the genesis of delusions", writes Freud, "a fair number of analyses have taught us that the delusion is found applied like a patch over the place where originally a rent had appeared in the ego's relation to the external world" (Freud, 1924b, p. 151). The gap, in time, can become the "split" in the ego. However, this is more complicated than it seems, as the German for "split" is *Einreiss*, which leans more to a meaning of a "tendency to tear". This adds another perspective onto Freud's meaning because a "tendency" includes the idea that, despite being fragile, the tear may not worsen. It is not a break. This is less critical than a *Reiss*, which is an actual tear and is more a term to delegate to psychosis (Danckwardt & Wegner, 2007, p. 1118). This is the first recognition by Freud that the ego itself can be ill rather than healthy, being unable to stave off the other agencies of the mind. The split in the ego can mean that things are both really known and quite unknown simultaneously, like a life lived in a concurrent parallel way. Intellectually, one might prefer to think that if a person knows one and the other in parallel, then both states are known and the one knows the other, as it were. In severe mental illness, this is often not at all true. In addition, a sense of persecution from the tear in the mind can exist beneath the patch that is designed to cover it up. An *Einreiss* moving to a *Reiss* really does mean a deep gap between a mind knowing things on one side of the

canyon, but hardly, if at all, beyond, on the other side. The patch covering the tear in the mind like a dream is a symptom that attempts reconnection with reality. That "which we take to be the pathological product, is in reality an attempt at recovery, a process of reconstruction", writes Freud (1911b, p. 71).

4. The following quote introduces the mother into the infant's early psychic life, as well as the infant's own capacity to use motor activity to begin to obtain its needs.

> It will rightly be objected that an organization which was a slave to the pleasure principle and neglected the reality of the external world could not maintain itself alive for the shortest time, so that it could not have come into existence at all. The employment of a fiction like this is, however, justified when one considers that the infant—provided one includes with it the care it receives from its mother—does almost realize a psychical system of this kind. (Freud, 1911b, p. 220, n4)

5. Polonius is in fact there at that very time and place to observe the young Danish prince for evidence that his madness was real and to report his findings back to the king and queen. Hamlet plays on this, to be at a better advantage to get revenge on Claudius for killing his father.

6. A reference to the previous mention of his life and then his mother as a raft in the sea.

7. *Flectere si nequeo superos Acheronta movebo*. Virgil, *Aeneid*, Book VII, 312. "If I cannot have the overworld I will have the underworld." Quoted on the front sheet of Freud's *Interpretation of Dreams*.

Chapter 9: Early Covid writings

1. My essay was translated into Chinese and posted here: https://mp.weixin. qq.com/s/TSEm–akN87cTRean6Uy9ng

2. A version of this essay is published in *Mind in the Line of Fire: Psychoanalytic Voices to the Challenges of Our Times*. IPA, 2023.

Chapter 10: Bloomsbury and the early evolution of British psychoanalysis

1. Sharpe was interested in Froebel and Pestalozzi, whose work centred on the individual's freedom to grow.

2. Following analysis with Freud, 31 March to June 1922 and late 1923 to summer 1924, in 1925 Sir Arthur Tansley, the eminent Cambridge ecologist, became a psychoanalyst at the BPAS.

3. To be clear, much of the clinic's work was far from what we might recognise as psychoanalysis, although immediately post WWI, knowledge of analytic technique was not very great either. The interest in war trauma does seem to be an important strand in analytic understanding.

4. In John Forrester's view, Keynes' 1936 work contained anxiety about the future rather than hope—an inversion leading to lack of trust in the future, due to the aggression of two world wars, leading to anxiety around the future.

5. Moore and Russell were Apostles but not Bloomsbury.

6. Between March and June 1922, forty per cent of Freud's patients were from Cambridge. This meant that Freud became an expert in Cambridge academe, especially science, for which subject it was the leading university in the country. Not only did this lead to the seeding of psychoanalysis in the UK and the Empire, but it attached analytic insights to scientific endeavours. An example was Tansley's botany.

7. Alix loved dancing in Berlin: "she attended a number of balls, always on the lookout, usually in vain, for a suitable partner to match her height and skill. The spectacle of Alix and Melanie, the one in a silk nightgown with a wickerwork basket for a hat, the other decked out as Cleopatra, cruising the dance floor at 4 A.M. and occasionally crossing paths with Sachs and Rado on similar errands is enough to give a latter–day analyst pause" (Meisel & Kendrick, 1986, pp. 38–39).

8. Russell argued that the genuine pacifist neither seeks peace for its own sake or order and security, nor for his own tranquillity or comfort. He strives for peace in order that all human lives may flourish freely, because what motivates a pacifist is the brotherhood of men.

9. Adrian and Karin Stephen were both in analysis with James Glover. When Glover died in 1926, Adrian went into analysis with Ella Freeman Sharpe. Karin continued with Edward Glover, then with Clara Thompson on her visit to the United States in 1927, where she met Ferenczi and enjoyed his lectures, and finally went into analysis with Sylvia Payne. Karin's work as a philosopher was supervised by her uncle, Bertrand Russell. Karin wrote *Psychoanalysis and Medicine—A Study of the Wish to Fall Ill* (1933).

10. Jones was President of the BPAS for the extraordinarily long period 1919 to 1944.

11. Karin Stephen's deafness may have meant that she preferred to make a written rather than verbal contribution. The vigour of her mind was a powerful counterpoint to her hearing difficulties. See Forrester and Cameron, 2017, p. 554.

12. Freud (1923a), "Two Encyclopaedia Articles", which Strachey had just finished translating, publishing it in the *International Journal of Psycho–Analysis*.

13. Women only received the vote on the same terms as men, aged twenty-one, in 1928.

14. Really, the Ladies' Agreement between Melanie Klein and Anna Freud.

15. *Independent Women in British Psychoanalysis: Creativity and Authenticity at Work*, eds Elizabeth Wolf & Barbie Antonis, London: Routledge, 2023.

16. Melanie Klein's first analysis was with Ferenczi in Budapest, commencing around 1914 and lasting until 1919. She travelled to Berlin in 1921 and had a brief analysis with Karl Abraham during 1924–25 until his early death.

17. Enid Balint went into analysis with Winnicott following the death of Rickman. Rickman was interested in learning about psychoanalysis in his own analyses—starting with having his first analysis with Freud in Vienna, then going to Budapest to be analysed by Ferenczi and lastly having analysis in London with Klein.

Chapter 11: Apocalyptic times and the missing debate

1. In Freud's *Group Psychology* (1921c), even a religion that declares itself to be about love is hostile to those who are not a part of the community of believers.

2. An important reason is that Armageddon (Megiddo), a town in Israel, is cited in the *Book of Revelation* as the prophecies' location of a gathering of armies for a battle during the *end of times* that brings on the fight between God and the Satan-led unrepentant sinners.

3. In 1529 Pizzaro conquered an Inca population of twenty million, and fifty years later it had been reduced to only 900,000. It is only in recent times that the number has returned to its earlier number (personal communication, Dr. M. Lemlij). Peru has the worst official Covid death rate (Lanchester, 2021).

4. The idea of democracy being delivered to the people in the setting up of the soviets as a consequence of the Russian revolution depended on who controlled their agenda; in time Lenin, and then to a greater extent Stalin, took power and control of what had started off as a citizens' democracy.

Postscript

1. How Putin's war destroyed a golden age of Russian culture. *Financial Times*, 16 March 2023, https://www.ft.com/content/4228c0df-4928-4639-a8b0-a22387f48ab2 (last accessed 23 August 2023).
2. Conversation between Shostakovich and members of the Emerson String Quartet from the liner notes of their 1999 recording of the work on Deutsche Grammophon.
3. The Professional Artist in Russia: The Evolution of Status. *Heritage 2*, 2022 (75), https://www.tretyakovgallerymagazine.com/articles/2-2022-75/professional-artist-russia-evolution-status#:~:text=The%20social%20and%20cultural%20biography,national%20psyche%20and%20self%2Dawareness (last accessed 23 August 2023).
4. RASHID International (2017). The intentional destruction of cultural heritage in Iraq, https://rashid-international.org/publications/reports/ (last accessed 23 August 2023). RASHID International e.V. is a worldwide network of archaeologists, cultural heritage experts and professionals dedicated to safeguarding and promoting the cultural heritage of Iraq. They collect and share information, research and expert knowledge, work to raise public awareness, and both develop and execute strategies to protect heritage sites and other cultural property through international cooperation, advocacy and technical assistance.
5. Final Report on Damage assessment in Babylon by International Coordination Committee for the Safeguarding of the Cultural Heritage of Iraq, UNESCO26/06/2009.
6. Schwarm, Betsy. Leningrad Symphony No. 7 in C Major, Op. 60. *Encyclopædia Britannica*, 3 February 2017, https://www.britannica.com/topic/Leningrad-Symphony-No-7 (last accessed 16 August 2023).
7. A former Azov emblem featured a combination of a Wolfsangel and the black sun, two symbols associated with the Wehrmacht and the SS. The flag of the Patriot of Ukraine party, whose members formed the core membership of Azov in 2014 had the Wolfsangel, which is similar to the swastika. zov emblem featured a combination of a Wolfsangel and the black sun, two symbols associated with the Wehrmacht and the SS. The flag of the Patriot of Ukraine organisation, whose members formed the core membership of Azov in 2014 had the Wolfsangel, which is similar to the swastika. It was established originally as a far-right militia. After the union with the National Guard, the

Ukrainian government's first act was to root out two groups within Azov: foreign fighters and neo-Nazis (see Mironova & Sergatskova, 2017).

8. In the Jedwabne massacre in 1941, Polish villagers rounded up their Jewish neighbours and burnt them alive in a barn seemingly without any German orders or prescience. This history continues to be totally rejected by much of the Polish public. See Gross (2000).

9. Freud quoted by Richard Sterba (1978). Sterba attended the Psychological Wednesday Society evenings in Freud's study between 1928 and 1937.

10. The attack on Guernica had to be postponed for six days due to logistic problems. See Richardson (2022).

References

Abraham, N., & Torok, M. (1994). *The Shell and the Kernel: Renewals of Psychoanalysis* (Ed., trans. and with an introduction by N. T. Rand). Chicago, IL: University of Chicago Press.

Abram, J. (2023). The exceptional contributions of Marjorie Brierley: Affects, mediation and countertransference. In: E. Wolf & B. Antonis (Eds.), *Independent Women in British Psychoanalysis: Creativity and Authenticity at Work*. London: Routledge, 2023.

Acocella, J. (2021). Francis Bacon's frightening beauty. *The New Yorker*, 24 May 2021.

Alley, R., & Rothenstein, J. (1964). *Francis Bacon: Catalogue Raisonné and Documentation*. London: Thames & Hudson.

Alster, E. (2023). Paula Heimann, 1899–1982: Becoming Independent. In: E. Wolf & B. Antonis (Eds.), *Independent Women in British Psychoanalysis: Creativity and Authenticity at Work*. London: Routledge, 2023.

Appignanesi, L., & Forrester, J. (1992). *Freud's Women*. London: Weidenfeld & Nicholson.

Arendt, A. (1968). Walter Benjamin. In: *Men in Dark Times*. New York: Harcourt Brace, 1983.

Arendt, H. (1963). *On Revolution*. London: Penguin, 2006.

Balint, E. (1990). Unconscious communication. In: *Before I was I. Psychoanalysis and the Imagination*. London: Free Association, 1993.

Balint, E. (1993). *Before I was I: Psychoanalysis and the Imagination*. Free Association.

Balint, M. (1968). *The Basic Fault—Therapeutic Aspects of Regression*. London: Tavistock.

Barratt, B. (2016). *Radical Psychoanalysis—An Essay on Free-Associative Praxis*. London: Routledge.

Becker, E. (1973). *The Denial of Death*. New York: Free Press.

Benjamin, W. (1927–1940). *The Arcades Project*, (Trans. H. Eiland & K. McLaughlin). Cambridge, MA: Belknap Press, 2002.

Benjamin, W. (1940). Theses on the philosophy of history. In: H. Arendt (Ed.), *Illuminations: Essays and Reflections*. London: Bodley Head.

Benjamin, W. (1970). H. Arendt (Ed.), *Illuminations: Essays and Reflections*. London: Pimlico, 1999.

Besserman Vianna, H. (1994). Politique de la psychanalyse face à la dictature et à la torture. N'en parlez à personne. [Psychoanalysis, Dictatorship and Torture: Don't Talk About It]. Paris: L'Harmattan, 1997.

Bion, W. R. (1966). Catastrophic change. In: C. Mawson (Ed.), *The Complete Works of W. R. Bion. Standard Edition, Volume 6*. London: Routledge, 2014.

Bion, W. R. (2014). *The Complete Works of W. R. Bion. Standard Edition, Volume 6*. C. Mawson (Ed.), London: Routledge.

Bollas, C. (1987). *The Shadow of the Object: Psychoanalysis of the Unthought Known*. London: Free Association.

Bollas, C. (1989). *Forces of Destiny: Psychoanalysis and the Human Idiom*. London: Free Association.

Bollas, C. (1992). *Being and Character*. New York: Hill and Wang.

Brabant, A., Falzeder, E., & Giampieri-Deutsch, P. (Eds.) (1993). *The Correspondence of Sigmund Freud and Sándor Ferenczi*. Cambridge, MA: Harvard University Press.

Bratby, R. (2018). *"Metamorphosen"—Study for 23 Strings*. Royal Opera House Programme, orchestra of the Royal Opera House in concert, Monday 23 April 2018.

Brecht, K., Volker, F. Hermanns, L., Jülich, D. H., & Kaminer, I. J. (1985). *"Here Life Goes on In a Most Peculiar Way …": Psychoanalysis Before and After*

1933 (English ed. prepared by Hella Ehlers, trans. Christine Trollope). London: Karnac.

Butler, J. (2019). Genius or suicide. *London Review of Books*, vol. 41, no. 20, 24 October 2019.

Carroll, L. (1865). *The Adventures of Alice in Wonderland*. London: Macmillan, 2016.

Caygill, H. (2019). Bacon's cynegetic visions. In: Ben Ware (Ed.), *Francis Bacon: Painting, Philosophy, Psychoanalysis* (Francis Bacon Studies 2) (pp. 20–41). London: Thames & Hudson.

Clark, C. (1939). *Positioning in Radiography* (Fifteenth edition). London: CRC Press, 2015.

Clark, T. J. (2022). *If These Apples Should Fall: Cézanne and the Present*. London: Thames & Hudson.

Cohn, N. (1972). *The Pursuit of the Millennium*. London: Paladin.

Czaplicka, E. A. (1914). *Aboriginal Siberia*. Oxford: Oxford University Press.

Danchev, A. (2012): *Cézanne: A Life*. London: Profile, 2013.

Danckwardt, J. F., & Wegner, P. (2007). Performance as annihilation or integration? *International Journal of Psychoanalysis*, 88(5): 1117–1133.

Davies, H. M. (2001). *Francis Bacon: The Papal Portraits of 1953*. San Diego, CA: Museum of Contemporary Art.

Davies, H. M., & Yard, S. (1986). *Francis Bacon*. NYC: Abbeville Press.

Deleuze, G. (1951). *Francis Bacon: The Logic of Sensation*. London: Bloomsbury, 2005.

Eisenstein, S. (Director) (1925). Battleship Potemkin. Vimeo: https://vimeo.com/353600419?ref=em–share

Eliot, T. S. (1940). East Coker, *Four Quartets*. In *Collected Poems 1909–1962*. London: Faber, 1974.

Eliot, T. S. (1975): Sweeney Agonistes. In: *The Complete Poems and Plays*. London: Faber.

Ferenczi, S. (1924). *Thalassa: A Theory of Genitality*. New York: Norton, 1968.

Ferenczi, S. (1925a). Psychoanalysis of sexual habits. In: M. Balint (Ed.), *Final Contributions to the Problems and Methods of Psycho-analysis* (pp. 259–297). London: Hogarth, 1950.

Ferenczi, S. (1925b). The problem of acceptance of unpleasant ideas—advances in knowledge of the sense of reality 1. In: M. Balint (Ed.), *Final Contributions to the Problems and Methods of Psycho-analysis* (pp. 366–379). London: Hogarth, 1950.

Ferenczi, S. (1926). Gulliver phantasies. In: M. Balint (Ed.), *Final Contributions to the Problems and Methods of Psycho-analysis* (pp. 41–60). London: Hogarth, 1950.

Ferenczi, S. (1931). Child-analysis in the analysis of adults. *International Journal of Psycho-Analysis*, 12: 468–482.

Ferenczi, S. (1932). Confusion of tongues between adults and the child—the language of tenderness and of passion. In: M. Balint (Ed.), *Final Contributions to the Problems and Methods of Psycho-analysis* (pp. 156–167). London: Hogarth, 1950.

Ferenczi, S. (1988). *The Clinical Diary of Sándor Ferenczi* (Ed. J. Dupont, J., Trans. M. Balint & N. Z. Jackson). Cambridge, MA: Harvard University Press.

Forrester, J. (2017). On holding as metaphor: Winnicott and the figure of St Christopher. In: *Thinking in Cases*. London: Polity Press.

Forrester, J., & Cameron, L. (2017). Bloomsbury analysts. In: *Freud in Cambridge* (pp. 505–612). Cambridge: Cambridge University Press.

Foucault, M. (1966). *The Order of Things: An Archeology of the Human Sciences*. Routledge: London, 2001.

Fredheim, R. (2014). The memory of Katyn in Polish political discourse: A quantitative study (2014). *Europe-Asia Studies*, 66(7): 1165–1187.

Freud, A. (1936). *The Ego and the Mechanisms of Defence*. London: Karnac, 1992.

Freud, A. (1949). Notes from the 1949 IPA Congress, *International Journal of Psycho-Analysis*, 31.

Freud, S. (1896c). The aetiology of hysteria. *S. E.*, 3: 187–221. London: Hogarth.

Freud, S. (1900a). *The Interpretation of Dreams*. *S. E.*, 4. London: Hogarth.

Freud, S. (1909d). Notes upon a case of obsessional neurosis. *S. E.*, 10: 153–252. London: Hogarth.

Freud, S. (1910c). Leonardo da Vinci and a memory of his childhood. *S. E.*, 11: 59–138. London: Hogarth.

Freud, S. (1911b). Formulations on the two principles of mental functioning. *S. E.*, 12: 213–226. London: Hogarth.

Freud, S. (1913c). On beginning the treatment. (Further recommendations on the technique of psychoanalysis, I). *S. E.*, 12: 121–144. London: Hogarth.

Freud, S. (1913f): The theme of the three caskets. *S. E.*, 12: 289–302. London: Hogarth.

Freud, S. (1915e). *The Unconscious*. *S. E.*, 14: 159–190. London: Hogarth.

Freud, S. (1919e). A child is being beaten: A contribution to the study of the origin of sexual perversions. *S. E.*, 2: 175–204. London: Hogarth.

Freud, S. (1920g). *Beyond the Pleasure Principle. S. E.*, 18: 1–64. London: Hogarth.

Freud, S. (1921c). *Group Psychology and the Analysis of the Ego. S. E.*, 18: 65–144. London: Hogarth.

Freud, S. (1923a [1922]). Two encyclopaedia articles. *S. E.*, 18: 235–259. London: Hogarth.

Freud, S. (1924b [1923]). Neurosis and psychosis. *S. E.*, 19: 147–154. London: Hogarth.

Freud, S. (1925d [1924]). An autobiographical study. *S. E.*, 20: 1–70. London: Hogarth.

Freud, S. (1925h). Negation. *S. E.*, 19: 235–240. London: Hogarth.

Freud, S. (1930a). *Civilization and Its Discontents. S. E.*, 21: 57–146. London: Hogarth.

Freud, S. (1933a). *New Introductory Lectures on Psycho-Analysis. S. E.*, 22: 1–182. London: Hogarth.

Freud, S. (1933b [1932]): Why war? *S. E.*, 22: 199–215. London: Hogarth.

Frosch, S. (2005). *Hate and the "Jewish Science"*. London: Palgrave Macmillan.

Goggin, J. E., & Goggin, E. B. (2001). *Death of a "Jewish Science": Psychoanalysis in the Third Reich*. West Lafayette, IN: Purdue University Press.

Gross, J. G. (2000). *Neighbors: The Destruction of the Jewish Community in Jedwabne, Poland*. Princeton, NJ: Princeton University Press.

Grosskurth, P. (1985). *Melanie Klein*. London: Hodder and Stoughton.

Hall, C. (2014). *Legacies of British Slave-Ownership 1763–1833*. Cambridge: Cambridge University Press.

Heimann, P. (1989). *Paula Heimann: About Children and Children-No-Longer: Collected Papers 1942–80*. M. Tonnesman (Ed.). London: Tavistock/Routledge.

Houdini, H. (2011). *A Magician Among the Spirits*. Cambridge: Cambridge University Press.

Huysmans, J. K. (1903). *Against Nature* (Trans. Theo Cuffe, with illustrations by William Tillyer). London: 21 Publishing, 2018.

Jacobson, B. (2018). *William Tillyer: The Loneliness of the Long Distance Runner*. London: 21 Publishing.

James, M. (Director) (2022). *William Tillyer: The Golden Striker*. [Film, available on Vimeo].

Jansen, L., Luitjen, H., & Bakker, N. (2009). *Vincent van Gogh, The Letters. Volume 3*. London: Thames & Hudson.

Jones, E. (1951). The Madonna's conception through the ear. In: *Essays in Applied Psycho-Analysis, Volume 2* (pp. 266–357). London: Hogarth Press.

Joyce, A. (2016). Introduction. In: *The Collected Works of D. W. Winnicott, Volume 6 (1960–1963)*. Oxford: Oxford University Press.

Joyce, A. (2019). *Health: Dependence towards Independence in Twelve Essays on Winnicott*. Oxford: OUP.

Kafka, F. (1975). The *Diaries of Franz Kafka, 1910–1923*. M. Brod (Ed.). Entry, 19 October 1921. Harmondsworth: Penguin.

Kavvadias, N. (2006). *The Collected Poems of Nikos Kavvadias*. Athens/Riverdale, NJ: Cosmos Publishing.

Keats, J. (1817). *Selected Letters of John Keats*. Letter to George and Thomas Keats, 21 December 1817. Harmondsworth: Penguin, 2014.

Keynes, J. M. (1919). *The Economic Consequences of the Peace*. London: Macmillan.

Keynes, J. M. (1936). *The General Theory of Employment, Interest and Money*. London: Macmillan.

Keynes, J. M. (1939). My early beliefs. In: *Essays in Biography, Volume X*, (pp. 433–450). London: Macmillan & Cambridge University Press for the Royal Economic Society, 1972.

Khan, M. M. R. (1979). Role of the "collated internal object" in perversion-formations. In: *Alienation and the Perversions*. London: Hogarth.

King, P., & Steiner, R. (Eds.) (1991): *The Freud–Klein Controversies 1941–45*. London & New York: Tavistock/Routledge.

Kirchkheli, M. (2023). Marion Milner: The pliable self. In: E. Wolf & B. Antonis (Eds.), *Independent Women in British Psychoanalysis: Creativity and Authenticity at Work*. London: Routledge, 2023.

Klee, P. (1966). *Paul Klee on Modern Art*. With an introduction by Herbert Read (Trans. Paul Findlay). London: Faber.

Lanchester, J. (2021, 16 December). Lost in Covid. *London Review of Books*, 43(24). Available at: https://www.lrb.co.uk/the-paper/v43/n24.

Langer, M. (1989). *From Vienna to Managua: Journey of a Psychoanalyst* (Trans. M. Hooks). London: Free Association.

Langer, M., & Bauleo, A. (1973). Algo más sobre la tortura. *Cuestionamos*, 2: 93–94.

Lear, J. (2006). *Radical Hope: Ethics in the Face of Cultural Devastation*. Cambridge, Mass.: Harvard University Press.

Lemlij, M. (2021). Personal communication.

Linderman, F. (1962). *Plenty-Coups: Chief of the Crows*. Lincoln, NE: University of Nebraska Press.

Meisel, P., & Kendrick, W. (1986). *Bloomsbury/Freud. The letters of James and Alix Strachey 1924–1925*. London: Chatto & Windus.

Mironova, V., & Sergatskova, E. (2017). How Ukraine reined in its militias: The lessons for other states. *Foreign Affairs* (1 August), https://www.foreignaffairs.com/articles/ukraine/2017-08-01/how-ukraine-reined-its-militias (last accessed 23 August 2023).

Mitscherlich, A., & Mitscherlich, M. (1967). *The Inability to Mourn*. NYC, New York: Grove, 1975.

Nietzsche, F. W. (1886). *The Birth of Tragedy*. London: Penguin, 1993.

Nobus, D. (2016). Psychoanalytic violence: an essay on indifference in ethical matters. *Psychoanalytic Discourse/Le discours psychanalytique*, 2016, 1(2): 1–21.

Novick, J., & Novick, K. K. (1997). Not for barbarians: An appreciation of Freud's "A Child is Being Beaten". In: E. S. Person (Ed.), *On Freud's "A Child is Being Beaten"* (pp. 31–46). New Haven, CT: Yale University Press.

Ottinger, D. (2019). *Francis Bacon: Books and Painting*. London: Thames & Hudson.

Parker, S. (2014). *Bertolt Brecht: A Literary Life*. London: Methuen.

Parsons, M. (2014). An Independent theory of clinical technique. In: *Living Psychoanalysis: From Theory to Experience* (pp. 184–204). Hove: Routledge.

Paskauskas, R. A. (1993). *The Complete Correspondence of Sigmund Freud and Ernest Jones 1908–1939*. Cambridge, MA: Harvard University Press.

Peppiatt, M. (2008). *Francis Bacon: Anatomy of an Enigma*. Edinburgh: Constable.

Phillips, A. (1988). *Winnicott*. Cambridge, MA: Harvard University Press.

Raitt, S. (2004). Early British psychoanalysis and the Medico-Psychological Clinic. *History Workshop Journal*, 58: 63–85.

Read, H. (1951). Review of artists in the British Pavilion, Venice Biennale.

Reward, J. (Ed.) (1995). *Paul Cézanne, Letters*. Boston, MA: Da Capo Press.

Richardson, J. (2022). *A Life of Picasso Volume IV: The Minotaur Years 1933–1943*. London: Jonathan Cape.

Rickman, J. (1951). Number and the human sciences. In: P. King (Ed.), *No Ordinary Psychoanalyst: The Extraordinary Contributions of John Rickman*. London: Karnac, 2003.

Robinson, K. (2023a). Ella Sharpe: Being Independent, following Freud. In: E. Wolf & B. Antonis (Eds.), *Independent Women in British Psychoanalysis: Creativity and Authenticity at Work*. London: Routledge, 2023.

Robinson, K. (2023b). Doing things differently: Pearl King's independence. In: E. Wolf & B. Antonis (Eds.), *Independent Women in British Psychoanalysis: Creativity and Authenticity at Work*. London: Routledge, 2023.

Róheim, G. (1952). *The Gates of the Dream*. New York: International Universities Press.

Schama, S. (2022). Art against tyranny. *The Financial Times* (Life and Arts section), 3 December 2022.

Schrenck-Notzing, A. von (1920). *Phenomena of Materialisation. A Contribution to the Investigation of Mediumistic Teleplastics*. London: Kegan Paul, Trench, Trübner & Co.

Schwirtz, M. (2020). "Nurses Die, Doctors Fall Sick and Panic Rises on Virus Front Lines", *The New York Times*, March 30, 2020, updated 5 May 2020.

Searles, H. (1975). The patient as therapist to his analyst. In: P. Giovacchini (Ed.), *Tactics and Techniques in Psychoanalytic Therapy, Volume 2* (pp. 95–151). NY: Jason Aronson.

Sklar, J. (2011). *Landscapes of the Dark: History, Trauma, Psychoanalysis*. London: Karnac.

Sklar, J. (2019). *Dark Times: Psychoanalytic Perspectives on Politics, History and Mourning*. London: Phoenix.

Sklar, J. (2020a). Meditation on death.

Sklar, J. (2020b). "Atish-oo, Atish-oo".

Sklar, J. (2020c). It takes our breath away.

Snyder, T. (2017). Germany must own up to its past. *Kyiv Post* (7 July). https://archive.kyivpost.com/article/opinion/op-ed/timothy-snydergermany-must-past-atrocities-ukraine.html (last accessed 15 August 2023).

Somaini, P. (2023). Nina Coltart's colourful ways of listening. In: E. Wolf & B. Antonis (Eds.), *Independent Women in British Psychoanalysis: Creativity and Authenticity at Work*. London: Routledge, 2023.

Stephen, A. (1936). On defining psychoanalysis. *The Psychoanalytic Review*, 23: 101–116.

Stephen, K. (1933). *Psychoanalysis and Medicine—A Study of the Wish to Fall Ill*. Cambridge: Cambridge University Press.

Sterba, R. F. (1978). Discussions of Sigmund Freud. *The Psychoanalytic Quarterly, 47*(2): 173–191.

Strozier, C. (1994). *Apocalypse: On the Psychology of Fundamentalism in America.* Boston, MA: Beacon.

Strozier, C. (2021). Private correspondence.

Subotić, J. (2020). *Yellow Star, Red Star: Holocaust Remembrance after Communism.* New York: Cornell University Press.

Sylvester, D. (1975). *Interviews with Francis Bacon.* London: Thames & Hudson, 1988.

Sylvester, D. (2000). *Looking Back at Francis Bacon.* London: Thames & Hudson.

Sylvester, D. (2016). *The Brutality of Fact: Interviews with Francis Bacon.* London: Thames & Hudson.

Szabłowski, W. (2014). *Dancing Bears: True Stories of People Nostalgic for Life Under Tyranny* (Trans. Antonia Lloyd-Jones). London: Penguin.

Tausk, V. (1919). On the origin of the "Influencing machine" in schizophrenia. In: R. Fliess (Ed.), *The Psychoanalytic Reader: An Anthology of Essential Papers with Critical Introductions.* London: Hogarth, 1950.

Tillyer, W. (1958). Catalogue, end of year art show, Middlesbrough Art College.

Tillyer, W. (2002). *Hardware: Variations on a Theme of Encounter. (Bernard Jacobson Gallery, London 11 September–19 October 2002).*

Tóibín, C. (2021). Open in a scream. Review of *Francis Bacon: Revelations,* by M. Stevens & A. Swan. *London Review of Books* 43(5), 4 March 2021.

Troianovski, A., & Hopkins, V. (2023). One year into war, Putin is crafting the Russia he craves. *New York Times,* 19 February. https://www.nytimes.com/2023/02/19/world/europe/ukraine-war-russia-putin.html (last accessed 15 August 2023).

Tuymans, L. (2022). *The Breaking Point in The EY Exhibition CÉZANNE.* Chicago: The Art Institute of Chicago.

Winnicott, D. W. (1949). Hate in the countertransference. In: *Through Paediatrics to Psycho-analysis* (pp. 194–203). London: Hogarth, 1975.

Winnicott, D. W. (1952). Anxiety associated with insecurity. In: L. Caldwell & H. Taylor Robinson (Eds.), *The Collected Works of D. W. Winnicott, Volume 4 (1952–1955)* (pp. 55–58). Oxford: Oxford University Press, 2016.

Winnicott, D. W. (1953). Transitional objects and transitional phenomena: A study of the first not-me phenomena. In: L. Caldwell & H. Taylor Robinson

(Eds.), *The Collected Works of D. W. Winnicott, Volume 4 (1952–1955)* (pp. 159–174). Oxford: Oxford University Press, 2016.

Winnicott, D. W. (1958a). The capacity to be alone. In: *The Maturational Processes and the Facilitating Environment*. London: Hogarth.

Winnicott, D. W. (1958b). Psycho-analysis and the sense of guilt. In: L. Caldwell & H. Taylor Robinson (Eds.), *The Collected Works of D. W. Winnicott, Volume 5 (1955–1959)* (pp. 135–148). Oxford: Oxford University Press, 2016.

Winnicott, D. W. (1960a). Letter to Michael Balint 5/2/1960. In: L. Caldwell & H. Taylor Robinson (Eds.), *The Collected Works of D. W. Winnicott, Volume 6 (1960–1963)* (p. 44). Oxford: Oxford University Press, 2016.

Winnicott, D. W. (1960b). Ego distortion in terms of true and false self. In: L. Caldwell & H. Taylor Robinson (Eds.), *The Collected Works of D. W. Winnicott, Volume 6 (1960–1963)* (pp. 159–172). Oxford: Oxford University Press, 2016.

Winnicott, D. W. (1963a). Communicating and not communicating, leading to a study of certain opposites. In: L. Caldwell & H. Taylor Robinson (Eds.), *The Collected Works of D. W. Winnicott, Volume 6 (1960–1963)* (pp. 433–466). Oxford: Oxford University Press, 2016.

Winnicott, D. W. (1963b). Fear of breakdown. In: L. Caldwell & H. Taylor Robinson (Eds.), *The Collected Works of D. W. Winnicott, Volume 6 (1960–1963)* (pp. 523–532). Oxford: Oxford University Press, 2016.

Winnicott, D. W. (1966a). The split-off male and female elements to be found in men and women. In: L. Caldwell & H. Taylor Robinson (Eds.), *The Collected Works of D. W. Winnicott, Volume 7 (1964–1966)* (pp. 217–330). Oxford: Oxford University Press, 2016.

Winnicott, D. W. (1966b). The location of cultural experience. In: L. Caldwell & H. Taylor Robinson (Eds.), *The Collected Works of D. W. Winnicott, Volume 7 (1964–1966)* (pp. 429–436). Oxford: Oxford University Press, 2016.

Winnicott, D. W. (1967). Mirror-role of mother and family in child development. In: L. Caldwell & H. Taylor Robinson (Eds.), *The Collected Works of D. W. Winnicott*, vol 8 (pp. 211–218). Oxford: Oxford University Press, 2016.

Winnicott, D. W. (1971). *Playing and Reality*. London: Tavistock.

Winnicott, D. W. (1988a). *Human Nature*. London: Free Association.

Winnicott, D. W. (1988b). *Babies and Their Mothers*. London: Free Association.

Winnicott, D. W. (1989). *Psycho-Analytic Explorations* (C. Winnicott, R. Shepherd & M. Davis (Eds.)). London: Routledge, 2010.

Wolf, E., & Antonis, B. (Eds.) (2023). *Independent Women in British Psychoanalysis: Creativity and Authenticity at Work*. London: Routledge.

Wulff, M. (1946). Fetishism and object choice in early childhood. *Psychoanalytic Quarterly*, 15: 450–471.

Wullshager, J. (2019). Sex and death: how Francis Bacon reinvented art history around his essential themes. *The Financial Times/Gagosian*, 22/23 June 2019.

Yau, J. (2021). Catalogue essay, *William Tillyer—A Retrospective*. New York: Rizzoli Electra.

Young-Bruehl, E. (1982). *Hannah Arendt: For Love of the World*. 2nd Edition. Newhaven: Yale University Press, 2004.

Index